First World War
and Army of Occupation
War Diary
France, Belgium and Germany

2 DIVISION
6 Infantry Brigade
Royal Fusiliers (City of London Regiment)
17th Battalion and Machine Gun Company
4 January 1916 - 28 February 1918

WO95/1363

The Naval & Military Press Ltd
www.nmarchive.com
Published in association with The National Archives

Published by

The Naval & Military Press Ltd

Unit 10 Ridgewood Industrial Park,

Uckfield, East Sussex,

TN22 5QE England

Tel: +44 (0) 1825 749494

www.naval-military-press.com

www.nmarchive.com

This diary has been reprinted in facsimile from the original. Any imperfections are inevitably reproduced and the quality may fall short of modern type and cartographic standards.

© **Crown Copyright**
Images reproduced by permission of The National Archives, London, England, 2015.

Contents

Document type	Place/Title	Date From	Date To
Heading	2 Division 6 Brigade 17 R. Fusiliers 1919 Jan-1919 Feb		
War Diary	Duren	01/01/1919	11/02/1919
War Diary	Leichlingen	12/02/1919	28/02/1919
Heading	2nd Division 6th Infy Bde 1-17th Battalion Royal Fusiliers Feb-Dec 1918		
Heading	6th Brigade. 2nd Division. Battalion Came From 5th Brigade 6.2.18. 1/17th Battalion Royal Fusiliers February 1918		
War Diary	Divisional Reserve Metz	01/02/1918	04/02/1918
War Diary	Ref 57c D2 & Lavacquerie Metz	05/02/1918	06/02/1918
War Diary	La Vacquerie (left)	06/02/1918	09/02/1918
War Diary	Lavacquerie (Left) Support	10/02/1918	12/02/1918
War Diary	La Vaquerie Left	13/02/1918	15/02/1918
War Diary	Metz	16/02/1918	17/02/1918
War Diary	Support Line Villers Plouich	18/02/1918	21/02/1918
War Diary	Frontline Lavaquerie Center	22/02/1918	26/02/1918
War Diary	Metz Tent Camp	27/02/1918	28/02/1918
Miscellaneous			
Operation(al) Order(s)	Operation Order No. 10 By Major S.J.M. Hole M.C. Commanding 17th Royal Fusiliers		
Operation(al) Order(s)	Operation Order No. 11 By Major S.J.M. Hole M.C. Commanding 17th Royal Fusiliers.	07/02/1918	07/02/1918
Miscellaneous	C Form. Messages And Signals.		
Operation(al) Order(s)	Operation Order No. 12 By Major. S.J.M. Hole. M.C. Commanding 17th Royal Fusiliers.	08/02/1918	08/02/1918
Operation(al) Order(s)	Operation Order No. 13 By Major S.J.M. Hole M.C. Commanding 17th Royal Fusiliers.	11/02/1918	11/02/1918
Operation(al) Order(s)	Amendment No. 1 To Operation Order No. 13 By Major S.J.M. Hole M.C. Commanding 17th Royal Fusiliers.	12/08/1918	12/08/1918
War Diary	Operation Order No. 15 By Major S.J.M. Hole M.C. Commanding 17th Royal Fusiliers.	14/02/1918	14/02/1918
Operation(al) Order(s)	Operation Order No. 16 By Major S.J.M. Hole M.C. Commanding 17th Royal Fusiliers.	17/02/1918	17/02/1918
Operation(al) Order(s)	Operation Order No. 17 By Major S.J.M. Hole M.C. Commanding 17th Royal Fusiliers.	20/02/1918	20/02/1918
Operation(al) Order(s)	Operation Order No. 18 By Major S.J.M. Hole M.C. Commanding 17th Royal Fusiliers.	22/02/1918	22/02/1918
Operation(al) Order(s)	Operation Order No. 20 By Major. S.J.M. Hole. M.C. Commanding 17th Royal Fusiliers.	25/02/1918	25/02/1918
Heading	6th Brigade. 2nd Division. 17th Battalion The Royal Fusiliers March 1918		
War Diary	Metz Tent Camp.	01/03/1918	01/03/1918
War Diary	Support Line Mes Villers Plovich	02/03/1918	05/03/1918
War Diary	Frontline Lavacquerie Centre Sector	06/03/1918	09/03/1918
War Diary	Metz Camp P.30 D On Equancourt Road	10/03/1918	10/03/1918
War Diary	Metz Camp P.30 D	11/03/1918	13/03/1918
War Diary	Support Line R7d1.9. Vacquerie Centre Sector	14/03/1918	16/03/1918
War Diary	Support Line R7d1.9	17/03/1918	17/03/1918
War Diary	Frontline Vacquerie Centre Sector	18/03/1918	19/03/1918

War Diary	Frontline And Rocquigny Camp	20/03/1918	20/03/1918
War Diary	Rocquigny Camp	21/03/1918	21/03/1918
War Diary	0.3a Tank Camp & Mill Cross	22/03/1918	22/03/1918
War Diary	Mill Cross	23/03/1918	23/03/1918
War Diary	Sanders Camp	23/03/1918	23/03/1918
War Diary	Saunders Camp 0.4d	23/03/1918	23/03/1918
War Diary	Haplincourtwood 04c1.9.	23/03/1918	24/03/1918
War Diary	Red Line Villers-Av-Flos	24/03/1918	24/03/1918
War Diary	Beavlencourt	24/03/1918	24/03/1918
War Diary	Ligny-Thilloy	24/03/1918	24/03/1918
War Diary	Pys	25/03/1918	25/03/1918
War Diary	Beaucourt	25/03/1918	25/03/1918
War Diary	Auchonvillers Hamel Rd	26/03/1918	26/03/1918
War Diary	Mailly-Maillet-Beaussart Englebelmer	27/03/1918	28/03/1918
War Diary	Aveluy Wood Frontline	29/03/1918	29/03/1918
War Diary	Hedauville	30/03/1918	31/03/1918
Miscellaneous Diagram etc	A Form. Messages And Signals.		
Miscellaneous	Report On The Operation From March 21.1918 To March. 31.1918	21/03/1918	31/03/1918
Diagram etc Miscellaneous		01/04/1918	01/04/1918
Miscellaneous	V Corps.	20/04/1918	20/04/1918
Miscellaneous	Further Report On The Operation At Pys On March 25th, 1918	20/04/1918	20/04/1918
Miscellaneous			
Heading	6th Brigade. 2nd Division. 1/17th Battalion Royal Fusiliers April 1918		
War Diary	Hedauville	01/04/1918	01/04/1918
War Diary	Englebelmer	02/04/1918	03/04/1918
War Diary	Halloy	04/04/1918	05/04/1918
War Diary	Sibiville	06/04/1918	10/04/1918
War Diary	Sus St Leger	11/04/1918	15/04/1918
War Diary	Front Line Boisleux Sr Marc (South)	16/04/1918	20/04/1918
War Diary	Blaireville (Reserve)	21/04/1918	21/04/1918
War Diary	Front Line	22/04/1918	26/04/1918
War Diary	Blaireville	27/04/1918	30/04/1918
Heading	6th Brigade. 2nd Division. 1/17th Battalion Royal Fusiliers May 1918.		
War Diary	Front Line Boisleux Au Mont	30/04/1918	05/05/1918
War Diary	Blaireville	06/05/1918	07/05/1918
War Diary	Frontline Boiselux On Mont	08/05/1918	14/05/1918
War Diary	Barly	14/05/1918	31/05/1918
Heading	6th Brigade. 2nd Division. 1/17th Battalion Royal Fusiliers June 1918.		
War Diary	Barly	01/06/1918	06/06/1918
War Diary	Ayette	07/06/1918	07/06/1918
War Diary	Frontline Left Sub. Sector Ayette	08/06/1918	08/06/1918
War Diary	Monchy	09/06/1918	13/06/1918
War Diary	Frontline akette	13/06/1918	17/06/1918
War Diary	Monchy	18/06/1918	21/06/1918
War Diary	Adinfer Wood	22/06/1918	26/06/1918
War Diary	Ayette	27/06/1918	30/06/1918
Heading	6th Brigade. 2nd Division. 1/17th Battalion Royal Fusiliers July 1918		
War Diary	Monchy	01/07/1918	03/07/1918

War Diary	Adinfer Wood	04/07/1918	07/07/1918
War Diary	Ayette	08/07/1918	12/07/1918
War Diary	Monchy	13/07/1918	15/07/1918
War Diary	Adinfer Wood	16/07/1918	19/07/1918
War Diary	Ayette	20/07/1918	24/07/1918
War Diary	Monchy	25/07/1918	30/07/1918
War Diary	Adinfer Wood	31/07/1918	31/07/1918
Heading	6th Brigade. 2nd Division. 1/17th Battalion Royal Fusiliers August 1918.		
War Diary	Adinfer Wood	01/08/1918	03/08/1918
War Diary	Ayette	04/08/1918	09/08/1918
War Diary	Monchy	10/08/1918	13/08/1918
War Diary	Adinfer Wood	14/08/1918	18/08/1918
War Diary	Ayette	19/08/1918	23/08/1918
War Diary	Courcelles	24/08/1918	24/08/1918
War Diary	Ervillers	25/08/1918	25/08/1918
War Diary	Ayette	26/08/1918	31/08/1918
Heading	6th Brigade 2nd Division. 1/17th Battalion Royal Fusiliers September 1918		
War Diary	Ayette	01/09/1918	02/09/1918
War Diary	Vaulx-Vraucourt	03/09/1918	03/09/1918
War Diary	Doignies	04/09/1918	05/09/1918
War Diary	Beaumetz	06/09/1918	07/09/1918
War Diary	Morchies	08/09/1918	13/09/1918
War Diary	Hermies	14/09/1918	14/09/1918
War Diary	Demicourt	15/09/1918	16/09/1918
War Diary	Morchies	17/09/1918	17/09/1918
War Diary	Behagnies	18/09/1918	26/09/1918
War Diary	Flessuieres	27/09/1918	27/09/1918
War Diary	Noyelles	28/09/1918	30/09/1918
Miscellaneous	Record Of Operation-2nd/4th Sept., 1918.	08/09/1918	08/09/1918
Heading	6th Brigade. 2nd Division. 1/17th Battalion Royal Fusiliers October 1918.		
War Diary	Noyelles	01/10/1918	02/10/1918
War Diary	Flot Farm	03/10/1918	07/10/1918
War Diary	Forenville	08/10/1918	08/10/1918
War Diary	Lock 7	08/10/1918	13/10/1918
War Diary	Niergnies	14/10/1918	22/10/1918
War Diary	St. Hilaire	23/10/1918	23/10/1918
War Diary	St Python	24/10/1918	24/10/1918
War Diary	Vertain	26/10/1918	31/10/1918
Heading	6th Brigade. 2nd Division. 1/17th Battalion Royal Fusiliers November 1918.		
War Diary	Ruesnes	01/11/1918	02/11/1918
War Diary	Solsnes	03/11/1918	03/11/1918
War Diary	Escarmain	04/11/1918	06/11/1918
War Diary	Villers Pol	07/11/1918	07/11/1918
War Diary	Wargnies Le Petit	08/11/1918	09/11/1918
War Diary	Preux Au Sart	10/11/1918	16/11/1918
War Diary	La Saule	17/11/1918	18/11/1918
War Diary	Maubeuge	19/11/1918	20/11/1918
War Diary	Estinnes-Au-Mont (Belgium)	21/11/1918	24/11/1918
War Diary	Anderlues	25/11/1918	25/11/1918
War Diary	La Neuve Ville Montignies	26/11/1918	28/11/1918
War Diary	Vitrival	29/11/1918	29/11/1918
War Diary	Wepion	30/11/1918	30/11/1918

Heading	6th Brigade. 2nd Division. 1/17th Battalion Royal Fusiliers December 1918		
War Diary	Wepion	01/12/1918	04/12/1918
War Diary	Bonneville	05/12/1918	05/12/1918
War Diary	Huy	06/12/1918	06/12/1918
War Diary	Ellemelle	07/12/1918	07/12/1918
War Diary	Awyaille	08/12/1918	08/12/1918
War Diary	Basse Desnie	09/12/1918	09/12/1918
War Diary	Burnenville	10/12/1918	11/12/1918
War Diary	Elsenborn Lager	12/12/1918	12/12/1918
War Diary	Imgenbroich	13/12/1918	13/12/1918
War Diary	Drove	14/12/1918	14/12/1918
War Diary	Duren	15/12/1918	31/12/1918
Heading	2nd Division 6th Infy Bde Machine Gun Company Jan-Dec 1916		
Heading	6th Brigade. 2nd Division. 6th Brigade Machine Gun Company : January 1916.		
War Diary		04/01/1916	31/01/1916
Heading	6th Brigade. 2nd DIvision. 6th Brigade Machine Gun Company : February 1916		
War Diary		03/02/1916	28/02/1916
Heading	6th Brigade. 2nd Division. 6th Brigade Machine Gun Company : March 1916.		
War Diary	In the Fields	01/03/1916	19/03/1916
Heading	6th Brigade. 2nd Division. 6th Brigade Gun Company: April 1916.		
War Diary	In the Fields	02/04/1916	30/04/1916
Heading	6th Brigade. 2nd Division. 6th Brigade Machine Gun Company : May 1916.		
War Diary	In The Field	01/05/1916	30/05/1916
Heading	6th Brigade. 2nd Division. 6th Brigade Machine Gun Company : June 1916.		
War Diary	In The Field	02/06/1916	29/06/1916
Heading	6th Inf. Bde. 2nd Div. War Diary. 6th Machine Gun Company July 1916		
War Diary	In The Line	02/07/1916	31/07/1916
Heading	6th Brigade 2nd Division. 6th Brigade Machine Gun Company August 1916		
War Diary	Field	01/08/1916	31/08/1916
Miscellaneous	Fire Orders. By Lieut. M. Kavanagh, Commanding 6th. Machine Gun Coy.	07/08/1916	07/08/1916
Heading	6th Brigade. 2nd Division. 6th Brigade Machine Gun Company : September 1916.		
War Diary	In The Field Serre Sector	02/09/1916	20/09/1916
War Diary	Counceller All Bois	20/09/1916	23/09/1916
War Diary	Bus Au Artois	23/09/1916	29/09/1916
Heading	6th Brigade. 2nd Division. 6th Brigade Machine Gun Company : October 1916.		
War Diary	Hebuterne Sector Bus. Les. Artois	01/10/1916	04/10/1916
War Diary	Hebuterne Sector	05/10/1916	07/10/1916
War Diary	Puichvillers	08/10/1916	18/10/1916
War Diary	Bertrancourt	19/10/1916	23/10/1916
War Diary	Mailly Maillet	24/10/1916	28/10/1916
War Diary	Beaussart	29/10/1916	29/10/1916
War Diary	Mavily-Maillet	29/10/1916	31/10/1916

Heading	6th Brigade. 2nd Division. 6th Brigade Machine Gun Company ; November 1916.		
War Diary	Mailley Maillet	01/11/1916	12/11/1916
War Diary	Serre Sector	12/11/1916	14/11/1916
War Diary	Mailley Maillet	16/11/1916	16/11/1916
War Diary	Louvencourt	16/11/1916	16/11/1916
War Diary	Authieule	19/11/1916	19/11/1916
War Diary	Autheux	21/11/1916	21/11/1916
War Diary	Le Festil	22/11/1916	22/11/1916
War Diary	Noyelle En Chaussee	24/11/1916	24/11/1916
War Diary	Forest L" Abbaye	25/11/1916	26/11/1916
War Diary	Capennes	27/11/1916	30/11/1916
Heading	6th Brigade. 2nd Division. 6th Brigade Machine Gun Company : December 1916.		
War Diary	Gapennes	01/12/1916	31/12/1916
War Diary	Gapennes	09/12/1916	20/12/1916
Heading	2nd Division 6th Infy Bde 6th Machine Gun Company Jan-Dec 1917.		
Heading	6th Brigade. 2nd Division. 6th Machine Gun Company January 1917.		
War Diary	Gapennes	01/01/1917	08/01/1917
War Diary	Grimont	09/01/1917	09/01/1917
War Diary	Puchevillers	11/01/1917	11/01/1917
War Diary	Aveluy	12/01/1917	19/01/1917
War Diary	2 Sections In Line 2 Section Wallace Huts.	20/01/1917	27/01/1917
War Diary	Bouzincourt	28/01/1917	31/01/1917
Heading	6th Brigade. 2nd Division. 6th Machine Gun Company : February 1917.		
War Diary	Bouzincourt	01/02/1917	05/02/1917
War Diary	Usna Hill	07/02/1917	13/02/1917
War Diary	Line	14/02/1917	15/02/1917
War Diary	Trenches	15/02/1917	16/02/1917
War Diary	Line	16/02/1917	23/02/1917
War Diary	Albert	23/02/1917	28/02/1917
Miscellaneous	6th Inf Bde.	04/02/1917	14/02/1917
War Diary	6th Inf. Bde	15/02/1917	15/02/1917
Miscellaneous Diagram etc	For The Operation I understand You Will Hare		
Miscellaneous	6th Inf Bde	11/02/1917	11/02/1917
Miscellaneous	To Be Manned by 5th Bde		
Miscellaneous	A Form. Messages And Signals.		
Miscellaneous	Messages		
Miscellaneous			
Miscellaneous	18 Anal M15625		
Miscellaneous	Headquarters, 2nd Division.	12/02/1917	12/02/1917
Heading	6th Brigade. 2nd Division. 6th Machine Gun Company : March 1917.		
War Diary	Albert	03/03/1917	03/03/1917
War Diary	Usna Hill	08/03/1917	08/03/1917
War Diary	Line	08/03/1917	20/03/1917
War Diary	Usna Hill	21/03/1917	21/03/1917
War Diary	Warloy. Billon	22/03/1917	22/03/1917
War Diary	La Vicogne	26/03/1917	26/03/1917
War Diary	Occoches	27/03/1917	27/03/1917
War Diary	Nuncq	28/03/1917	28/03/1917
War Diary	Monchy Cayeux	30/03/1917	31/03/1917

Miscellaneous	A Form. Messages And Signals.		
Miscellaneous	H Q 6th Inf 13th		
Miscellaneous	6th Infantry Brigade.	07/03/1917	07/03/1917
Miscellaneous Diagram etc	A Form. Messages And Signals.		
Miscellaneous	MW143	15/03/1917	15/03/1917
Miscellaneous	Oc 6 M 6 Coy	16/03/1917	16/03/1917
Heading	6th Brigade. 2nd Division. 6th Machine Gun Company : April 1917		
War Diary	Monchy-Cayeux	01/04/1917	01/04/1917
War Diary	Ourton	07/04/1917	07/04/1917
War Diary	Acq	10/04/1917	10/04/1917
War Diary	Roclincourt	11/04/1917	11/04/1917
War Diary	W of Bailleul	18/04/1917	27/04/1917
War Diary	Front of Oppy	28/04/1917	29/04/1917
War Diary	Ecurie	30/04/1917	30/04/1917
Miscellaneous	H.Q. 6 Inf. Brig.	27/04/1917	24/07/1917
Miscellaneous			
Miscellaneous	H.Q. 6 Inf Brig	24/04/1917	24/04/1917
Miscellaneous	Guns For Barrage	24/04/1917	24/04/1917
Miscellaneous	Disposition of Guns	26/04/1917	26/04/1917
Miscellaneous	H.Q. 6 Inf Brig		
Heading	6th Brigade. 2nd Division. 6th Machine Gun Company : May 1917.		
War Diary	Ecurie	01/05/1917	01/05/1917
War Diary	1/2 Coy Bray 1/2 Coy Line	02/05/1917	02/05/1917
War Diary	1/2 Coy Echrie 1/2coy Bray	02/05/1917	02/05/1917
War Diary	Bray	04/05/1917	14/05/1917
War Diary	Camblain	17/05/1917	17/05/1917
War Diary	Chatelain	18/05/1917	18/05/1917
War Diary	Roclincourt	25/05/1917	31/05/1917
Heading	6th Brigade. 2nd Division. 6th Machine Gun Company June 1917.		
War Diary	Roclincourt	01/06/1917	01/06/1917
War Diary	2 Section In Line	02/05/1917	02/05/1917
War Diary	HQs And 2 Sections Roclincourt Line	04/05/1917	06/05/1917
War Diary	Line	06/05/1917	14/05/1917
War Diary	Ecoivres	16/05/1917	19/05/1917
War Diary	Bethune	19/05/1917	19/05/1917
War Diary	Line	20/05/1917	30/05/1917
Heading	6th Brigade. 2nd Division. 6th Brigade Machine Gun Company : July 1917.		
War Diary	Givenchy Sector	01/07/1917	31/07/1917
Heading	6th Brigade. 2nd Division. 6th Machine Gun Company : August 1917.		
Miscellaneous	H.Q. 6th Inf Bde		
War Diary	Givenchy Sector	01/08/1917	31/08/1917
Heading	6th Brigade. 2nd Division. 6th Machine Gun Company : September 1917.		
War Diary	Givenchy Sector	01/09/1917	05/09/1917
War Diary	Annezin Transport At Gorge	06/09/1917	07/09/1917
War Diary	Annezin	08/09/1917	18/09/1917
War Diary	Givenchy Sector	19/09/1917	30/09/1917
Heading	6th Brigade. 2nd Division. 6th Machine Gun Company ; October 1917.		
War Diary	Givenchy Sector	30/09/1917	06/10/1917

War Diary	Bethune	06/10/1917	06/10/1917
War Diary	Hurionville	07/10/1917	31/10/1917
Diagram etc			
Miscellaneous	Training Frogramme For Week Ending Sunday		
Miscellaneous	6th Machine Gun Company		
Miscellaneous	Programme Of Having For Week Ending		
Diagram etc			
Heading	6th Brigade. 2nd Division. 6th Machine Gun Company : November 1917.		
War Diary	Hurionville	01/11/1917	01/11/1917
War Diary	Steenbecque	05/11/1917	05/11/1917
War Diary	Eecke Area	06/11/1917	06/11/1917
War Diary	Houtkerque Area	07/11/1917	24/11/1917
War Diary	Rocquigny Doignies	24/11/1917	28/11/1917
War Diary	Line	28/11/1917	30/11/1917
Miscellaneous	6th Machine Gun Company		
Heading	6th Brigade. 2nd Division. 6th Machine Gun Company ; December 1917.		
War Diary	Combrai Front Moeuvres Sector	01/12/1917	04/12/1917
War Diary	La Bucquiere	05/12/1917	08/12/1917
War Diary	Moeuvres Sector	09/12/1917	21/12/1917
War Diary	Velu Wood	21/12/1917	26/12/1917
War Diary	Moeuvres Sector	27/12/1917	31/12/1917
Miscellaneous	6th Machine Gun Company	06/12/1917	06/12/1917
Miscellaneous	B. G. C. 6th Infy Bde	07/12/1917	07/12/1917
Miscellaneous	6th Machine Gun Company		
Operation(al) Order(s)	6th Machine Gun Company Operation Order No M15	08/12/1917	08/12/1917
Miscellaneous	Relief Table 9/10 Dec 1917		
Operation(al) Order(s)	6th Machine Gun Company Operation Order No M6	26/12/1917	26/12/1917
Heading	2nd Division 6th Inf Bde No. 6 Machine Gun Coy. Jan-Feb 1918		
Diagram etc			
Heading	6th Brigade. 2nd Division. No. 6 Machine Gun Company January 1918.		
War Diary	Cambrai Front Moeuvres Sector	01/01/1918	03/01/1918
War Diary	Cambrai Front	03/01/1918	04/01/1918
War Diary	Racquigny	05/01/1918	23/01/1918
War Diary	Metz	24/01/1918	30/01/1918
War Diary	La Vacuerie Sector	31/01/1918	31/01/1918
Miscellaneous	6th Machine Gun Company		
Heading	6th Brigade. 2nd Division. Reorganised in March & Formed Part Of 2nd Divisional Machine Gun Battalion No. 6 Machine Gun Company February 1918.		
War Diary	La Vacquerie Sector	01/02/1918	28/02/1918
Operation(al) Order(s)	6th M.G. Coy. Operation Order No. VI	09/02/1918	09/02/1918
Operation(al) Order(s)	6th Machine Gun Company Operation Order No. 51		
Miscellaneous		02/03/1918	02/03/1918
Miscellaneous	Appendix A to accompany 6th M.G. Coy. O.O. No. 51		
Heading	2 Div 6 Inf Brigade-1/17 Royal Fusiliers. 1918 Feb To 1919 Feb. 6 Machine Gun Company. 1916 Jan To 1918 Feb.		

2 DIVISION

6 BRIGADE

17 R. FUSILIERS

1919 JAN - 1919 FEB

WAR DIARY
INTELLIGENCE SUMMARY

17th ROYAL FUSILIERS

39

Place	Date	Hour	Summary of Events and Information	Remarks
DÜREN	1919 JAN 1		Companies were at the disposal of their commanders for P.T., D.F. games Platoon Drill, any Educt. mcontry Duties. Classes were held at which instructors who were given on the following subjects, viz: Elementary Mechanics, Arithmetic and English. A football match was played against the 1st King's Regiment in the afternoon.	
	2		All Companies conducted under Company arrangements. A lecture was delivered by Major J.A.F. OZANNE on "AMERICA OF TO-DAY".	
	3		Companies were at the disposal of their commanders for P.T., Games, Close + Arms Drill. Teachers were received on instruction in Board Duties and the R.S.M. Educational classes were held - Elementary Arithmetic, English + Arithmetic. A Battalion parade was held on Brig. Drill Avenue. A football match was played during the afternoon v the 3rd Bn. LTH. gro.	
	4		Church, England and non conformist services were held which were well attended.	
	5		Companies were at the disposal of their commanders for B.F. Arms Sabiting Drill. Classes were held in English, Shorthand, Arithmetic + Elem. Mechanics. A football match was played during the afternoon v the R.A.F. - Result 2 goals to 1 in favour of the 17th R.Fus.	
	6		The Bn. was moved out of a Route march. The Bend attended. A football match was played against the 3rd Bn. M.G.C. during the afternoon - Result. The Battalion, 14 pts. 3rd Bn. M.G.C. nil.	

WAR DIARY or INTELLIGENCE SUMMARY

Army Form C. 2118.

Place	Date 1919 JAN	Hour	Summary of Events and Information	Remarks and references to Appendices
DÜREN	8		The Battalion carried on with the usual training. P.T. Games and Company Drill. Classes were held at which instruction was given in English, Shorthand and Elementary Mathematics. A lecture was delivered on Civics. A football match was played v 2nd SOUTH STAFFS. REGT. Result 8 goals to 2.	
	9		Company were at the disposal of their Commanders. Classes were held as in accordance with those of previous day. Company were at the disposal of their Commanders. Classes were being held at which instruction was given in English, History and Elementary Mathematics.	
	10		The Battalion carried on with the usual training. P.T. Games and Coy. Drill Classes were held - Arithmetic, Shorthand and Elementary Mathematics.	
	11		The Battalion trained by Coys. the Remainder in attendance. A football match was played v the 2nd DIV. Hd Qrs. Result - 5.0 in favour of 2nd DIV. H.Q. Church of England and Non-conformist represencee's were held. Wich were will attended. "A" Coy provided the Guard for the grinsing of the Railway.	
	12			
	13		Companies were at the disposal of their commanders for P.T. Arms Drill, Henry Drill and Gas March. B. Coy provided the Ridistry Joseph. Blences were held in Arithmetic, Shorthand, English and Elem. Mathematic. Lecture from E.J. THOMAS from the Battalion and took up the appointment of Coy. trainer.	
	14		The Battalion carried was at Ron. Kirch von ROLSDORF and LENDENSDORF KRAUTASM. The Railway Guard was furnished by "C" Coy. A football match is played against the 5th FIELD Coy R.E. - Resulting in a draw, 3 all. The drawing down arrived and who collected, with the necessary guard by 2Lt. H. ENNIS. The Battalion Butler were met at the Station by the Battalion Band an provided by D. Coy. New Coy Commander - The Railway Guard was provided by D. Coy.	

WAR DIARY
or
INTELLIGENCE SUMMARY.
(Erase heading not required.)

Army Form C. 2118.

Place	Date 1919 JAN	Hour	Summary of Events and Information	Remarks and references to Appendices
DÜREN	15		Classes were held in English, Shorthand, Arithmetic & Elem. Mathematics.	
	16		Companies were at the disposal of their commanders. Remainder of same were commenced. Classes were held – Elem. Mathematics Arithmetic & etc. The Railway Guard was provided by "A" Coy. A fatigue was supplied against the 10th D.C.L.I. Reunion so was the 11th Battalion F.S. mess!	
	17		Companies were at the disposal of their commanders. The Railway Guard was furnished by B. Coy. Classes were held in English, Shorthand, Arithmetic and Elem. Mathematics too. 2/Lieut. H.S. GILL and a draft of 78 O.R. joined the Battalion. 2/Lt. GILL was posted to "A" Coy. A guard of 1 & 8 was given to the Regimental Concert Party at DÜREN THEATRE which was conducted by the Commanding Officer. Companies	
	18		The New Staff of N.C.O's appointed by the Commanding Officer Companies were at the disposal of their commanders. Classes were held as before, and the Function of "Alleluia" march was played behind the 1st HINGS Recruiting... a draft – 1 all.	
	19		Church Parade, Service outside of recruits was never even held. The Railway Guard was supplied by D. Coy.	
	20		A Battalion parade was held and Brevet-Lt.Col. HICKMAN being on command. The Riches provided the 2nd Bn't Guard. 2/Lt. HICKMAN being on command. The Riches guard was supplied by "A" Coy. A Reg't F.S. that match was played against the 3rd Batt. M.G.C. – Result 12 hits to an favor of the Batt. Classes	
	21		A Battalion parade was held and Command Drill practiced. The Railway Guard was furnished by B. Coy. A draft of 25 O.R. joined the Battalion. The Batt. F.S. Football Battalion Cease/Confed. was held at 12.00. The Railway Guard was furnished by C. Coy. A further draft of	
	22			

Army Form C. 2118.

WAR DIARY
or
INTELLIGENCE SUMMARY.
(Erase heading not required.)

Instructions regarding War Diaries and Intelligence Summaries are contained in F. S. Regs., Part II. and the Staff Manual respectively. Title pages will be prepared in manuscript.

Place	Date 1919 JAN	Hour	Summary of Events and Information	Remarks and references to Appendices
DÜREN	23		The KING'S COLOUR was presented to the Battalion by the G.O.C 2nd DIV.	
	24		The Burying ground was provided by D. Coy. Bayonets at the shoulder at their funeral arranged by Pt. Arrangements carried out smoothly in the 30 yds range. The Railway guard was furnished by A Coy. Stretcher bearers in the Stand Ambulance English & Belum Mutinnes by Coy. Corporals at the moment of their internment. The Burying ground was furnished by O.R.H. Classes were held in the verbal subjects.	
	25		Church of England, R.C. & Non-conformist services were held.	
	26			
	27		Bayonets at the shoulder. The Burying guard was furnished by D. Coy. to A Coy for musketry. The Burying guard was furnished by D. C.M. Classes were held in the verbal subjects	
	28		Boys were at the shoulder of their Commander, the 30 yds range was allotted to A and D Coy. The Railway guard was furnished by A Coy. The Battalion paraded. The Burying guard was furnished by B Coy.	
	29		Strews were held in the verbal subjects. eg: Stretcher, English, Arithmetic and Elem Mechanics.	
	30		The Carparty at the shoulder of their Commander, rifle and attention by and to the tune of musketry. The Burying guard was supplied by C Coy. Classes were held in the verbal subjects.	
	31		The Expences of the discharge of their Commander Pt. B.F. Expenders English and Musketry. The Fly guard was supplied by D Coy. Classes were held in the verbal subjects.	

Army Form C. 2118.

WAR DIARY
or
INTELLIGENCE SUMMARY.
(Erase heading not required.)

January 1919

Place	Date	Hour	Summary of Events and Information	Remarks and references to Appendices
			RATION STRENGTH. 34 Offrs. 568 O'ranks	
			AWARDS	
			Capt. J. Spencer MM.	
			Lieut. Col. W.C. Smith D.S.O., M.C. — D.S.O. Bar to D.S.O. Gaz. 1/1/19.	1/1/19
			No. 1458 Sgt. E. White — D.C.M.	
			Lieut. Col. W.C. Smith D.S.O., M.C. — D.S.O.	
			Capt. J.H. Moir M.C. — D.S.O	
			MILITARY CROSS	
			Capt. J.G. Sword	
			L/C. Norrington MM.	
			Lieut. H.B.J. Rofe	
			2nd Lieut. F.G. Waters	
			" A. Easson	
			" F. Harris	
			D.C.M.	
			61690 CSM. W.J. Kerry MM. 672 L/C. D. Lowry MM.	
			13175 L/C. H.E. Harvey MM. 48510 Pte. Irvine MM.	
			M.S.M.	
			S/424 CQMS. Mitchell HG.	
			S/343 Sgt. A.H. Fox (deceased)	
				W.C. Smith Lieut Col
				Comdg 17th Royal Fus

Army Form C. 2118.

WAR DIARY
or
INTELLIGENCE SUMMARY.

17th ROYAL FUSILIERS

JR 40

39a

Place	Date 1919 FEB	Hour	Summary of Events and Information	Remarks and references to Appendices
DÜREN	1		Companies were at the disposal of their commanders. The Rubery Guard was provided by A Coy. Lecturers & Lecture givers received instructions as usual.	
	2		Church of England, Roman catholic and Nonconformist services were held at Düren. Guard was provided by B Coy.	
	3		Companies were at the disposal of their commanding officers. All men not in the 30 yds range to Musketry practice. The Rly guard was mounted by C Coy. Lectures held on the subjects continue to interest and Elementary Subjects. (The Battalion carried out a Route March in the morning where there still remain & B Cos.) The Rly Guard was provided by D Coy.	
	4			
	5		Companies were at the disposal of their commanders. Lectures & other employments were provided by A Coy. The Rly Guard was provided by A Coy. Lectures were held on the usual subjects.	
	6		On arrival at the disposal of their commanders the Rly guard was mounted by B Coy. Lectures were held on the usual subjects.	
	7		Coys were at the disposal of their commanders. The Rubery Guard was supplied by C Coy. Cold wet snow was held during the evening which was well attended by all ranks.	
	8		Coys were at the disposal of their commanders. As every day directly to lectures & platoon commanders. The Rubery guard was provided by D Coy. Lectures were held on the usual subjects.	

WAR DIARY or INTELLIGENCE SUMMARY

Army Form C. 2118.

Place	Date 1919 FEB	Hour	Summary of Events and Information	Remarks and references to Appendices
DÜREN	9		Church of England R.C. and Nonconformist services were held. The Divisional General was inspected by the Corps.	
	10		Conference held at the disposal of their commander for entertainment.	
	11		The Battalions entrained Billets in DÜREN and moved at 07.45. The Battalion entrained at DÜREN STATION and arrived at OPLADEN at 11.40. The Battalion and Hot meal was served. The Bn moved at 13.25 arriving at LEICHLINGEN at 14.30. Battalion Hd qr were established in the TANNENHOF HOTEL.	
LEICHLINGEN	12		Companies arms at the disposal of the Commander. The C.O. and staff all ranks	
	13		Coys were at the disposal of their commander for P.T. and Steady drill. Classes were held in Shorthand, Arithmetic, English & Elem. Mathmn.	
	14		The Battalion bathed at LEICHLINGEN SANATORIUM. men not so engaged were at the disposal of their Commanders.	
	15		A Battalion parade was held at which Battalion Drill was practised.	
	16		Church of England services were held in the LUTHEREN CHURCH, LEICHLINGEN	
	17		A Battalion musketry parade was held. of the Bayoneteers, experts (attending courses) passed to the 6th Division were in the ranks and inspected.	
	18		The Battalion carried out a route march. Refreshments were Bde HQ T Nd go 17th Royal Sussex was reported owing to influenza — Rank 5 grade 2 — to quarters of the Brigade.	

Army Form C. 2118.

WAR DIARY
or
INTELLIGENCE SUMMARY.
(Erase heading not required.)

Instructions regarding War Diaries and Intelligence Summaries are contained in F. S. Regs., Part II. and the Staff Manual respectively. Title pages will be prepared in manuscript.

Place	Date 1919 FEB	Hour	Summary of Events and Information	Remarks and references to Appendices
LEICHLINGEN	19	—	The Battalion Lectures. Classes were held in the several subjects. The Medical Officer lectured at men of "C" Coy.	
	20		Men were at the disposal of their Commander for Platoon or Section drill. The M.O. lectured the men of "D" Coy. Classes were held as the usual subjects.	
	21		Men were at the disposal of the Coy. Commander for P.T. arm and physical drill. The M.O. lectured the men of "A" Coy. Classes were held in the usual subjects.	
	22		Men were at the disposal of the Coy. Commanders for P.T. Bayonet & Arms drill etc. Lectures by Coy. Commanders. Coy. Schemes at Ruse & footballs Regimental Rugby at 2nd SH & Stephensmin Rugby at LANGENFELD. Rosub Regtl Rugby	
	23	1-1		
	24		Church of E. & R.C. that served were held at R. LUTHERAN CHURCH LEICHLINGEN & Battalion Orders Re-established. Command Drill. H.Q. Coy. Coys. Chaseman Adjutant & General subjects.	
	25		Coy. & Company Platoon were to march & were excellent. Men were employed in cleaning up equipment and were lectured by Platoon Commanders.	
	26		A Battalion Parade was held in full ceremonial order & attended by Battalion & Adjutant. Was followed by Battalion STUART in the Repetition in Infantry. Competitions were at the disposal of their Commanders. Classes were held in the usual subjects.	
	27			
	28		Men were at the disposal of their Coy Commanders for P.T. Fire orders & control, and Musketry. Platoon Commanders. Coy Commanders exercised their Coys...	

WAR DIARY
or
INTELLIGENCE SUMMARY.

Army Form C. 2118.

Place	Date	Hour	Summary of Events and Information	Remarks and references to Appendices
LEICHLINGEN	1919 FEB 28		To 2nd and 3rd Class Army Schools. The M.O. lectures the men engaged on the Transport and Telegraphs.	
			RATION STRENGTH 31 Offrs 508 O.Ranks	
			AWARDS	
			No 1129 Sgt. SPENCER G.M. ⎫	
			57464 C.Q.M.S. A. J. NEWMAN ⎬ M.M.	
			2064 " B. PIDDOCK ⎭	
			1636 L/C. BARROW H.G. Decoration Militaire (Belgian)	

H.C. Small Lieut. Col.
Cmdg. 17th Royal Fusiliers

2ND DIVISION
6TH INFY BDE

1-17TH BATTALION
ROYAL FUSILIERS
FEB - DEC 1918

FROM 5 BDE 2 DV

6th Brigade.
2nd Division.

Battalion came from 5th Brigade 6.2.18.

1/17th BATTALION

ROYAL FUSILIERS

FEBRUARY 1918.

Army Form C. 2118.

17th ROYAL FUSILIERS

WAR DIARY
or
INTELLIGENCE SUMMARY.

Place	Date	Hour	Summary of Events and Information	Remarks and references to Appendices
Around Fins METZ	7.7.18		LARGE working parties employed on new Transport lines at FINS, and in burying cables. Battn. allotted Battalion at METZ. Lectures by O.C. Companies on Trend Warfare.	
"	7.7.18	—	**Battalion Sports.** In connection with the sports a marching competition by selected parties from companies took place in the morning. This included an inspection by Brigadier Gen. Bullen-Smith CB. G.S.O. This was won by "C" Company. The Brigadier also judged a Company competition in the best turned out privates from the alarm actions. All Companies produced smart appearing men, including some nice delicacies. The Brigadier who expressed his high approval pronounced D & B Company decidedly the best, and their cooks shared the prize.	
		1:30	In the afternoon a sports programme of 16 events, including 5 open events & a horse jumping competition, was carried out. The Regimental Band played selections throughout the afternoon, & the twenty included events drew a number of spectators from all over the division. The Brigadier commanded the 5th Infantry Brigade, who was present thought trust, consented to distribute the prizes.	28.W.

Army Form C. 2118

WAR DIARY
or
INTELLIGENCE SUMMARY. 17th ROYAL FUSILIERS

(Erase heading not required.)

Place	Date	Hour	Summary of Events and Information	Remarks and references to Appendices
Divisional Reserve SOUZEAUCOURT METZ	Feb 3	1:20 am 10:30 AM	A voluntary church parade was held - B Company billet	
		11 am	The G.O.C. 5th INFANTRY Brigade inspected the Battalion on the Sports ground. He informed us that it was the last time he would address the 17th Royal Fusiliers as this Brigade, as the breaking up of certain units in the Army necessitated our transfer as a Battalion to the 6th Brigade. He spoke of the very high esteem he felt for the battalion, and expressed gratitude to all ranks for the way they had supported him while under his command. He was greatly moved at parting with the 17th Royal Fusiliers, & his good wishes either of the 5th Infantry Brigade would always be with us.	
			The Divisional Commander recognised the hardships and briefly expressed his regret at the circumstances that necessitated this change of Brigades.	
		5:30 pm	Battalion working party employed wiring LINCOLN RESERVE trench from R.17.C.7.3. to R.24.C.0.5.	
	Feb 4th		Training continued. Company officers paraded in the morning. Adjutants paraded for all NCOs in the afternoon.	

Army Form C. 2118.

WAR DIARY
or
INTELLIGENCE SUMMARY. 17th ROYAL FUSILIERS
(Erase heading not required.)

Place	Date	Hour	Summary of Events and Information	Remarks and references to Appendices
R45/c D 2 LA VACQUERIE & METZ	July 5th	10:00am	Training continued under Coy Commanders. In the evening an excellent concert in the Barn at the Pont Occupied by "A" & "B" Coys.	Sgn
"	July 6		The returns proves on the command of the S.O.C. 6th Infantry Brigade (Brigadier General WALSH). The arrival of the Belgian Croix-de-Guerre to 575 R.Q.M.S. (A/R.S.M.) BRUNTON. T.	Sgn
			Was approved by H.M. the King.	
"			S.O.C. Battn left METZ and moved to the front line (Left Bn, Left Brigade) LA VACQUERIE (left) Relieving the 1st KINGS (LIVERPOOL) Regt (R10 a 50.75 — R9 b 50.15) "D" Coy on left, "C" Coy on right, "A" Coy Support "B" Coy in reserve at Battn HQ (R 3. 5.75. 10) (L satisfactory Relief was carried out without casualties.	
LA VACQUERIE (left)	July 7	8.30pm	Dark bombs carried up and posts & trenches improved.	Sgn
"			Work continued improving front line. Fair communications established between B.H.Q.—SORREY Rd, and Soup Kitchen Posts. New A.I.D. Post established at B.H.Q.—SORREY Rd, also Soup Kitchen. Hot drinks 4 hours every 24 hours carried to front line.	

Army Form C. 2118

WAR DIARY
or
INTELLIGENCE SUMMARY.

17th R. NORTH'd FUSILIERS

(Erase heading not required.)

Instructions regarding War Diaries and Intelligence Summaries are contained in F.S. Regs., Part II. and the Staff Manual respectively. Title pages will be prepared in manuscript.

Place	Date	Hour	Summary of Events and Information	Remarks and references to Appendices
LA VACQUERIE (Left)	Feb 14th		Mounted post built in VICTORY LANE (R.9.b.75.15) gives excellent observation over BONAVIS Ridge. General situation quiet. Enemy artillery	
	Feb 15th		Activity amounts to much above Bn. normal by 1st Royal Liverpool Regt. & moved into support on HIGHLAND RIDGE. Bn. HQ (R.7.d.6.35). Lorries brought up to VILLERS PLOUICH.	
LA VACQUERIE (Right) Support	Feb 16th		Working parties found for ROBIN TRENCH (R.9.b.4.2 – R.9.b.9.8).	
	Feb 17th		Working parties found noon 10th inst.	
	Feb 18th		Battn. relieved the 1st Kings (Liverpool) Regt. in Left Brigade Sector (Rgtl Disposn R.10.a.5.8). B by in centre A by on right "D" coy in support by the with 2 Platoons (2 Lt. Staffordshire Regt) attached for work and technical purposes. Bn. H.Q. into in SURREY RD. (R.4.b.30.13). A further company & 2 S. Staffordshire Regt. for technical reasons were attached to the Battn. into established in SURREY RD. Relief carried out very promptly without casualties.	
LA VACQUERIE Left	Feb 18th		Work improving front line trenches, ROBIN Trench & VICTORY LANE. Both Woytho had approaches & some reference by SAPPING Platoons. Enemy very active. Four Germans killed & wounded by them.	

A.F.O.P.2 Wt.W.128 9/17 1293 750,000 1/17. D. D. & L. Ltd. Forms/C2118/14.

Army Form C. 2118.

WAR DIARY
or
INTELLIGENCE SUMMARY. 17th ROYAL FUSILIERS
(Erase heading not required.)

Instructions regarding War Diaries and Intelligence Summaries are contained in F.S. Regs., Part II. and the Staff Manual respectively. Title pages will be prepared in manuscript.

Place	Date	Hour	Summary of Events and Information	Remarks and references to Appendices
LAVACQUERIE (X21) 57cSW2	Feb 14		Movement of enemy considerably less in front system owing to snipers activity. Considerable movement of enemy small parties observed in our front line of LAVACQUERIE from our Coy OP.	See [appx]
		10.15	Left company snipers shooting to harrassment of garrison snipers.	
		11.15	ARTILLERY retaliation called for, registration of shells series. Wiring carried out by all three companies in front line.	
	Feb 15		SAPPING Platoon found wiring party for NAVAL SUPPORT Trench in afternoon. A number of shells circled by "E" Company occupying NAVAL SUPPORT. Both it is believed to Snr & Stokes Shrap Regt and enemy 4.2 bullets nr METZ. A fine night and moonlight enabled a complete with relief of garrison to be carried out. They occupied their new quarters by 10 p.m.	See [appx]
METZ	Feb 16		Cleaning up. Repair & clothes requirement. 1500 Company inspected by C.O. METZ. 9d Commanding officer received the following letter from the Gen. Com. 2 Bn. "I am proud to see that Cpl STONE who was killed in the German attack of 30th November 1917 when the 17th Btn Royal Fusiliers, forming to one of my Bns has been awarded the VICTORIA CROSS. I congratulate the Regt on the great honour which has been bestowed upon it, and on having so gallant particularly. A.H.[?] G. Gerelé." Signed C.E. PEREIRA Major Gen. comd. 2 Div.	

WAR DIARY
INTELLIGENCE SUMMARY. 1/7 Batt⁴ R.S war F05/2/1/E7/5

Army Form C. 2118.

(Erase heading not required.)

Place	Date	Hour	Summary of Events and Information	Remarks and references to Appendices
METZ	15/7/15	7pm 10pm	Metz area bombed by enemy aircraft.	J.M.
	17th		Usual Sunday service. Heavily bombed by aircraft at night, a few bombs landing outside Canteen. Several gas shells thrown into the village. A draft of 30 O.R. arrived — nearly all of 17th Batt⁴ men.	J.M.
Support line VILLERS PLOUICH	18th		New draft 130 O.R. arrived 10 P.M. having been d/f in railway trucks all night, delayed by their engine on account of bombing raid. Marched to Support Line and relieved 2nd South Staffs: Trench strength of companies now 100 O.R.	
	19th		Gas S.O.S. Working parties to front line etc daily.	J.M.
	20th		A direct hit on shelter in Village ("A" Coy) will gas shell. Four men evacuated to hospital suffering from mustard gas poisoning. Six men not on working party returning late took their equipment to another billet but were affected by the gas through following day, and evacuated to hospital the following day.	J.M.
	21st		All London papers full of little description of battle fought by the 2/?	J.M.

Army Form C. 2118.

WAR DIARY
or
INTELLIGENCE SUMMARY. 17th (S) Batt: R.W. Fusiliers

(Erase heading not required.)

Instructions regarding War Diaries and Intelligence Summaries are contained in F. S. Regs., Part II. and the Staff Manual respectively. Title pages will be prepared in manuscript.

Place	Date	Hour	Summary of Events and Information	Remarks and references to Appendices
	21st		Division at BOURLON WOOD giving particular mention of this battalion, photographs of Captain S. & N.E. etc.	See
FRONTLINE LAVACQUERIE CENTER	22nd		Relieved 1st King's Regiment. Frontage 1900x.	See
	23rd		In early morning our extreme right (NEPTUNE SAP) bombarded by three batteries. Punishment N.O.I. asked for and obtained at 20 o'clock. We suffered two casualties wounded. During the night a deserter came over from the 80th Regiment 211th Div. This Division has come from the Russian front and mostly comprises ALSATIANS. Prisoner states he does not consider that there will be an attack on this front.	See
	24th		Much good work done by Battalion and practically whole system duck-boarded, latrines made etc.	See
	25th		Quiet.	
	26th		Bombardment by T.M.'s and S.p.S. There dug-out entrance blown	See

Army Form C. 2118.

WAR DIARY
or
INTELLIGENCE SUMMARY. 17th ROYAL FUSILIERS
(Erase heading not required.)

Place	Date	Hour	Summary of Events and Information	Remarks and references to Appendices
	26th		Mr. Stephen was eventually cut. We rebuilt with Punishment No II, but the front was very much tilt off gas. We had few casualties. Relieved by 2nd South Staffs and marched to tent camp outside METZ.	5pm 5pm
METZ	27th		Large working parties. Weather very bad. Lecture by Capt Glasson on salvage. Inspection of staffs, kit inspection and baths.	
TENT CAMP	28th		Lt. Col S.V.P. WESTON returns from leave and resumes command. Football against 2nd Coy. Pioneers L.N.L.R. Companies at disposal of Coy. Commanders.	5pm

Following Officers joined the Battalion during the month:-
2nd Lts. H.W. FISH. T.H. BACON. A.W. WOODCOCK. G. COTTON. C. FORD. J. SWORD
R.j. and Capt: J. AYLMER.
Ration strength 26 — 638. French strength 23 — 528.
Casualties. 2/Lt A Kidd. Wounded not passed 39 O.R.

[signature]
17th R. Fus.

(2)

LEWIS GUNS 7	Lewis Guns will go up under Sgt. BEALE and will be picked up by companies at R.8.c.95.70.
ADVANCE PARTY 8	2 Lieut. H.M. HART, the R.S.M., Sgt. GRIMES M.M., and 1 Sgt. per Coy will go up in advance to take over Trench Stores etc. Receipts will be given and duplicates sent to Battn. Hqrs by 9 a.m. 7th inst. 2 Lieut. HART will take over all work in progress, O.P.s and Snipers Posts.
Hq. Qr. PARTY 9	2 Lieut. R.L. PELTON will be in charge of the Hd. Qr. Party.
PACKS & BLANKETS 10	Packs and blankets will be outside Coy Hqrs. by 9 a.m.
OFFICERS VALISES 11	Officers' valises will be outside Coy. Hqrs. by 2 pm.
OFF. TRENCH KITS MESS GEAR 12	Officers' trench kits and mess gear will be stacked at Battn. Hqrs. by 3 pm.
TRANSPORT 13	The Quartermaster will arrange for all necessary transport.
WATER 14	One Water Cart, filled, will come up nightly, and in addition 40 petrol tins will be taken up.
Fd. CONTAINER PACKS 15	All Food Container Packs will be taken up.
COOKING ARRANGEMENTS 16	Four Sawyer Stoves are at R.8.b.3.9. and Sgt. SPENCER will arrange for 1 Cook per Coy. to go up with the battalion. Cooking arrangements will be the same as during the last tour.
RATIONS 17	Rations will be taken up by limber to R.8.c.95.70 and the usual Ration Parties will report to the R.S.M. @ 7.30 pm. nightly.
SGT. MATTOCKS 18	Sgt. MATTOCKS will remain at the Transport with "B" Coys. Lewis gun and he will continue the course of instruction with the u/m:-

No. 68905 Pte. LOVEDAY. R "A" Coy   No. 69546 Pte. ANDERSON R.P. "B" Coy
" 51789 " SADLER D "   " 69638 " PETERS E.A. "
" 81279 " WILKINS C "C" Coy   " 69667 " VINCENT F. "D" Coy
" 81265 " BELL G "   " 69640 " PEARLE W.S. "

The "B" Coys. Lewis gun team will return to the Company tomorrow morning.

SAPPING PLATOON 19	The Sapping Platoon will remain at the Transport Lines.

Opp. 16

SECRET.
OPERATION ORDER No. 10.
BY
MAJOR S.J.M. HOLE M.C.
Commanding 17TH Royal Fusiliers

Reference GOUZEAUCOURT 1/20,000

TRANSFER 1 The 17TH ROYAL FUSILIERS is transferred to the 6TH INF. BDE. as from the 6TH inst.

RELIEF 2 The Battalion will evacuate billets and will relieve the 1ST KINGS LIVERPOOLS in the LEFT SUB-SECTOR on the night 6TH/7TH. Inter-company boundary R.10.c.15.85.
Companies will be disposed as follows:—

"D" Coy. 17TH R.F. relieves "A" Coy. 1ST KINGS on the LEFT. Coy. Hqrs. R.10.a.0.5
"C"   "   "   "   "   "B" "   "   "   "   " "RIGHT.   "   " R.9.d.70.80
"A"   "   "   "   "   "C" "   "   "   "   " SUPPORT. "   " R.9.b.75.15
"B"   "   "   "   "   "D" "   "   "   "   " RESERVE   "   " R.8.b.8.1

BATTN. HQRS. at R.8.b.8.1.
"C" & "D" Coys. will establish combined Posts on their respective flanks.

GUIDES 3 The order of relief will be as follows:— "D", "C", "A", "B", Hq. Qrs. and guides will be at R.8.b.3.8 at 6.30 pm as follows:—
"D" Coy. L9(L.G.) L8. L7(L.G.) L6. L5. L4(L.G.) L3. L2(L.G.) L1.
"C"   " R5a(L.G.) R5. R.4a(L.G.) R.4. R.3b. R.3a(L.G.) R.3. R.2a(L.G.) R.2. R.1.
"A"   " 2 guides.
"B"   " 2   "
One guide for Aid Post and Relay Post in WOOD AVENUE.

RELAY POST 4 Sgt. GRIMES M.M. will detail 1 N.C.O, 3 Signallers and 4 Runners to man the Relay Post.

ROUTE 5 Companies will move off at 10 mins. interval commencing at 4.15 pm. Order of March:— "D", "C", "A", "B", Hd. Qrs. ROUTE Overland Track crossing BEAUCAMP – VILLERS PLOUICH ROAD Q.18.b.8.8 – SUPPORT BATTN. SECTOR R.7.d – ROAD in R.8c – R.8.b.3.8.

ATTACHMENT 6 "B" Coy. will detail 1 Lewis gun section and 1 Rifle section to be attached to "A" Coy. These 2 sections will march up with "B"

BILLETS 20	Billets will be left scrupulously clean, and "Billets Clean" certificates rendered to Ord. Room.
WARNING 21	No troops will cross the TRESCAULT — HERMIES ROAD before 5.15 pm.
TRENCH FOOT PRECAUTIONS 22	Coy. Commanders will pay great attention to the rubbing of feet, and all precautions will be taken to avoid Trench Feet.
RELIEF COMPLETE 23	Code Word for relief complete "MESS." ACKNOWLEDGE.

Issued at 10 pm.   (Sgd) A.C. Felton 2/Lieut.
                                                             a/Adjt.

Copies to:—
- No 1. 6th Inf. Bde. Hqrs.
- " 2. 1st Kings. Regt.
- " 3. 2nd S. Staffs.
- " 4. "A" Coy
- " 5. "B" "
- " 6. "C" "
- " 7. "D" "
- " 8. Quartermaster.
- " 9. R.S.M.
- " 10. File.
- " 11. War Diary.

SECRET

OPERATION ORDER No. 11.
BY
Major S.J.M. Hole. M.C.
Commanding 17th Royal Fusiliers

Reference LA VACQUERIE Map 1/10,000 & Air Photo of R.10.a.

1. The following minor operation will be undertaken tonight on the Left Sub-sector.

DETAIL OF PARTY. 'D' Coy will detail a Fighting Patrol of 3 N.C.Os and 12 men under command of Capt. BEAUFORD. The patrol will be formed into 3 groups of 1 N.C.O and 4 men each. Capt. BEAUFORD will accompany the centre party.

OBJECT OF PATROL. The object of the patrol is to ascertain if the trench running from R.10.a.75.45. to SUNKEN ROAD at R.10.a.45.37 is occupied and if so, to kill the enemy, capture prisoners, obtain identifications and destroy dug-outs.

EQUIPMENT. Each other rank will be equipped with rifle with bayonet fixed, 10 rounds in magazine, 40 rounds in tunic pocket & 4 Mills bombs. In addition 20 P. Bombs will be distributed between the patrol.

MODE OF APPROACH. The patrol will leave the front line at the point where light railway touches it at R.10.a.4.5. and will move along the railway at 15 yards interval between groups for a distance of 50 yards. The party will then half right turn & will line up parallel with the trench, they will get up as close and noiselessly as possible and then rush the trench. The bayonet will be used as far as possible.

MODE OF WITHDRAWAL. If the SUNKEN ROAD running through R.10.a. is unoccupied, the withdrawal will be effected through it, otherwise the patrol will withdraw by the same route as going in.

LEWIS GUN CO-OPERATION. Lewis Guns on both flanks will engage known Machine Guns in the event of the latter opening fire.

WOUNDED. 'D' Coy will have a Stretcher Bearer party ready to effect the removal of any wounded if necessary.

REPORTING POINT. O.C. 'D' Coy will arrange for all ranks to report to his Hd Qrs on return from the patrol. Prisoners, identifications etc to be sent to Batt. Hd Qrs at once.

(2)

IDENTIFICATION. All identification will be removed from all ranks taking part in the patrol and men should be warned that in the event of being captured, they can only be required to give their name and rank.

DETAIL. On the return of the patrol it will be accommodated for the night at Batt. Hd. Qrs and a hot meal provided.

CODE WORD. The following code will be employed:—

Trench unoccupied	TINKER
Trench occupied, garrison overcome, and identifications procured	TAILOR
Patrol unable to reach objective	SOLDIER
Dug-outs destroyed	SAILOR

ZERO. Zero hour will be 11. p.m.

Acknowledge.

(Sgd) A Whitley Lavarack
Major for O.C.

7/2/18.

Issued to
6th Inf. Bde.
9th Cheshire Regt.
2nd South Staff.
O.C. 'D' Coy.
O.C. 'C' Coy (for information)
File.

"O" Form.
MESSAGES AND SIGNALS.

Army Form C. 2123.
(In books of 100.)

No. of Message ....

Prefix......Code.......Words.......	Received	Sent, or sent out	Office Stamp.
£ s. d.	From..................	At.................m.	
Charges to collect	By....................	To....................	
Service Instructions.		By....................	

Handed in at................ Office.........m. Received ....m.

TO

*Sender's Number	Day of Month	In reply to Number	A A A
R51			
TINKER			

FROM CK 3

PLACE & TIME

*This line should be erased if not required.

OPERATION ORDER No. 12.
BY
MAJOR. S.J.M. HOLE. M.C.
Commanding 17th Royal Fusiliers

SECRET

Reference Map LA VACQUERIE 1/10,000.

RELIEF.   The Battn will be relieved from the front line on the
I   evening of the 9th/10th by the 1st KINGS REGT. & on completion of relief will move into the Support area R.7.c. and d. at present occupied by the 1st KINGS.

DETAIL   Coys will be relieved as follows:—
II

'D' Coy. 17th R.F. will be relieved by 'C' Coy. 1st KINGS.
'C'   "   "   "   "   "   'D'   "   "
'A'   "   "   "   "   "   (2 platoons) 'A'   "   "
'B'   "   "   "   "   "   (2 platoons and drums) 'A'   "   "
H.Q.   "   "   "   "   "   H.Q.

NOTE Each Front Line Coy. of the 1st KINGS will have 1 platoon in VICTORY LANE.

GUIDES will not be required. Relief will commence about 6.30 pm. On completion of the relief, Coys will move independently to the Support area and will take over the dispositions they held on the previous occasion, with the exception of 'A' Coy. who will take over accommodation from 'C' Coy. 1st KINGS.

ADVANCE   2nd Lieut. FELTON, R.S.M., + 1 N.C.O. + 1 man per Coy. will report to
PARTY.   present Hd Qrs of 1st KINGS at 2 pm tomorrow to take over
III   accommodation, stores, etc.

COOKERS.   The Quartermaster will arrange for the Cookers to come up to
IV   the Support area + for a hot meal to be ready for all ranks on arrival after relief.

RATIONS.   Rations will be delivered in the Support area along with the
V   Cookers and will occupy the position previously held.

TRANSPORT   The Quartermaster will arrange for the removal of the WATER
VI   CART + for the Ration limbers, after dumping rations to come along and collect Officers French Kits, Mess Gear, Lewis Guns and Magazines.

OFFICERS   All Officers Kits, Mess Gear, etc will be dumped at the
KITS.   present Ration Dump by 6.30. pm.
VII

(2)

LEWIS GUNS — VIII
Lewis Guns and Ammunition will be dumped at present Ration Dump by Coys on their way out.

WATER TINS AND FOOD CONTAINER PACKS — IX
All Petrol Tins taken over will be handed over and all Food Container Packs will be taken out by the Battn.

WARNING — X
No movement is allowed in the Support area above ground by daylight & the police have been ordered to take the names of any officers or other ranks not complying with this order. All names being sent to Divl. Hd Qrs for disciplinary action.

TRENCH STORES — XI
Trench Stores will be handed over, receipts obtained and duplicates sent to Orderly Room by 10.am on the 10th inst.

WORK — XII
The Intelligence Officer will hand over all work in progress, dispositions, O.Ps, Maps, Aeroplane Photos, etc & obtain receipts for same.

CODE — XIII
Code word for relief complete "GREAT"
     "   "   arrival in new area "BRITAIN."
Acknowledge by wire.

(Sgd) A. Shirley Lavarack
Major for O.C.

8-2-18.

Issued to
6th Inf. Bde.
1st King Regt.
O.C. 'A' Coy.
  "   'B' "
  "   'C' "
  "   'D' "
Quartermaster
R.S.M.
File.

SECRET

OPERATION ORDER No. 13
BY
MAJOR S.J.M. HOLE M.C.
Commanding 17th Royal Fusiliers

Reference Map. LA VACQUERIE 1/10,000
and 6th Inf. Bde. Order No. 347.

RELIEF
I
The 17th Royal Fusiliers will relieve the 1st KINGS REGt. on the Front Line of the Left Bde. Sector on the night of 12th/13th and on completion of relief, dispositions will be as follows:—
"B" Coy 17. R.F. on the Right relieving "B" Coy 1st KINGS.
"A" " " " " Centre " "C" " "
"D" " " " " Left " "D" " "
"C" " " " in SUPPORT with 1 Platoon in VICTORY LANE relieving Platoon of "C" and "D" Coys 1st KINGS, 1 Lewis Gun Section in Post 30, 1 Rifle Section in Post 29 (both in WELSH SUPPORT) and the balance of Coy in NAVAL RESERVE relieving "A" Coy. 1st KINGS

BOUNDARIES
II
Inter-Company Boundaries will be as follows:—
Right Inter-Company Boundary — R.q.d.4.3.
Left " " " — R.10.a.05.00.
Battalion Boundaries will be R.15.a.8.8. on the RIGHT and R.10.a.4.8. on the LEFT.
Coys will move off as follows:— "D","A","B","C" & Hd.Qrs commencing at 6.30 p.m.

VICTORY LANE PLATOON
III
The Platoon in VICTORY LANE will have permanent posts at R.q.b.50.00. and R.q.b.8.5. which will be held to the last.

2ND S. STAFFS
IV
1 Coy of the 2nd S. STAFFS will be located in VICTORY LANE and will be under O.C. 17th R.F. for work and tactical purposes 2 Platoons of 2nd S. STAFFS will be located at BATT. H.Q. and will be under O.C. 17th R.F. for tactical purposes only, these detachments will wire (in position) by code word "STAFF."

LEWIS GUNS
V
Lewis Guns and Ammunition will be carried into the line.

OFFICERS KITS
VI
Officers Kits and Mess Gear will be carried over by hand.

TRENCH STORES
VII
All Trench Stores will be taken over, receipts given and duplicates handed to Orderly Room by 10 am on the 13th.

(2)

TRENCH STORES IN SUPPORT VIII.	All Trench Stores here will be handed over to 2nd S. Staffs and receipts obtained which will be rendered to Orderly Room by 10 am. on the 13th.
DEFENCE SCHEME IX	Defence Schemes, Maps, Sketches and Work in progress will be taken over by the Intelligence Officer.
DEFENCE SCHEME IN SUPPORT X	All Defence Schemes, Maps, Sketches and Work in progress will be handed over to the 2nd S. Staffs & receipts obtained.
RATIONS & WATER XI.	The Quartermaster will make the usual arrangements for rations and water. Coys will furnish their own ration and hot food parties
HOT FOOD. XII.	Arrangements for hot food will be the same as during the previous tour.
DISPOSITIONS. XIII	Coys will forward to Orderly Room by 10 am on the 13th a sketch map, giving their dispositions.
ADVANCE PARTY XIV	The R.S.M., Sjt. Gaines and 1 N.C.O. per Coy will go over in advance and take over Trench Stores, Work, etc.
RELIEF COMPLETE XV	Code word for relief complete "FORD". Acknowledge by wire.

(Sgd) A Whitley Lavarack.
Major for O.C.

Issued at 9. pm
to
6th Inf. Bde.
1st Kings
2nd S. Staffs
O.C. "A" Coy
  " "B" "
  " "C" "
  " "D" "
Quartermaster
R. S. M.
File.
War Diary.

SECRET

AMENDMENT No 1
TO
OPERATION ORDER No. 13
BY
MAJOR S. J. M. HOLE M.C.
Commanding 17th Royal Fusiliers.

Reference Map LA VACQUERIE 1/10000
and 6th INF. BDE. ORDER No. 347

RELIEF.
I.
Para 1 is amended as follows:—
"B" Coy 17th R.F. will take over from "B" Coy 1st KING'S from R.g.d.25.40.(C.T. exclusive) to R.g.b.50.00. Coy. H.Q at R.g.d.75.85.
"C" Coy. 1 platoon in NAVAL RESERVE (NORTHERN END) with 1 post S. of road R.g.c.65.60. and 1 platoon in VICTORY LANE (relieving supporting platoons of "C" and "D" 1st KING'S.)
"A" Coy. as per O.O. No.13, but with Coy. H.Q. at R.g.d.90.75.

BOUNDARIES.
II.
Boundaries are altered as follows:—
Right Battn. Boundary R.g.d.25.40.(C.T. exclusive) thence westwards to junction of FARM AVE. and SURREY ROAD, thence to junction NEWPORT AVE. and SURREY ROAD.
Right Inter-Coy. Boundary R.g.b.50.00.
Left   "   "   "   as per O.O. No.13.
Left Battn. Boundary   "   "   "   "

VICTORY LANE PLATOON.
III.
This para. is cancelled.

(Sgd) A. Whitley Lavarack,
Major for O.C.

Issued at 2-30 p.m.
To:—
All recipients of O.O. No.13.

SECRET.   OPERATION ORDER No. 15
                     BY
            MAJOR S.J.M. HOLE M.C.
            Commanding 17th Royal Fusiliers.

Reference Sheet LA VACQUERIE 1/10,000   4/2/18.

RELIEF.   The Battalion will be relieved in the front line on the night 15th/16th
   I.   by the 2nd S. STAFFS REGT. and on completion of relief Companies will
            march independently to billets in METZ, at present occupied
            by 1st KING'S REGT.

DETAIL.   "B" Coy. 17th R.F. will be relieved by "B" Coy. 2nd S. STAFFS REGT.
   II.   "A"   "   "   "   "   "   "   "   "C"   "   "   "   "   "
            "D"   "   "   "   "   "   "   "   "D"   "   "   "   "   "
                                                                 Overflow of "B" Coy. 2nd S. STAFFS. in NAVAL
                                                                                                    RESERVE.
            "C" Coy. {   "   "   "   "   "   "   "   "C"   "   "   "   " in ROBIN
                                                                                    TRENCH S.
                         "   "   "   "   "   "   "   "D"   "   "   "   " in ROBIN
                                                                                    TRENCH N.

            Battn. H.Q. 17th R.F. will be relieved by Battn. H.Q. 2nd S. STAFFS REGT.
            "A" Coy. 2nd S. STAFFS REGT. will remain in its present position in
            VICTORY LANE.

GUIDES   Guides will be furnished as follows:-
  III.   "A" "B" & "D" Coys. 17th R.F.   1 guide per post numbered as per post.
            "C" Coy. 17th R.F.   1 guide for NAVAL RESERVE.
                                            1   "   " ROBIN TRENCH SOUTH.
                                            1   "   "   "   "   NORTH.
            Signallers   1   "   " RELAY POST.
            Rendezvous for all guides EXCEPT "B" Coy. 17th R.F. junction of NEPHEW
            DUMP with Road R.8.b.5.9.
            "B" Coy. guides will rendezvous at S.E. end of Ravine R.14.b.2.7.
            Hour of rendezvous for all guides will be wired to Coys. tomorrow.
            On completion of relief "B" Coy. will march out via Ravine R.14.b.2.7.

LEWIS GUNS. Lewis Guns & Ammunition will be dumped at NEPHEW DUMP
   IV.   by Coys. on their way out, EXCEPT "B" Coy. who will dump their
            guns under a N.C.O. on road in R.8.c.6.4.

OFFICERS' KITS. Officers' Kits & Mess gear will be dumped at NEPHEW DUMP.
    V.
TRENCH STORES. Trench stores will be handed over on relief and receipts
    VI.   obtained will be submitted to O. Room by 10 am 16th inst.

DEFENCE SCHEME. VII.	Defence Schemes & maps will be handed over by Intelligence Officer.
PETROL TINS ETC. VIII.	All petrol tins & hot food containers surplus to Trench Stores will be taken out of the line.
BILLETS. IX.	The Quartermaster will take over the billets in METZ & arrange for H.Q. & Coy. guides to be at X roads by Bde. Hd. Qrs.
HOT MEAL. X.	The Quartermaster will arrange for a hot meal for all ranks on arrival in billets.
PACKS & BLANKETS. XI.	The Quartermaster will arrange for packs & blankets to be ready in billets on arrival of troops.
OFFICERS' VALISES. XII.	Officers' valises to be ready at Battn. & Coy. Hd. Qrs' on arrival.
SALVAGE. XIII.	All possible salvage will be brought out on relief & dumped at NEPHEW DUMP.
TRANSPORT. XIV.	The Quartermaster will arrange for all necessary transport.
CODE WORD. XV.	Code word for relief complete "THANKS".

Acknowledge.

Issued at 7 p.m.

(Sgd.) A. Whitley Lavarack.
Major for O.C.

To:-
6th Inf. Bde.
1st King's Regt.
2nd S. Staffs Regt.
24th R.Fus. (For information).
O.C. "A" Coy.
  " "B" "
  " "C" "
  " "D" "
Quartermaster.
R.S.M.
File.
War Diary.

SECRET.

OPERATION ORDER Nº 16.
BY
MAJOR S.J.M. HOLE M.C.
Commanding 17th Royal Fusiliers

17/2/18

Ref: Map LA VACQUERIE 1/10,000 & B.O.O. 349.

RELIEF. I
The Battalion will evacuate billets tomorrow and will relieve the 1st Kings Regt in the Support area. Coys will move off in the following order A, B, C, D, Hd Qrs, commencing at 4.30 pm.

DETAIL II
Coys will take over the same positions as previously occupied. "C" Coy will have 1 Officer & half Company in SURREY ROAD. Front Line Battn. Hd Qrs.

ADVANCE PARTY. III
2nd Lieut HART, R.S.M., and 1 N.C.O. per Coy. will go up in advance and take over Trench Stores, etc.

A.A. POSITIONS IV
"A" & "B" Coys will each find 1 Lewis Gun & team to relieve teams of 1st Kings at Q.11.d.2.8. and Q.12.a.6.5. respectively. Reliefs to be complete by 2.30 pm.

VISUAL STATION V
Sjt. GRIMES will detail 1 N.C.O. & 3 Signallers to take over the Bde. Visual Station at R.7.d.15.87. (5th Field Coy. H.Q.) Relief to be complete by 2.30 p.m. Completion of relief to be reported direct to Bde Signals Officer by code word "VISUAL".

TRENCH STORES ETC. VI
Standing Orders regarding Trench Stores, Defence Schemes, etc will be observed.

PACKS & BLANKETS. VII
Packs & Blankets will be outside Coy. H Qrs by 9. am tomorrow.

OFFICERS. VALISES. VIII
Officers Valises will be outside Coy. H Qrs by 2. pm tomorrow.

OFFICERS TRENCH KITS & MESS GEAR IX
Officers Trench Kits & Mess Gear will be outside Batt. H Qrs at 4. pm.

TRANSPORT. X
The Quartermaster will make the usual arrangements for Transport, Rations, Water, etc.

HOT FOOD XI
The arrangement for hot food will be the same as during last tour.

BILLETS. XII
Billets will be left scrupulously clean & a certificate to that effect handed in to Orderly Room.

CODE WORD XIII
Code word for relief complete "MOON"

Acknowledge.

Issued to

6th Inf Bde.   All Coys.
1st Kings Regt.   Quartermaster
2nd S. Staffs.   R.S.M.
File.   War Diary.

(Sgd) A Whitley Lavarack
Major for O.C.

SECRET.

OPERATION ORDER No 17
BY
MAJOR S.J.M. HOLE. M.C.
Commanding 17th Royal Fusiliers.

20/2/18

Ref: Map GOUZEAUCOURT 1/20,000
& 6th Inf: Bde: Order N°350.

RE-ARRANGEMENT OF BDE. FRONT.
I

On the night of February 21st/22nd the following re-arrangement of the Brigade Front will take place:—
The Northern Brigade Boundary will remain as at present.
The Southern Brigade Boundary will be R.15.a.8.3 – R.15.a.5.5 – R.13.b.3.3 – Q.18.b.7.4 – Q.18.b.4.3. – Q.17.a.1.5.
The 99th Bde. will be on our right & the 5th Bde. on our left.

BDE. H.Q.
II

The 6th Inf. Bde. H.Q. will be established at Q.17.d.6.5.

SUPPORT BATTALION.
III

In order to carry out the above re-adjustment, the Support Battn (17th R.F.) will be disposed as follows:—

Batt. H.Q.   in RHONDDA TRENCH.
'D' Coy.   "   TRENT AVENUE.
Half of 'C' Coy   "   MERTHYR TRENCH.
  'C'   "   FRONT LINE BATT. H.Q. (SURREY ROAD)
'A' Coy.   "   NAVAL RESERVE (South of FARM AVENUE)
                      Coy. H.Qrs. MONUMENT RAVINE.
'B' Coy.   "   MONUMENT RAVINE.

NOTE. 'A' Coy will arrange to have 1 Officer permanently stationed in NAVAL RESERVE.
'A' & 'B' Coys will each send a sketch map to Batt. H.Qrs showing their exact dispositions by 9 a.m. on the 22nd.
The above moves will take place tomorrow commencing at 6 p.m.

FRONT BATTALION.
IV

On completion of above re-arrangement the Front Battn will be disposed as follows:—

H.Q. – SURREY ROAD.
3 Coys, each with 3 Platoon Posts in Front Line and 1 Platoon in Support.
1 Coy in Reserve in VICTORY LANE.

TACTICAL DISPOSITIONS
V

"A". "B" & "C" Coys will be at the disposal of the Front Line Battn Commander for tactical purposes.

A.A. LEWIS GUNS
VI

Any Anti-Aircraft positions in NAVAL RESERVE or MONUMENT RAVINE will be taken over by 'A' & 'B' Coys respectively.

(2)

ADVANCE PARTY
VII
'A' & 'B' Coys will each send an Advance Party of 1 Officer, 1 Sjt. & 4 men to take over Dispositions, Trench Stores, etc. All receipts for Trench Stores will be forwarded to Orderly Room by 10. am on the 22nd.

RATIONS
VIII
The Quartermaster will arrange that rations for 'A' & 'B' Coys & 46 of 'C' Coy to be dumped at Western end of MONUMENT RAVINE (R.8.C.6.4) & rations for Hd Qrs, 'D' Coy & remainder of 'C' Coy to be dumped as at present.

COOKERS.
IX
Both Cookers will return to Transport Lines tomorrow night.

WATER CART
X
The Water Cart will be dumped in present situation & all Water Tins will be dumped with 'A' & 'B' Coys rations. Sjt. MATTOCKS will be responsible for the distribution of rations to 'A', 'B' & 46 of 'C' Coy.

CODE WORD
XI
Code word for relief complete "HAPPY VALLEY".

INTER-BATTN RELIEF
XII
On the night of 22nd/23rd the 17th R.F. will relieve the 1st KINGS in the Front Line & will be disposed as follows:—
'A' Coy on the RIGHT. 'B' Coy in the CENTRE
'C' " " " LEFT. 'D' " " SUPPORT (VICTORY LANE).
Coy Cmdrs will send Officers to reconnoitre the dispositions held by the 1st KINGS on the morning of the 22nd.

<u>ORDERS FOR THIS RELIEF WILL BE ISSUED SEPARATELY</u>

Acknowledge.

(Sgd) A Whitley Lacarack.
Major for O.C.

Issued to
6th Inf. Bde.
2nd S. Staffs.
1st Kings.
All Coys.
Quartermaster.
R.S.M.
War Diary.
File.

SECRET

OPERATION ORDER No. 18
By
MAJOR S.J.M. HOLE. M.C.
Commanding 17th Royal Fusiliers

22/2/18

Ref: Map LA VACQUERIE 1/10,000 & 6th I.B. Order No. 350.

RELIEF. The 17th R.F. will relieve the 1st KINGS in the Front Line on the night 22nd/23rd. Relief to commence at dusk.

DISPOSITIONS II "A" Coy 17th R.F. will relieve "A" Coy 1st KINGS on the RIGHT FRONT.
"B" " " " " "C" " " " in the CENTRE.
"C" " " " " "D" " " " on the LEFT.
"D" " " " " "B" " " " in SUPPORT.

On completion of relief the Battn will be disposed as follows:-

RIGHT - "A" Coy. Platoon Posts. No.1. R.15.a.q.t. No.2. R.15.a.85.80.
No.3. R.q.d.15.15., 1 Platoon in NAVAL RESERVE. S. H.Q - R.q.c.45.05.

CENTRE - "B" Coy. Platoon Posts. No.4. R.q.d.30.55. No.5. R.q.d.75.35.
No.6. R.10.c.15.65., 1 Platoon in ROBIN TRENCH. S.
Accommodation. VICTORY LANE. H.Q - R.q.d.60.95.

LEFT - "C" Coy. Platoon Posts. No.7. R.10.a.15.05. No.8. R.10.a.35.45.
No.9. R.10.a.50.75. 1 Platoon in ROBIN TRENCH. N.
Accommodation. VICTORY LANE. H.Q - R.10.a.25.50.

SUPPORT - "D" Coy. VICTORY LANE. H.Q - R.q.b.45.45.

BATTALION H.Q. - SURREY ROAD.

NOTE. "A" Coy will have one officer permanently in dug-out at R.q.d.15.15.

GUIDES. III No guides will be supplied.

OFFICERS KITS & MESS GEAR. IV Officers Kits & Mess Gear will be taken over by hand.

LEWIS GUNS & AMMUNITION. V Lewis Guns & Ammunition will be taken over by hand.

RATIONS. VI Rations for Hd Qrs, "B" "C" & "D" Coys will be brought to Battn. H.Q. dump. "A" Coy rations will be dumped at Western end of MONUMENT RAVINE.

HOT FOOD. VII Arrangements for hot food will be issued separately.

ADVANCE PARTY TRENCH STORES, ETC. VIII 2nd Lieut HART, R.S.M. & 1 Officer & 2 N.C.O's per Coy will go up in advance to take over Dispositions, Trench Stores, etc. Lists of Trench Stores will be forwarded to Orderly Room by 10 am on 23rd

TRENCH STORES. IX 2nd Lieut HART will hand over Trench Stores, Dispositions, etc. in Support position to 2nd S. STAFFS.

WATER X	Water arrangements will be as during previous relief.
A.A. LEWIS GUNS XI	The 2 Lewis Guns now found by "B" & "D" Coys will be relieved by 2nd S. STAFFS at 5 pm this evening.
COMMAND XII	The Coys of the 2nd S. STAFFS relieving "A", "B" & "C" Coys will be under the command of O.C. 17th R.F. for tactical purposes.
CODE WORD	Code word for relief complete "KIPPER". Acknowledge.

[signature] MAJOR.
for O.C.

Issued at 3.30 pm
to
6th Inf. Bde.
1st Kings
2nd S. Staffs.
O.C. "A" Coy
O.C. "B" Coy
O.C. "C" Coy
O.C. "D" Coy
Quartermaster
R.S.M.
File
War Diary

SECRET

OPERATION ORDER No. 20.
BY
MAJOR S.J.M. HOLE. M.C.
Commanding 17th Royal Fusiliers

25/2/18

Ref. Map Contour Day 1/20,000

RELIEF	On the night 26th/27th the Battalion will be relieved in the front line by the 2nd S. Staffs. and on completion of relief will move into Divisional Reserve at Camp F.30.d. Companies will march independently. Relief will commence at dusk.
DETAIL II.	Coys. will be relieved by their opposite numbers under arrangements between Coy. Commanders concerned.
TRENCH STORES III.	Trench Stores (Defence Scheme etc) will be handed over, receipts obtained and handed in to Orderly Room by 10 a.m. 27th inst.
LEWIS GUNS & AMMUNITION IV.	Lewis Guns & Ammunition will be dumped as follows:- "A" Coy at Western end of MONUMENT RAVINE under a Cpl. who will take charge of same until loaded on limber. The remainder will be dumped at Ad Lus dump under Sgt. MATTOCKS by Coys on their way out.
OFFICERS KITS & MESS GEAR V.	All Officers Kits & Mess Gear will be dumped at Bath Ad Lus dump by 7 p.m.
TRANSPORT VI.	The Quartermaster will arrange for the usual Transport and will also arrange for Kits, Blankets, Packs, etc to be moved across to the camp tomorrow.
BILLETS VII.	The Quartermaster will arrange for parties to go over to the camp early tomorrow morning & take over all accommodation & will arrange for guides to meet the Batn at Cross Roads METZ.
HOT MEAL VIII.	The Quartermaster will arrange to provide a hot meal for all ranks on their arrival in camp.
BATHS IX.	The Quartermaster will arrange for Baths on the 27th and make arrangements for drawing clean clothing.
CODEWORD X.	Code word for relief complete "REPOSE". Acknowledge.

Issued to:-
6th Inf Bde.   All Coys.
2nd S. Staffs.   R.S.M.
1st Kings.   etc.
Quartermaster War Diary.

Major for O.C.

6th Brigade.
2nd Division.

17th BATTALION

THE ROYAL FUSILIERS

MARCH 1 9 1 8

Attached:-

Report on Operations 21st-31st March.
Report on Operations at PYS 25th March.

Army Form C. 2118

WAR DIARY
INTELLIGENCE SUMMARY

17th (S) Batt. Royal Fusiliers

1918.

Place	Date	Hour	Summary of Events and Information	Remarks and references to Appendices
METZ Tent Camp	MARCH 1st		Expected Enemy Attack — Practice turn outs in Sunken Rd East of HAVRINCOURT WOOD — Played 2nd & 3rd & Bucks at football & lost by 1-2 — Wettest day	$1/u$ SPU.
SUPPORT LINE Ma Villar's Plough	2nd		Took over new HQ's in PLOUGH SUPPORT R7.21.9 — formely occupied by 226th Field Coy R.E. — Relieved the 1st KINGS REGT — A Coy gassed — in the evening, several men sent down the line — A Coy were in SNAP RESERVE. Enemy shelled us with gas for 4 hours & also shelled RIBECOURT & TRESCAULT causing several hundred casualties in the Division —	$1/u$ SPU
	3rd		Very quiet day — except for occasional gas shelling all over RIDGE & BEACAMP by the enemy — Visibility fine — much enemy movement up HIGHLAND in MIERONIES & 3 guns spotted firing in GONNELIEU. R.A.S. HALESORTH. E. wounded.	SPU
	4th		Quiet day — Observation bad — Enemy looks hard on his defence lines — gas shelling ceases —	$1/u$ SPR
	5th		This day left Observations — Enemy movement increased in a southerly direction. Slight shelling of ASHBY AVENUE — 2 men wounded — Enemy battery at VAUCELLES WOOD detected & silenced.	$1/u$ SPR.
FRONT LINE LAVACQUERIE CENTRE Sector	6th		In front line — relieved 1st Kings Regt — a very quiet day — Much wiring done by the battalion	SPU

WAR DIARY

INTELLIGENCE SUMMARY.

(Erase heading not required.)

Army Form C. 2118.

Place	Date	Hour	Summary of Events and Information	Remarks and references to Appendices
FRONTLINE VACQUERIE CENTRE Sector	March 7th		Snipers active — Pte AYRES killed one Hun opposite NEPTUNE SAP. We were badly shelled by T.M.s — Heavy shelling of by 4.2"s & 5.9"s — Casualties 2 killed & 2 wounded D.R.s — Chief targets seemed to be WOOD AVENUE — VICTORY LANE — NAVAL RESERVE & WELSH SUPPORT — Sgt ELLIS killed by german sniper — Several Hun T.M. emplacements spotted	Appx
	8th		Enemy again worries us with T.M.s Medium only — Our observers warned our artillery of enemy heavy T.M. emplacements — 2 of which were silenced accordingly. Our Snipers active — Pte AYRES claimed 2 hits & Pte RIDDELL one —	Appx
	9th		Snipers again active 3 hits claimed by Pte MARSH - AYRES & RIDDELL German Snipers more active we had one man wounded by their fault — Enemy attitude quieter — 50 coils of wire put out by the Battalion — We were relieved by the 2nd South STAFFS Regt & went back to the old camp — during the out going we was put out as follows A Coy 22 coils B " 26 " C " 35 " D " 26 "	Appx
METZ CAMP P.30.d or EQUANCOURT ROAD	10th		Enemy shelled Front line & WOOD AVENUE & VICTORY LANE with 4.2s & 5.9s We had about 4 Casualties — 1 man killed —	Appx

Army Form C. 2118.

WAR DIARY
INTELLIGENCE SUMMARY
(Erase heading not required.)

Instructions regarding War Diaries and Intelligence Summaries are contained in F. S. Regs. Part II. and the Staff Manual respectively. Title pages will be prepared in manuscript.

SHEET 57C 40500

Place	Date	Hour	Summary of Events and Information	Remarks and references to Appendices
METZ CAMP P.30d	MARCH 11th		Nice easy day in Camp - METZ shelled by H.V. gun - Working party on digging new Cable trench -	French Sqn.
"	12th		Still on rest - Parades under Coy Commanders & working parties on Cable trench & cleaning up of METZ continued - Engagement accepted by Regiment yesterday - FOOTBALL 1st KRRF 2 goals v 10th DCLI. 1 " also B Coy 17th RF 0 goals v D " 0 "	French Sqn.
"	13th		Still on rest - usual fatigues etc - & firing on range - FOOTBALL. A Coy 6 goals v B Coy 0 " C Coy 0 " v D " 0 " OFFICERS 0 goals v SERGEANTS 1 "	French Sqn.
SUPPORT LINE R7d1.9. VACQUERIE Centre Sector	14th		Relieved the 1st King's Regt in Support - gas shelling at night - Battalion worked hard on improving ASHBY AVENUE 2/Lt LEATHER (Lt. 5th RB.) joined	French Sqn.
"	15th		Splendid day for observation - Enemy movement plentiful from North to South - Several Enemy Aeroplanes about - gun spotted firing from MERGNIES WOOD - 2/Lt GREEN wounded	French Sqn.
"	16th		Observation again unfortunately good - Large bodies of enemy seen entering MARCOING - Battalion hard at work on Highland Ridge Defences - Enemy artillery normal but AIRCRAFT very active - movement again plentiful -	French Sqn.

Army Form C. 2118.

WAR DIARY
~~INTELLIGENCE~~ SUMMARY

(Erase heading not required.)

Instructions regarding War Diaries and Intelligence Summaries are contained in F. S. Regs., Part II. and the Staff Manual respectively. Title pages will be prepared in manuscript.

SHEET 57C / in 4000

Place	Date	Hour	Summary of Events and Information	Remarks and references to Appendices
SUPPORT LINE R7d19.	MARCH 17th		Battalion still busy wiring generally improving HIGHLAND defences. Fighting Patrol sent out under 2/Lt PANTING to gain identification — The patrol tried to capture some of the enemy in NEPTUNE & VICTOR SAPS — The enemy were to be seen — the party brought back a notice board with them — Enemy movement again abnormal —	Appx. SR2
FRONT LINE VACQUERIE CENTRE South.	18th		Battalion relieved the 1st Kings Regt in the Front line — A Raid was carried out by 2/Lt FISH 417.GR3 taping out etc arranged by 2/Lt PANTING — The party entered the enemy front line opposite A VICTOR SAP to gain identification — Several enemy were killed and shoulder straps of 3 men of the 88th R.I.R. 21st Reserve Division (NORMAL) were obtained — No live Huns were taken owing to the keenness of our men in the raid, who actually shot a prisoner in their excitement. Congratulations were received from 2nd Div —99th — 6th & 5th Brigades as so many other units had failed to gain identification — our casualties were 1 missing — which is 80/10 Germans are known to have been killed — Much Salvage collected —	Appx. CPR3
"	19th		Preparation for Relief — Enemy movement normal — in the front line — Snipers active on both sides — we had 1 man wounded — Enemy Artillery normal — Break in the weather — T.M. activity slightly more active —	Appx. SR3

Army Form C. 2118.

WAR DIARY
or
INTELLIGENCE SUMMARY.
(Erase heading not required.)

Instructions regarding War Diaries and Intelligence
Summaries are contained in F. S. Regs., Part II.
and the Staff Manual respectively. Title pages
will be prepared in manuscript.

57c/1/1000

Place	Date	Hour	Summary of Events and Information	Remarks and references to Appendices
FRONT LINE and ROCQUIGNY CAMP	MARCH 20th		Enemy movement very abnormal – Several Staff officers seen around La VACQUERIE & a relief seemed certain. Several hundreds of enemy seen entering & leaving the trenches in full pack – Brigade warned – signs of enemy offensive – Several enemy machine guns taken into their front support lines – Battalion was relieved on the night (viz. B.Coy) by the 1/17th LONDON REGT (POPLAR & STEPNEY RIFLES) & in Centre left position by the 1/18th LONDON REGT. (LONDON IRISH) the 2nd Divn was relieved by the 47th Division & the 17th RF entrained at METZ for ROCQUIGNY – The last Coy of Battn HQ arrived at ROCQUIGNY at 6AM on the 21st inst –	Hurst orr
ROCQUIGNY CAMP	21st "		The German Offensive begins – Battn on arrival at ROCQUIGNY immediately stands to – remains standing to all day – ROCQUIGNY shelled by HV gun & bombed at night – German barrage very heavy –	Hurst orr
0.3a TANK CAMP & MILLCROSS.	22nd "		Battalion moves up to TANK Camp on the BAPAUME Road at 0.3a & stands to in a field until 5PM when it moves up to MILL CROSS on the FREMICOURT–LEBUCQUIERE Road – the Battn is in Support to the 9th Gloucesters 19th DIVN	General orr orr
MILL CROSS	23rd "	1AM	Moved to Green line – HQ at S.E. SAUNDERS Camp – HAPLINCOURT – BERTINCOURT Rd –	
SAUNDERS CAMP	" "	2AM	STOOD TO – Expected Enemy attack – Colonel WESTON appointed Outpost Commander of	orr
" "	" "	5AM	Grade – Position said to be or	yes

WAR DIARY
INTELLIGENCE SUMMARY

Army Form C. 2118.

Place	Date	Hour	Summary of Events and Information	Remarks and references to Appendices
SAUNDERS CAMP O.4.d.	MARCH 23rd	10 AM	Heavy shelling of front line.	MP
HAPLINCOURT WOOD O.4.c.1.9.		12 Noon	Moved HQ to HAPLINCOURT WOOD	
		1 PM	Shelled out of HQ by 8 inch + 5.9 - moved HQ to O.4.c.1.9	
		3.30 PM	Gap reported of 1000 yds between 18 Kings + 2 SA.L.I reported nearer to Brigade	+ Loss
		4.30 PM	Enemy seen entering VELU WOOD in large numbers - reported to Brigade	
		5 PM	Heavy bombardment opens all round - Heavy shelling of Back Area - Enemy reported in Bus	
	24th	9 AM	Enemy Barrage opens - Bde informed of anticipated attack -	
		9.50 AM	S. STAFFS on our left report enemy forming up on Railway embankment between FREMICOURT and BEUGNY - asked Bde for Artillery	
		9.55 AM	Left Post of 18 Kings blown up - one platoon of our D.Coy moves up in support + 1 Platoon of our A Coy ordered tasked to	
		10.5 AM	Brigadier informs us that H.L.I. are coming to fall back on our right suggested that they should be rallied	
		10.15 AM	H.L.I. reported to be reforming - D.C.L.I. reported to have bolted - asked Bde that they should be rallied	
		10.20 AM	9th Cheshires (19th Divn) seen bolting on our left - N.C.O. sent out to rally same	
		10.30 AM	Large number of Cheshires seen bolting Kings form defensive flank - Right flank O.K.	
		10.45 AM	Our A Coy sent to reinforce 2 S. STAFFS to form defensive flank	
		10.55 AM	Cheshires reported to be counter attacking from MILL CROSS - informed M.G. officer -	
		11.15 AM	Aeroplane action asked for by on S. STAFFS front	
		11.30 AM	S.O.S. put up on Right front - 2/Lt CAMPBELL KILLED	
		2.5 PM	Right flank gave way we were forced to retire to red line - the 17th were the last to go - Major FAREWELL wounded - Enemy M.G.s very active	PM

Army Form C. 2118.

WAR DIARY
INTELLIGENCE SUMMARY

(Erase heading not required.)

Instructions regarding War Diaries and Intelligence Summaries are contained in F.S. Regs., Part II. and the Staff Manual respectively. Title pages will be prepared in manuscript.

Place	Date	Hour	Summary of Events and Information	Remarks and references to Appendices
Red Line VILLERS-AU-FLOS	March 24th	4 PM	Battalion reformed here – but owing to shortage of ammunition plenis guns & according to brigade orders were forced to retire to the BAPAUME – PERONNE ROAD at BEAULENCOURT – Col WESTON – Stripp disarms a TANK taking all M.G.s & ammunition. Enemy in HAPLINCOURT WOOD & enfilade us with M.G. fire	SM / HWS sgt.
BEAUVENCOURT	"	5 PM	Battalion collected – Enemy in LETRANSLOY – we retire through 51st DIVISION – Ordered to retire to LIGNY-THILLOY LINE. Enemy Aircraft dominate the situation & do wonderful work for the enemy artillery	HWS sgt.
LIGNY-THILLOY	"	8 PM	Batt arrive at LIGNY-THILLOY – very fatigued – Bde formed up as follows:– 15 Kings 10off 160 ORs – STSTAFFS. 2 off 210 ORs – 17th KRF – 4 Offrs 26 ORs – B.Cy 26 ORs. C.Cy 10 offrs 180 ORs. D.Cy. 2 offrs 110 ORs.	SM
PYS	25th	3-15AM	Ordered to move along ALBERT–BAPAUME Road towards ALBERT	
PYS	"	4-30AM	Arrived at PYS held a line N.W. of the VILLAGE	
		2-10 PM	Enemy through LESARS advancing under cover of smoke barrage in COURCELETTE appeared to be retiring on the left – late enemy seen advancing in jungle file towards our Right	
		4 PM	Ordered by BRIGADIER of 5th DIV to hold line at all costs as follows:– PYS – MIRAUMONT – COURCELETTE – Right gives way – Kings & Staffs move off to unknown destination – the WELSH & RIFLES COUNTER ATTACK with about 40 ORs. Enemy in enemy broke over the Railway forced to retire – our Right flank gives – Major High pretty killed – old party their retire	SM

CORPS Commander Corps Cmd r MIRAUMONT

Army Form C. 2118.

WAR DIARY
INTELLIGENCE SUMMARY.
(Erase heading not required.)

Instructions regarding War Diaries and Intelligence Summaries are contained in F. S. Regs., Part II. and the Staff Manual respectively. Title pages will be prepared in manuscript.

Place	Date	Hour	Summary of Events and Information	Remarks and references to Appendices
BEAUCOURT	Aug 25th	—	Battalion files along main road & halted at BEAUCOURT. Thrown do of Officers & men are & gathered together here. We move on to spot between ARCHONVILLERS & held line from South of the ANCRE. New HAMEL Artillery falling short on 63rd DIVN — Brigade informed. Quiet evening —	hurry Init
AUCHONVILLERS — HAMEL	26th	9.50AM	Enemy seen advancing in direction of BEAUMONT HAMS - with east flank guard advancing along the BEAUCOURT Road into Artillery etc —	hurry
		11AM	Enemy seen in large numbers in the valley — his guns seen firing at us — Brigade informed — Enemy Snipers very active — he suffers a few casualties — The day passes quietly — 12th Divn relieved 63rd Divn on our right — we have 30 truck Lewis guns attached two —	hurry Init
		11PM	Relieved by 1st (CANTERBURY Rifles — NEW ZEALAND REGT) & went to MAILLY - MAILLET - Coys re-organised — ARB Corps eliminated — ARB Corps reorganised —	hurry
MAILLY-MAILLET	27th	1AM	Arrived MAILLY — Coys re-organised — Shelled slightly	hurry Init
BEAUSSART		3.15PM	Moved to BEAUSSART	Init
ENGLEBELMER		8.40PM	Moved up to ENGLEBELMER & relieved a Brigade of the 63rd DIVN — on 1 hours notice —	hurry Init
	28th		Quiet day — occasionally shelled devoted to re-organisation	hurry Init
	29th		Relieved 99th Brigade — Under Closed Winter — in Aveluy Wood — Front Line — ALL QUIET.	hurry Init
AVELUY WOOD FRONT LINE			Captain Green wounded — Enemy Shell MARTIN SART & AVELUY WOODS. Our patrol shoots a German Officer & man 9 sets identifications (M.T.R.) - We were relieved by the Composite Battalion	hurry Init
HEDAUVILLE	30th		under Lt-Col MURRAY LYON & go to HEDAUVILLE	hurry Init

Army Form C. 2118.

WAR DIARY
INTELLIGENCE SUMMARY
(Erase heading not required.)

Place	Date	Hour	Summary of Events and Information	Remarks and references to Appendices
HEDAUVILLE	March 31st	—	Resting :- In Brigade Reserve — Still under 1 hour's notice — Hedauville Shelled — Nothing of importance happens — During the month 2/Lt FLEMING & 2/Lt SPICER joined the battn — CASUALTIES for the month OFFICERS 2 Killed 7 Wounded 1 Wounded / Missing, NIL MISSING — TOTAL OFFICERS 10 + 3ˣ O.R.s 22 " 158 " 16 " 167 " O.R.s 363 Killed MAJOR PRETTY, M.C. & 2/Lt F/C CAMPBELL Wounded — MAJOR LAVARACK, M.C. — Capts. AYLMER — GLASSON & TAYLOR — Lt S.D. ANTILL. & 2/Lts — HARVEY — PANTING — "Wounded / Missing 2/Lt FISH — x Wounded before the Retirement — 2/Lt H.S. HAVELOCK, M.C. 2/Lt V H GREEN 2/Lt AS. LEATHER (GASSED) Ration Strength 12 Officers, 463. O.Ranks.	[illegible] Aug 1/5 R [illegible] April 5 1918

"A" Form.
MESSAGES AND SIGNALS.

Army Form C. 2121.
(In pads of 100.)

No. of Message..............

Prefix......... Code........... m	Words.	Charge.	This message is on a/c of:	Recd. at ....m.
Office of Origin and Service Instructions.	Sent			Date......
Report	At........m.		.............Service.	From......
	To......			
	By......		(Signature of "Franking Officer.")	By ....

TO { 9th Inf Bde

| Sender's Number. | Day of Month. | In reply to Number. | A A A |
| D 8 | 1 | | |

Herewith Report on Operations from March 21st to March 31st 1918, please

From 17th R Fus
Place
Time

The above may be forwarded as now corrected.   (Z)   A Pelly 2 Lt
                                    Censor.   Signature of Addressor or person authorised to telegraph in his name.

* This line should be erased if not required.

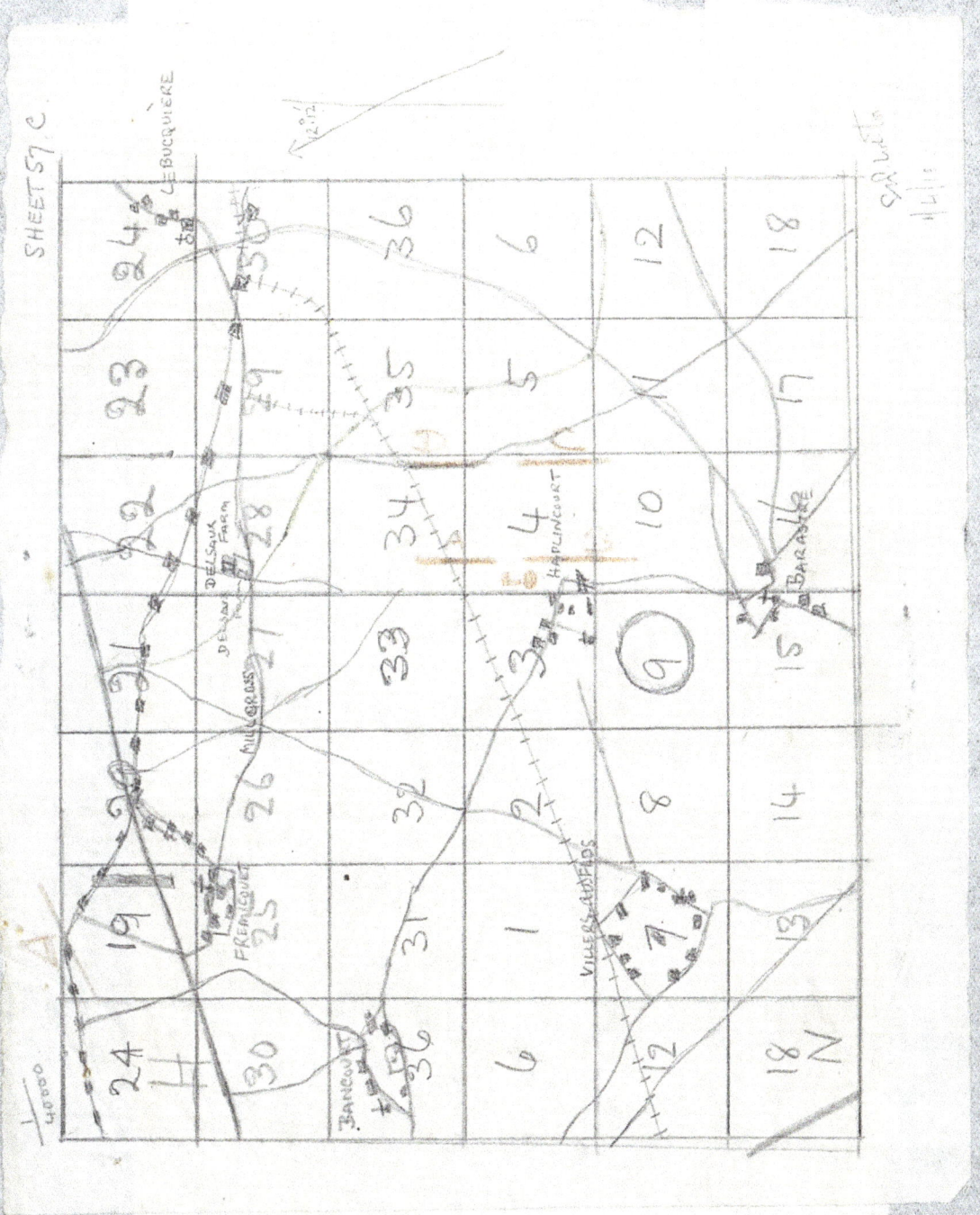

I.

Report on the operations from March 21. 1918 to March 31. 1918.

Ref. 57⁂. 1/40.000.

On the morning of Thursday, March 21, at 1.30 AM the Batt was relieved in the line by the 1/17 & 1/18 Londons. From the line the Batt marched to METZ & thence entrained to ROCQUIGNY.

At 6 AM. The Batt was in billets.
At. 5.2 AM. Ordered to "Stand To".

March 22.

    5 AM. Batt marched to an open field in O.2.a.

    5 P.M. Batt marched to MILL CROSS & took up position in support to 2nd S. Staffs.

March. 23.

    1 AM. Batt moved to Green Line & encamped about O.4. Central.

    2 AM. Ordered to "Stand To" owing to threatened enemy attack & established outpost line on the Green line.

    6.30 AM. Ordered to Consolidate the Green line.

    9.30 AM. I again went round the line with Lt Col. MURRAY LYON. 1st Kings & Lt Col ALBAN. 2nd S. Staffs & carefully fixed boundaries by daylight. At the same time there was a vast amount of work going on. The 10th D.C.L.I. & the 225th Field Coy. were digging the line & tools having been secured all the three Batts in the Bde joined in the consolidation.

    10. AM. Green line heavily shelled.
Arrangements made for the distribution of ammunition.
Telephone & Visual established with Bde.

ctd. 11

March. 23.

5 pm to dusk. The Line & Rear Areas were
heavily shelled.

The position of the Bde in the Front Line
was 1st Kings in the Right Sector of the Bde Front.
2nd S. Staff in the Left Sector of the Bde Front.
17th R. Fusiliers with 2 Coys in Support
& 2 Coys in Reserve. See Map attached
marked. "A".

End of 1st phase.

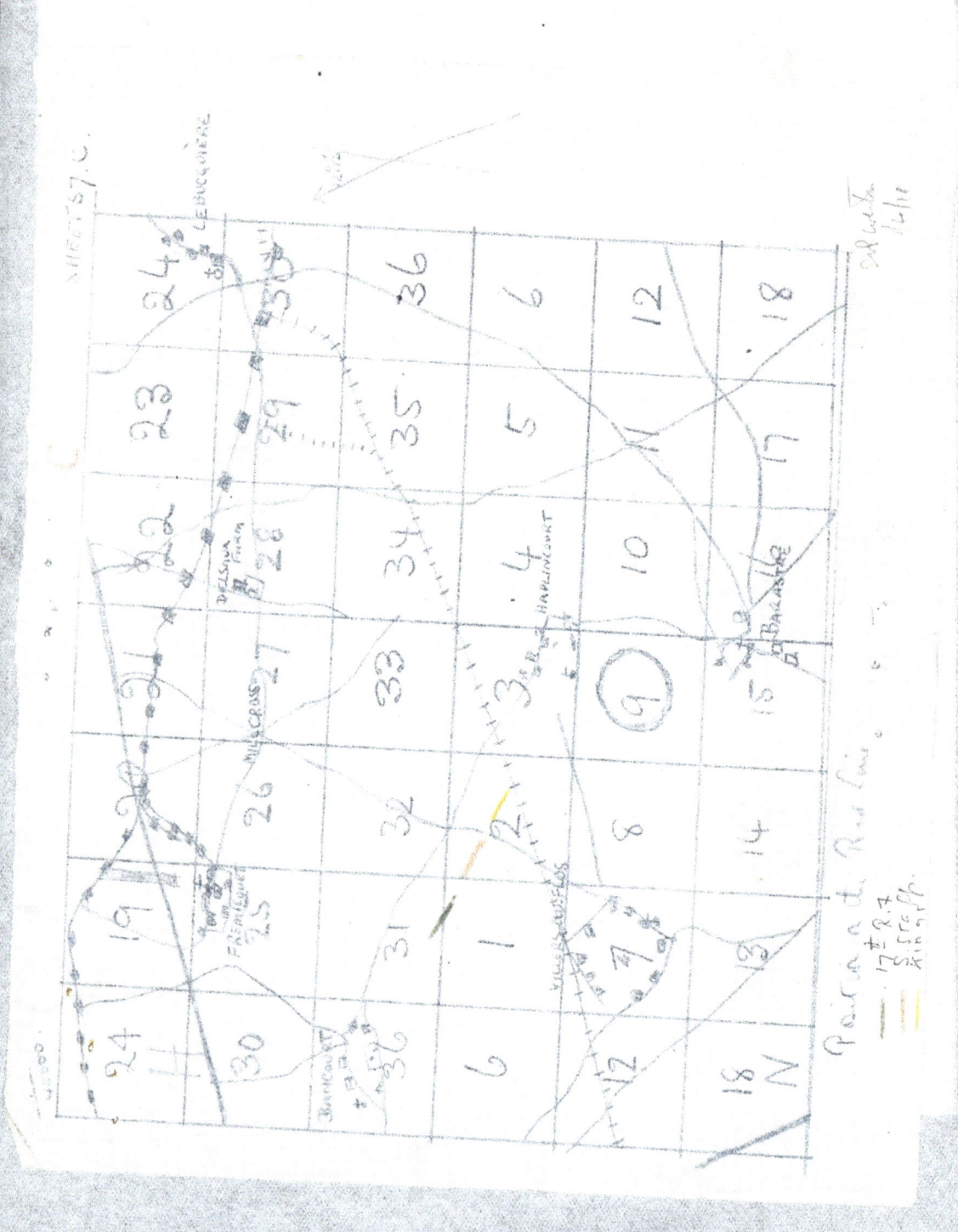

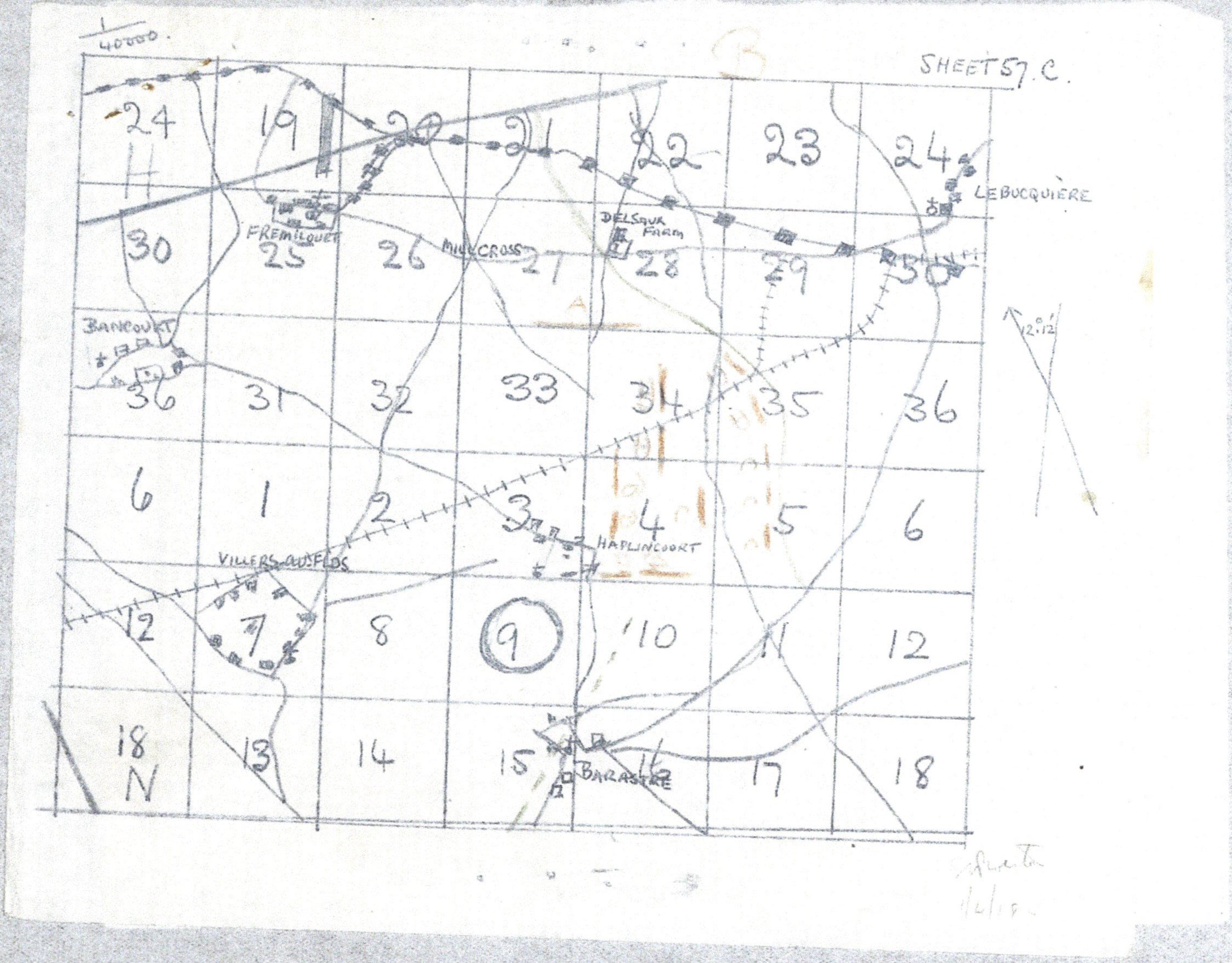
1/40000.
SHEET 57.C.
H
N
LEBUCQUIÈRE
FREMILQUET
MILLCROSS
DELSAUX FARM
BANCOURT
HAPLINCOURT
VILLERS-AU-FLOS
BARASTRE
A
B
12°12'
24
19
20
21
22
23
24
30
25
26
27
28
29
30
36
31
32
33
34
35
36
6
1
2
3
4
5
6
12
7
8
9
10
11
12
18
13
14
15
16
17
18

iii

March. 24th

During the night the enemy was reported by Bde
to be in Bus.

8.40 AM. Informed by Bde that H.L.I on the Right
were moving to a new position. I warned
O.C. 1st Kings & Machine Gunners.

9 AM. Heavy enemy Barrage.
Bde informed that attack was expected.

9.50 AM. S..taff ask for our Barrage.
attack developing on the left.

9.55 AM. Left Coy of 1st Kings blown up.
"D" Coy. 17th. R. Fusiliers move up
2 platoons to fill gap.
Capt GLASSEN. 17th. R.F. reports attack
developing on Left. not a Right.

10.5. AM. Brigadier informs me that H.L.I
were coming back too far on the Right.
I suggested that they be rallied
as I was being attacked on the left
& had not sufficient Reserves to support
both flanks.

10.20. AM. Cheshires on left seen to be coming back

10.30. AM. Large numbers of Cheshires seen to be
retreating.

10.45. AM. Sent "A" Coy 17th R.F. under Capt. AYLMER
to form defensive flank on Left & place
himself at the disposal of Lt Col. ALBAN.

iv

CO.

March. 24ᵗʰ.

11.30 A.M. SOS reported from Right Front.

12.30 P.M. Hearing from O.C 1ˢᵗ Kings that the gap on the Right Flank had not been filled, I went up to clear up position & found a gap of from 1000 to 1500 yards. Our Right was about O 5 d 3.5 the Left of the H L I was about O.4 c 3.7. On asking the H L I officer on the Left why he did not fill in the gap, he replied that his orders were to remain where he was. I proceeded to H.L.I H.Q & told O.C. Batt of the position on my Right this aft. He expressed himself unable to remedy the situation as his Right Flank was being drawn back in conformity to movements of 1ˢᵗ Ox & Bucks on his Right.

1 P.M. Signal for Reinforcement sent up from front line. Capt Bean O.C "C" Coy. 17ᵗʰ R.F in Support sent up 3 platoons.

1.30 P.M. Enemy fire had become intense.

I returned to H Q & sent up 2 platoons B Coy. 17ᵗʰ. R.F to fill in gap & making a defensive flank. The officer in charge 2ⁿᵈ. Lᵗ Campbell was unfortunately killed on the way up & these platoons did not reach their objective.

2.7 P.M. Information received from the front that the Right Flank had gone & that a general retirement had set in.

V.

March. 24th

Finding that the movement had become general I arranged with O.C. 1st Kings that he should go back to O.2.a with my adjutant & there we should re-form about the Red Line. At the same time I ordered Capt. Taylor with two platoons to hold Sunken Road running through O.4.a & c to cover retirement.

I also informed O.C. 2nd. H.L.I. & O.C. 2nd. S.Staff. of my movements. The message was acknowledged by the former but not by O.C. 2nd S.Staff, who was severely wounded about this time.

Meanwhile I remained with the Rear guard to keep in touch with the situation.

From about. 1.30 P.M onwards the telephone line to Bde was broken.

At about 2.45.P.M. I came back to O.2.a & found an order awaiting me to hold the Red line if possible & failing that to rally at BEAULIN COURT. At the same time I found some of the Bde forming up on the Red line & then retiring.

Meeting Capt DUFF I arranged with him to try & hold the Red Line and at 4.15 P.M sent an orderly to Bde reporting that we were established with the 1st Kings on the Right, the Staff in the Centre & the 17th R. Fusiliers on the left.

Unfortunately I was unable to establish touch on the flanks & was very short of ammunition.

VI

March 24

But with the assistance of 2 Machine guns
very severe casualties were inflicted on the
enemy as he deployed from HAPLINCOURT
WOOD, & 1 enemy flying Machine was
brought down in flames.

A Tank that had counter-attacked then
returned & I secured its Lewis guns & ammunition
but before this could be distributed the
enemy pushed home his attack and
a general retirement again set in.
This continued through the 51st Div.
who were entrenched round BEAULINCOURT.
Here the Batt rallied about 6.P.M. together
with the new 9th Bde.

———

End of 2nd phase.
See attached Map Marked "B" for position
of Batt just prior to retirement.
See attached Map Marked "C" for approximate
position of Bde on the Red Line

vii

March. 24/5.

Midnight. Formed up in —IGNY TILLOY line.

March. 25

3.30 A.M. Received orders to form up on the
ALBERT-BAPAUME Road.

5. A.M. Ordered to retire to line round PYS.

12. noon Went forward under orders & took up position.
W of LE SARS

1.30 P.M. Ordered to retire to AUCHONVILLERS

2.10 P.M. Stopped on PYS MIRAMONT Road
to try & get the Batt together.
While waiting a Brigadier rode up
who said that the 51st Div on the left
were holding on & that the orders were
to hold the IRLES-PYS-COURCELETTE
line at all costs. I told him that
almost the entire Bde had gone & that
I doubted if I could get the men to hold
so large a frontage.
However having gathered about 200 men
I formed them in small posts about
M.7 a & c (off the map) but I was
unable to get touch on either flank as
the frontage proved too long.
At the same time I reported to Bde & the orders
received asked for re-inforcements.
Immediately the line was heavily bombarded
& attacked. Again & again the men were
rallied by their officers. MAJOR PRETTY.
Capt DUFF & Capt PALMER rendered
conspicuous service.

viii

But first the Right Flank & then the Left
Flank gradually dwindled & this in addition
to heavy casualties reduces the Survivors
to about 40.

At 4·PM. The enemy were seen working round
the Right Flank So I took all available
men. Servants & Signallers to that quarter
but the Left Flank then began to give.
Ammunition had now completely given out.
there were no reinforcements in sight so about
4·30 PM I ordered the remnant of about 40
to retire to AUCHONVILLERS as originally
ordered.

Major PRETTY stopped behind with a small
Rear-guard but he was unfortunately killed
soon after.

End of 3rd phase.

HH IX

March 26.

The Batt. was now reduced to 6 officers & 205 men

It was allotted a sector from S.18.c.3.2. to q.17.d.55. with the 13 Corps on their share Div on the Right. Reference Map. 57.D.SE. Edition. 4A.

March 27.
2 A.M. Relieved by New Zealand Batt.
Billetted in MAILLY-MAILLET WOOD.
Coy re-organises. A & B Coys eliminated.

3.15. P.M. Moved to BOISSART.

8.40 P.M. Marched back to ENGELBELMER.

March 28. Quiet day devoted to re-organisation.
29. Relieved 99th Inf Bde in the line.
30. Relieved by Composite Batt.
31. Billetted in HEDAUVILLE.

The approximate casualties of the Batt. for the 10 days were.

- 2 Officers killed.
  8 do   Wounded.
 22 O R's Killed
 100 O R's Wounded.
  8 O R's Wounded & Missing
 177 O R's Missing

5

The difficulties of Re-forming in the face of the enemy were very pronounced & worked by all the qualities of very highly trained troops.

The losses in Officers who repeatedly & fearlessly exposed themselves were severely felt.

During the operations no less than 10 out of 15 became casualties.

Ammunition proved a great source of anxiety. It was difficult to check the men from shooting at long range, & so wasting what they had. Shooting at aeroplanes especially accounted for an enormous number of rounds.

The extremely exhausting series of moves at the commencement of the operations following on a tour in the line, when many of the Batt had been gassed to a greater or lesser degree, told heavily on the physical powers of the men.

Of the 8 wounded Officers only one fell into the hands of the enemy. This was largely due to the heroic conduct of Capt the Rev. H. Gibson whose great physical strength enabled him to rescue several who otherwise must have been left.

After the initial fight the enemy barrage was never heavy but the co-operation between their aeroplanes & artillery was extremely good & their fire was most accurate. Their machine guns worked round to the flanks & brought severe enfilade fire to bear.

XI

At no stage was the retirement conducted in an otherwise than orderly manner and at the points where the enemy advance was checked severe casualties were inflicted on him as long as the supply of ammunition lasted.

April 1. 1918.

S.W. Weston
Capt.
Cmdg. 7th R. Irish Reg.

V Corps.

    I attach a report by Lieut.Colonel WESTON Commanding 17th Battalion Royal Fusiliers.
    From the report it is evident that he did his utmost to assist the Corps on our left and his small party appears to have only begun their retirement after the 51st Division had begun to go back.
    This Battalion has a magnificent fighting record and I have a great feeling of pride when I read the account.

20th April, 1918.

Major-General,
Commanding 2nd Division.

Further Report on the Operation at PYS on
March 25th, 1918.

At 1.30 p.m. the Battalion formed part of a Rear Guard facing LE SARS.

At this time the order was received that the Brigade would withdraw to AUCHONVILLERS.

My dispositions were two companies in the front line and two in support.

I ordered the two front coys. to withdraw through the Support; this process to be continued.

On the PYS - MIRAUMONT Road I halted with the Rear-Guard, then 'A' and 'B' Coys. to collect stragglers and re-organise. My 'C' and 'D' Coys. had gone back.

'A' and 'B' consisted of about 100 men and 2 officers.

There were also about 100 men 24th R.Fusiliers marching away. The time was about 2.10 p.m. At this time a Bde. General rode up and asked for the senior officer.

Addressing me he said " The Corps Commander's orders are that the IRLES - PYS - COURCELETTE Line is to be held at all costs". "Officers are, if necessary, to use their revolvers to keep the men back". "The 51st Division are on your left".

I pointed out (i) That the whole Bde. certainly and I believed the whole Division had gone back to AUCHONVILLERS. (2) That I had practically no men for such a stretch of line and very little ammunition but that I would do all that I could and try to get reinforcements.

The Brigadier rode off.

We were not in touch with the 51st Division but I could see them on the hill to the North through my glasses.

With me I had a cyclist orderly so I sent a most urgent message to Bde. stating my position, the orders I had received and asking for reinforcements and ammunition.

At the same time I sent an officer to fetch back the Coy. of the 24th R.F. which I had just seen pass.

I then strung out my own two Coys. on the Left flank in a series of posts in shell holes at the top of the ridge. 'B' Coy. under Sec.Lt.PANTING I put on the left and ordered him to try and get in touch with the 51st Division. Next to him I put 'A' Coy. under Captain AYLMER.

The Coy. of the 24th R.F. then came up so I got them in position on the Right. On my Right Flank I could see no troops of ours for miles.

Shortly after 2.30 p.m. the enemy concentrated a heavy barrage on the ridge, enfiladed the position with heavy machine gun fire and advanced. For half an hour we held him in check. But trouble began when first one flank and then the other began to give way. All the officers by rushing along the top of the ridge with their revolvers and exposing themselves without fear, magnificiently rallied the men and the line held.

I could see the 51st Division wavering in the same way through my glasses, but they too were being rallied.

About this time my two officers on the left flank were both wounded but gallantly refused to withdraw.

This process of rallying continued without intermission until about 4 p.m. Our casualties were very heavy, but the line held.

About 4 p.m. MAJOR PRETTY, my acting Second-in-Command, who had conducted himself with the highest gallantry, dashed up to say that the enemy were round our right flank.

I collected all the Headquarters, Signallers and Runners and dashed over with them.

We formed a defensive flank and kept the enemy back and thus covered the MIRAUMONT Road.

The left flank then began to give; as I found out after-

wards....

from 2nd. Lieut PANTING, owing to the 51st Division having been driven back.

No re-inforcements were in sight.

Ammunition was now quite exhausted.

It was physically impossible to do any more. I could not shoot the remnant of the men now reduced to about 40 who had fought so well.

At 4.30 p.m. I ordered a retirement and left Major PRETTY with about 6 men to cover our retirement down the road leading to the bridge under the railway at MIRAUMONT.

Major PRETTY was unfortunately killed and the remainder either killed or wounded or taken prisoner as I afterwards learnt from the sole survivor - Sgt. BUTTERWORTH. The officers maintained the highest traditions of the 2nd Division. The men fought most gallantly, but as was natural in their exhausted state and in a completely isolated position, had to be rallied when they saw that there was a danger of their being surrounded.

Touch was never secured with either flank.

After the Brigadier-General rode away no word was received from the 51st Division.

Touch was never secured with my own Brigade.

All the lightly wounded were man-handled and got away.

The responsibility for all orders given on the Ridge is undoubtedly mine.

No blame can be attached to any other officer if it is considered that more could have been done.

(Signed) S.V.P.WESTON.

Lieut-Colonel.
Commanding 17th Royal Fusiliers.

20/4/18.

IV

and the line had
broken back the S.E. Div wavering
at same were doing my & cover our
try to were being rallied.
About this time my two officers on
the left flank were both wounded but
gallantly refused to fall down.
This precarious madly my continued
and intermission until about 4 P.M.
Our casualties were very heavy but
the line held.
About 4 P.M. Major PRETTY, my acting
Second in Command, who had conducted
himself with the highest gallantry
dashed up to say that the enemy
were round our wider flank
& erected all the Head quarters Section when
he formed a defensive flank & kept
the enemy back of then worked to keep
the left flank than began to give an
found no officers from 2nd Bn Coventry,
coming out S.E. Div having been driven back

V

he was in command were in sight.
Ammunition was now quite exhausted.
It was physically impossible to see any men.
I could not stop the command of the men
now moved to about 40 who had fought
to well.
At 4.30 P.M. I ordered a retirement
& left Major PRETTY with about 6 men
to cover the retirement down the road
leading to the Bridge under the Railway
at MIRAMONT.
Major PRETTY was unfortunately killed,
the remainder were killed or wounded
& rather became as I afterwards learnt
from the sole survivor L/C Butterworth.
The officer maintained the held and tradition
of the 2nd Div. The men fought most gallantly
& it was noticed in them and until
I felt I was completely isolated position
had to be rallied when the men
that otherwise were a change of others
being over resulted.

VI

Touch upon were secured on either flank.
O/Cs the Brigades I went rode over.
No word was received from the S.E. Div,
Touch was now resumed with my own
Bde.
All the lightly wounded were man-handled
& got away.
Re Regiment Lt. Jn all about 9 in
the Ridge is understood mine.
No blame can be attached to any
Officer if it is considered that more
could have been done.

S.R. Loftin
Lt.Col.
Cmdg. 17th R. Fusiliers

20/4/18.

I.

Further report on the operation at PYS.
on March 25th 1918.

At 1:30 p.m. the Batt formed part of a
Rear Guard Facing LE SARS.
At this time the order was received
that the Bde was to withdraw to AUCHON-
VILLERS.

My instructions were two companies in
the front line & two in support.
I ordered the two front Coys to withdraw
through the supports, the pattern then
continued.

At the PYS – MIRAMONT Road
I halted and the Reargued then A & B
Coys to called stragglers & reorganise
"C" & "D" Coys had gone back.
A & B counted of about 100 men
& 2 officers.
There were also about 150 men
24th R. Fusiliers marching with
The time was about 2.10 p.m.
At this time a Bde mounted rode up

II.

I knew as the Senior Officer. Addressing
me he said " The Corps Commanders
orders are that the IRLES – PYS –
COURCELETTE line is to be held
at all cost." Officers are, if necessary,
to use their revolvers to keep the men back.
"The S.f. Div are on your left."
"B" Coy under Lieut. Pantry I put
on the Left. I ordered him to try & get
in touch with the S.f. Div next to him
"A" Coy under Capt AYLMER.
The Coy of the 24th R.F. the came up
S. 9.95. them in position on the Right.
I my Right flank I could see no troops for
1/2 a mile.

Shortly after 2.30 p.m. the enemy commenced
a heavy barrage on the ridge, and put
the position under heavy machine gun
& advanced to half an hour we held
him in check. Two Tanks began to
fire on front of to the state before
to give us all the officers of using
along the top of the ridge, and then
ran than to fire in extended order
their magnificence rallied the men

III.

to fall back to Coy of the 24th R.F.
which I had just seen pass.
I then returned on my own two Coys
on the left flank in a series of short
individual heads at the top of the ridge.
"B" Coy under Lieut. Pantry I put
on the Left. I ordered him to try & get
in touch with the S.f. Div next to him
"A" Coy under Capt. AYLMER.
The Coy of the 24th R.F. the came up
S. 9.95. them in position on the Right.
& my Right flank I could see no troops for
1/2 a mile.

6th Brigade.

2nd Division.

1/17th BATTALION

ROYAL FUSILIERS

APRIL 1918.

Army Form C. 2118

6/7th ROYAL FUSILIERS

WAR DIARY
or
INTELLIGENCE SUMMARY.
APRIL 1918.

Vol 30

Place	Date	Hour	Summary of Events and Information	Remarks and references to Appendices
HEDAUVILLE	1st		Relieved 10th D.C.L.I. at ENGELBELMER and came into Divisional Reserve.	S/A
ENGELBELMER	2 & 3		Reconnaissance of Trenches in vicinity.	
HALLOY	4 & 5		Expected to be relieved by 6 N.F. but cancelled and relief delayed better hour. Relieved by Notson Batt. 63rd Divn. Marched here and had dinner on the way.	S/A S/A
SIBIVILLE	6th		Expect to remain here for short rest and training. Reorganisation as follows:- "A" Coy (in command) Capt. MATTHEWS. "B" Coy Capt HEWITT. "C" Coy. Capt. BEAK. "D" Coy Lt. FORBES MENZIES. Billets not good and men crowded - Training programme issued and special classes arranged.	S/A
	7th		Baths. Lewis Guns on the range - Major HOLES returns from a month's leave to England.	S/A
	8th		The Battalion draws similar Lewis Guns. Only four L.G. teams manned the retreat and special efforts made to replace the casualties.	S/A

30 W

WAR DIARY
or INTELLIGENCE SUMMARY.

Army Form C. 2118

17th ROYAL FUSILIERS

APRIL

Place	Date	Hour	Summary of Events and Information	Remarks and references to Appendices
SIBIVILLE	9th		The Divisional Commander inspected the camp. Attached to the battalion are now instructors from the L.G. School & N.C.O.'s to help. Also a musketry instructor from III Army and a field firing and bayonet practice is carried out daily. 2/Lt FELTON A/Adjutant is appointed O/s in and adjutant from this date. The battalion played the 5th Field Ambulance at football - later company matches played each of term.	
	10th		The Division moves into the Scotth Corps.	
Sub. ST-LEGER	11th		Marched to Sus-Saint-LEGER (12 Kilometres). The snow made officers and Coy. any commanders taken of the line for reconnaissance.	
	12th		Marched to BARLY (9 kilometres) and billeted with the Brigade at S/T in the Chateau.	
	13th			
	14th		The Fifth and Ninty-ninth Brigades move on to the ten marched to BLAIREVILLE and took over from from 1st WELSH GUARDS.	

Army Form C. 2118

WAR DIARY
or
INTELLIGENCE SUMMARY. 17th ROYAL FUSILIERS

(Erase heading not required.)

APRIL

Place	Date	Hour	Summary of Events and Information	Remarks and references to Appendices
Front Line BOISLEUX ST. MARC. (South)	15th		Reconnaissance of the PURPLE LINE by all officers and NCO's. This is the Reserve System in case the Division should have to retire.	S/Afs
	16th		Stood to in the Trenches. The 1st K.R.R.'s attacked but nothing materialised. Relieved 1st K.R.R.'s. Front line a good and deep trench with plenty of wire in front. The support and reserve trenches get more shelling than the front line which is hardly touched. The Canadians are on our left and the 2nd South Staff/s right.	S/Afs
	17th		Very heavy shelling from 3 to 5 AM. The Enemy came up three communication trenches in which we have made sap heads but did not attack on being fired at by "D" Company.	S/Afs
	18th		Quiet. We extend our front northwards for 100 x taking over part from the Staff/s	S/Afs
	19th		The line was too broken and snow about its sets in. It is impossible to get to the front line by day or use the front from Batt. H.Q.	S/Afs
	20th		Relieved by 2nd South Staff/s and marched to BLAIREVILLE.	S/Afs

Army Form C. 2118

WAR DIARY
or
INTELLIGENCE SUMMARY.   17th ROYAL FUSILIERS.   APRIL
(Erase heading not required.)

Place	Date	Hour	Summary of Events and Information	Remarks and references to Appendices
BLAIREVILLE. (RESERVE)	21st		Battalion arrived in billets at 2 A.M. Improvised baths and vermin with clean clothing. Church services at 11 A.M. and 7 P.M.	S/As
Front Line.	22nd		Relieved the 1st Bn King's Regiment in the right sub-sector and are opposite the village of BOISLEUX. Batt. H.Q. in a dug-out near cemetery at BOISLEUX-au-mont. The line is in as good and well wired as the left sector. Tour passed quietly.	S/As
	26th		Relieved by 2nd Bn. South Staffordshire Regiment. Two companies in the Purple Line.	S/As
BLAIREVILLE.	27th		Usual arms and baths at BRETENCOURT.	S/As
	28th		Batt: working party to dig communication trench in left sector. No casualties and men worked well under adverse conditions. The transport lines are at BAILLEULMONT, ten kilometres from BLAIREVILLE.	
	30th		Relieved 1st Bn KING'S REGIMENT in left sector and suffered casualties many in-	S/As

A7092. Wt. W1283g/M1293 750,000. 1/17. D.D.& L. Ltd. Forms/C2118/14.

WAR DIARY
or INTELLIGENCE SUMMARY.

17th ROYAL FUSILIERS

April 18

Army Form C. 2118.

Place	Date	Hour	Summary of Events and Information	Remarks and references to Appendices
			The following officers joined the Battalion during the month.	
			Capt. T.J.E. Blake. Posted to command B'n.	
			2/Lts. J.L. White, E.W. Patrick, G. Harris, T.H. Bennett, S.M.E. Davis, L.S. Milch, G.W. Atkinson, R.E. Austin, A.S. Martin, W.F. Williams, H. Vaizey, G.W. Sanders.	
			Casualties:- 14 O.R. killed. 24 O.R. wounded. 2 Lt. Fleming wounded.	
			Ration Strength 96 Offrs. 5th Bn. French Strength 23 Offrs. 1731 Bn.	
			The following decoration received.	The Distinguished Conduct Medal No 575 A/R.S.M. Brunton. S.d.b. (B.c.96). Bar to Military Medal 672 Z/Cpl Lowry M.M.
			Lt Col. S.V.P. Weston D.S.O.M.C. Second bar to D.S.O.	The Military Medal No 51646 Pte (L/Cpl) Bradley.
			T/Capt Moir M.C. Bar to M.C.	7010 Sgt Butterworth.
			T/Capt. Aylmer. The Military Cross.	68572 Pte Bichener.
			T/2/Lt Panting. "	3gr3 Sgt. Goddin.
			Rev. H. Gibson "	555 Cpl. Baynton.
			T/2/Lt F.W. Fish. "	52747 Pte Miles.
				51649 Sgt. Carr.

6th Brigade.

2nd Division.

1/17th BATTALION

ROYAL FUSILIERS

M A Y 1918.

Army Form C. 2118.

WAR DIARY
MAY INTELLIGENCE SUMMARY.
17th ROYAL FUSILIERS
Vol 3 }

(Erase heading not required)

Place	Date	Hour	Summary of Events and Information	Remarks and references to Appendices
FRONT LINE. BOISLEUX AU MONT.	30/1		Relieved 1st KINGS in left sub sector. Heavy Shelling on BLAIREVILLE-BOISLEUX-AU-MONT road and eighteen rounds and rafters wounded including Cpl HURLOCK. Trench strength 26 Officers and 540 O.R.	
	3rd		CANADIANS raided on our left and we co-operated with rifle and machine gun fire. Fairly heavy barrage in retaliation; but no casualties. Owing to our losses we have hitherto not up from the Draft School –	
	4th		At 9 A.M. the Germans opened a T.M. bombardment. It for BED- MENZIES D.S.O and Serjeant COLLETT killed. Slight readjustment of boundary. We bombarded BOTELLES with gas shells.	
	5th		Relieved by 2nd South Staffs. and reached billets without casualties – 17 O.R. reinforcement arrive at Draft School –	

Army Form C. 2118.

WAR DIARY
or
INTELLIGENCE SUMMARY.   17th R. FUS.
(Erase heading not required.)

Place	Date	Hour	Summary of Events and Information	Remarks and references to Appendices
BLAIREVILLE	6.		Baths, renewing equipment etc. Brigade Armourer inspects rifles.	
"	7.		Rifles shelled during night and our cookers slightly damaged. 1st Battalion of the (major standing to) in the last now stands for place. Major W.C. Smith 1st KRR assumes command of 1st Battalion during the temporary absence of Lt Colonel by June 9th	
FRONTLINE BOISLEUX au MONT-	8.		Relieved 1st Kings Regiment in night and next. Two Americans attached to us for instruction. Tour found quietly and without event.	
	11/12		Relieved by 16th Battalion L[an]. Fus, commanded by Col. STONE, and entrained to BARLY- from BLAIREVILLE. Not occupying same billets as when last here.	
	13.		Rest etc. (Bttn had training grounds and ranges)	
	14		Suitable range found and twenty targets made.	

Army Form C. 2118.

WAR DIARY
~~INTELLIGENCE SUMMARY~~
(Erase heading not required.)

17th R. Fus -

MAY

Instructions regarding War Diaries and Intelligence Summaries are contained in F. S. Regs., Part II. and the Staff Manual respectively. Title pages will be prepared in manuscript.

Place	Date	Hour	Summary of Events and Information	Remarks and references to Appendices
BARLY	14		The Divisional Commander lectures all officers on training to be carried out - platoon commanders commanding their own platoons - raising moral - ringing on line of march etc.	S.A.
	15.		Every man to fire 15 rounds per day. Heat wave begins - General WILLAN assumes command of the Brigade.	S.A.
	16.		Test alarm. Battalion marches to FOSSEUX in Route de march and inspected by Divisional Commander.	S.A.
	17.		Musketry the principle training. The Germans dropped bombs without damage near billets during the night -	S.A.
	18.		New draft arrives of 4 O.R. All young boys of satisfactory appearance and fairly trained.	S.A.
	19.		Football match against 6th Field Ambulance - Won - 3-1. No training. (Sunday)	S.A.

A7092. Wt. W12839/M1293 750,000. 1/17. D. D & I Ltd. Form/C2118/14.

WAR DIARY

17th ROYAL FUSILIERS

MAY

Place	Date	Hour	Summary of Events and Information	Remarks and references to Appendices
BARLY	20.		Carried out training programme.	
"	21.		One hours gun drill carried out daily in S.B.R. for next six days during training.	
	22.		Lecture by C.R.A. in chateau to fifty men per company. Excellent effort and well attended - Noted boxing competition.	
	23.		Paraded at 6.30 pm for inspection by Corps Commander - General HALDANE (VI CORPS). He presented V.C. ribbon to Pte CROWTHER (?) KINGS REGT.	
	24.		Weather breaks. Organised successful concert in the chateau grounds. Lieut Col. S.V.P. WESTON D.S.O. M.C. resumed command of the Battalion on his return from leave.	
	25.		The Divisional Commander inspects training.	
	26.		Usual routine. Short meeting in afternoon -	

Army Form C. 2118.

WAR DIARY
or
INTELLIGENCE SUMMARY.

17th Royal Fusiliers

(Erase heading not required.)

MAY

Place	Date	Hour	Summary of Events and Information	Remarks and references to Appendices
DARLY	27		Carried out Training Programme. The D.A.D.V.S. inspected the Transport Animals during the afternoon.	SYR
	28		Battalion Scheme carried out at LA BAZEQUE FARM V21	SYR
	29		Carried out Training Programme.	SYR
	30		Carried out Training Programme. The Commanding Officer and Adjutant attended the Divisional Scheme carried out in the neighbourhood of BAVINCOURT.	SYR
		5.0 pm	The Divisional Commander presented medal ribbons to recipients on the Chateau Green. A and B Companies attended the parade under Captain HEWETT.	SYR
	31		Carried out Training Programme.	
		6 Am	Rifle Competition for the best Platoon. Won by B Company.	
		10.30 am	Lewis Gun Competition won by D Company.	
			Mentioned in Kings Birthday Gazette	
			Lieut Col S.V.P. Weston D.S.O. M.C	
			Lieut A.F. Menzies D.S.O	
			Lieut G. Bengeery	
			2/Lieut J.Groves	
			Ration Strength 33 Officers 963 ORs Trench Strength 30 Officers 615 8 ORs	

6th Brigade.

2nd Division.

1/17th BATTALION

ROYAL FUSILIERS

JUNE 1918.

WAR DIARY or INTELLIGENCE SUMMARY. 17th ROYAL FUSILIERS

Army Form C. 2118.

Month: June

Place	Date	Hour	Summary of Events and Information	Remarks and references to Appendices
BARLY	1.		Brigade Horse Show. Private Hix's team of Mules won as usual. Colonel Watts' horse raced in Jumpers Competition. The Battalion is in VI Corps Reserve.	
	2.		Brigade boxing competition organised by the Battalion. A successful show and we won the middle weight, welterweight and light welter- and the 1st Batt 308th Regiment fought against us. The Americans from the 1st Batt 308th Regiment fought a z two Company marched to La Bazèque farm and carried out a	
	3.		scheme. The other two practised attacks in open and through up a barricade round the horse lines. Into Platoon football.	
	4.		Battalion field day at La Bazèque farm with others. The Battalion attacked through a wood. A cent attack in conjunction with the 3rd American Regiment was successful.	

32k

Army Form C. 2118.

WAR DIARY
or
INTELLIGENCE SUMMARY. 17th ROYAL FUSILIERS.

(Erase heading not required.)

June

Place	Date	Hour	Summary of Events and Information	Remarks and references to Appendices
BAPAUME	4.		Officer field-day C.O. and Company Commanders embus. and reconnoitre line.	
	5.		Inspections and preparations to relieve Guards Division. Played 13th King's at football and drew 2 all.	
	6.		Paraded at 6 p.m. and entrained on light railway. Arrived MONCHY at 10.30 p.m. and relieved 2nd Battn. Grenadier Guards. Marching to the line, one officer & 2 L. SPICER and nine men being killed and ten wounded. Relief completed 2.20 am.	
ACHIET.	7.		The Battalion holds the left sub-sector of the Brigade front, the 6th Brigade is in the centre of Divisional front. The relief was carried out well and trenches handed over in excellent condition. Our new post in front of the village of OKEOTE. We are about three miles north of the sector last held by the Battalion. Accommodation is good - water supply within a few yards of the front line, and a pleasant farm obtained be inspected. The go-W gest of Favreuil is opposed to us.	

WAR DIARY
or
INTELLIGENCE SUMMARY. 17th ROYAL FUSILIERS

Army Form C. 2118.

Month: June

Place	Date	Hour	Summary of Events and Information	Remarks and references to Appendices
Front Line Lt Sub Sector AVETTE.	8.		Lt. Colonel S.V.P. WESTON D.S.O. hands over command and goes to command the 122nd Battalion. Major W.C. SMITH M.C. 1st K.R.R. assumes command of the Battalion.	
	9.		Day passed without event.	
MONCHY.	10.		Relieved by 2nd Batt: Kings Regiment by 2 A.M. and marched to Reserve trenches S.W. of MONCHY. vacated by this battalion. Occasional fire.	
	11.		Baths. Lewis Gunners fired revolvers.	
	12/13		Relieved 1st Kings Regiment in Right Sub-sector without casualties. An excellent handing over.	
			SOUTH STAFFS	
FRONT LINE AVETTE.			The 2nd S.Staffs raided on our left at 10.30pm and lost 17. The attack killing an officer. A barrage on our front but no casualties.	
	14.		Day passed quietly.	
	15.		At dawn the enemy shelled AVETTE heavily for 3/4 hour in the [illegible]	

WAR DIARY
or
INTELLIGENCE SUMMARY. 17th ROYAL FUSILIERS

Army Form C. 2118

Place	Date	Hour	Summary of Events and Information	Remarks and references to Appendices
FRONT LINE. AYETTE	15.		2nd Lt. O. NEWTON STRAAF. during the night on one of their patrols. Luckily no damage to life. M.C. awarded to Captain GIBSON. C.F. honoured to rank of Major and Senior Chaplain & Divisional Infantry with much regret the loss of this gallant priest, who joined in May 1917.	
	16.		Test S.O.S. at 2 A.M.	
	17.		Day passed without event.	
MONCHY	18.		Relieved by 1st Kings and marched to reserve trenches at MONCHY without casualties.	
	19.		Baths, refitting etc.	
	20.		Co. and Coy. commanders reconnoitred PURPLE LINE System. The enemy put the Division near Battalion re-organised near Ayette. Officer the D. moved near. Battalion re-organised near Ayette. Officer estimate per Platoon two rifle sections and a Lewis gun section; each Lewis gun section to have 3 guns with gunners. 1 NCO and 10 men. Slight shelling of our trench at 9.15 P.M. was	

Army Form C. 2118.

WAR DIARY
or
INTELLIGENCE SUMMARY.
(Erase heading not required.)

Instructions regarding War Diaries and Intelligence Summaries are contained in F. S. Regs., Part II. and the Staff Manual respectively. Title pages will be prepared in manuscript.

Place	Date	Hour	Summary of Events and Information	Remarks and references to Appendices
MONCHY	21		Wiring instructions for new line to under supervision of R.E's	
ADINFER WOOD	22		Relieved the 2nd South Staffords in the Purple Line 5.30 p.m. Two companies in the Purple Front line & up on right, & one on left. Two companies in Purple Reserve line & up on right, D up on left. Resumption hunted large quantities of ammunition for ord and by water. R.E. supervising a great many men and parties from Div. That carried on in working shelters for the men and two hunting our communication trenches.	
	23		Two soldiers inspected machine and lewied on long-men weapons & facilities in the Purple Front line. The 23rd Royal Fusiliers blended activities on left of front line to strain identification.	
	24		did a raid on our right but failed. Shelling of B.H.Q. got 2.15 p.m.	
	25		Lieut. W.H. WINN wounded at H.Q. where to carry out raid on the night of 28/29th. The 1st Kings relieved us in support. I am senior.	
	26		The 2nd South Staffords in the front line 8.00 a.m. night relieved & in ready at 11.55 p.m. I am left and in support.	
AYETTE	27		Drew up orders for raid. Artillery & our own in more to manage out the barrage. Very quiet day 1 Sgt. 2 O.R.'s wounded	

WAR DIARY or INTELLIGENCE SUMMARY

Army Form C. 2118

Place	Date	Hour	Summary of Events and Information	Remarks and references to Appendices
AYETTE	28		At 10.55 PM 2/Lt L.C. NORRINGTON M.M. and 20 O.R's raided the enemy line. It Fll & 4.2 to obtain an identification. Raid was found under artillery and Stokes barrage. On reaching our own wire enemy opened out with M.G. then lifting to a back barrage of moderate intensity but no enemy wire at spots. Enemy wire was not excellent. If the enemy were seen whence the barrage more or less church for a distance of 30 yards. The men much more shaken for a few minutes and being unable to climb the enemy wire and not to caught as S.D. Raid was slightly later. Casualties 1st and several German were after the raid but fire fire and enemy artillery astonishingly fast. Casualties enemy artillery astonishingly nil.	
	29		Two quiet day	
	30		Relieved by 1st Kings Regt and on relieve moved into D. reserved position at MONCHY.	

Our casualties for the raid:
1/4409 (W.A. Bush armed) D.C.M.
4/77 Sjt — Joseph (armed) M.S.M.

Casualties:
Killed 2nd Lieut G.H. Spicer (6-6-18) 1 Other ranks 9
Wounded 2 Lieut W.H. Warn (27-6-18)
2 Lieut (W. Atkinson (27-6-18)
19 O.R's.

Ration Strength 24 Officers 626 O.R's Trench Strength 21 Officers 611 O.R's Sjt.

H.O. Smyth
Lieut Col
Comdg. 17 Royal Fusiliers

3-6-18

6th Brigade.

2nd Division.

-------- -----

1/17th BATTALION

ROYAL FUSILIERS

JULY 1918.

Army Form C. 2118.

WAR DIARY

INTELLIGENCE SUMMARY

(Erase heading not required.)

14th R.W.F. 232 ERS

July

33b

Place	Date	Hour	Summary of Events and Information	Remarks and references to Appendices
MAMETZ	1		Company training and clearing up	
	2		a certain amount of high explosive fire in vicinity of Bn. HQrs. One	
		11.30 pm	In retaliation for a raid carried out into the Division on our left. Major J.S.M. HOLE MC tired off twenty-two rounds of signal B. Station. Had a practice attack in vicinity of Brigade H.Q.C	
	3		The Divisional Commander came round the battalion areas to look at the billets. Returned the 2nd South Staffords in the support, and the 2nd D Coys in front. Double line, Bn. in right D on left and C top in purple trench C on right, A on left	
ADINFER WOOD	4		The enemy put down a 7 to 8 barrage with 5.9 shells on the CUCKOO VALLEY at 9.15 am. The O.C. went round the battalion area with	
	5		the commanding officer and went into the question of the outlying of Lewis Guns and the general want of defence by the outpost Brigade. Captain R.G.A. HENNIKER MC 2nd Duke of Wellington's Regt joined for a months attachment while battalion at rest in rear for first instruction while battalion not carrying under the R.E. of	
	6		division from 3 - 7 am. Battalion ordered to have up a scheme for a large raid on enemy.	

Army Form C. 2118

WAR DIARY
or
INTELLIGENCE SUMMARY.
(Erase heading not required.)

Instructions regarding War Diaries and Intelligence Summaries are contained in F. S. Regs., Part II. and the Staff Manual respectively. Title pages will be prepared in manuscript.

Place	Date	Hour	Summary of Events and Information	Remarks and references to Appendices
ADINFER WOOD	7		Still very hot. Battalion nothing under R.E. supervision from 3-7 am. Draw up plans for the raid.	
AYETTE	8		Bring men competition for the 2nd Lewis gun positions in the battalion. Relieved the 2nd & 4th Staffords in the front line. Coys in right front, D Coy centre, C Coy left, B Coy in rear. Relief complete 11.55 P.M.	
	9		Very quiet day. Enemy planes over flying very low indeed. Our guns did some wire cutting in centre of our front. Capt A.H.H.L.L. returned from leave and took over command of A Coy. One battery fired on its SOS lines at 10.30 P.M. At 4.30 am a new type of signal sent over reported to tell Brigade Signal Officer. He rang one to the Battalion as not at all good owing to so few men having any experience in the handling of the last wire. S.O.S. some continued wire cutting. There of our own bombed by our 18th arty. A touching item will number made to man have reasons for were he slay in a rest. Received information that the 10/7 Kings would carry out proposed raid. B & H & go shelled at intervals throughout the day with 4.2"	
	10			
	11			

WAR DIARY
or
INTELLIGENCE SUMMARY.
(Erase heading not required.)

Army Form C. 2118

Instructions regarding War Diaries and Intelligence Summaries are contained in F. S. Regs., Part II. and the Staff Manual respectively. Title pages will be prepared in manuscript.

Place	Date	Hour	Summary of Events and Information	Remarks and references to Appendices
AYETTE	12		2/Lt J.J. EVANS wounded on a fighting patrol. Orders came during the day for a further operation of trying to be confirmed in the evening. Battalion relieved by the York Rangers Regt in relief billets. Went into reserve. MONCHY.	
MONCHY	13		Battalion bathing and cleaning up. 2/Lt W.S. WARD and F.G. WATER joined the Battalion. MAY posted to A Coy. WATERS to D Coy.	
	14		Heavy rain prevented all parades	
	15		Companies practised an attack in the open with flags. 100 Officers and men employed on digging new trench. Major P.E.B.F. SMITH from the 2nd South Staffords posted as second in command. 2/Lt S. COKE and J.W. JAMES joined the battalion. COKE posted to A Coy, JAMES to D Coy	
ADINFER WOOD	16		Very hot thundery storm in early hours of the morning. All parades cancelled. Relieved 2nd South Staffords in support line. C Coy on right, A Coy on left in front line. B Coy in right D Coy on left in reserve line.	
	17		Whole battalion mining different localities and working in whole battalion mining different localities and working on new cut. Raid on Fort head during the day. Capt. D.G. GIBSON M.C. joined battalion and took over command of C Coy	

WAR DIARY
or
INTELLIGENCE SUMMARY.
(Erase heading not required.)

Army Form C. 2118

Place	Date	Hour	Summary of Events and Information	Remarks and references to Appendices
ADINFER WOOD	18		Whole battalion working on Wire and Dug-outs at 5.10 P.M the enemy began shelling DOUCHY very heavily with 2 shells about 15.00 were fired. One shell hit the front battalion AID POST	
	19		Battalion at work under the R.E from 3-7 P.M	
AYETTE	20		The enemy put down a barrage on AYETTE and DOUCHY from 2.30 - 3.30 a.m. Battalion relieved the 2nd South Staffords on the front line, A Coy on right front, B Coy centre, C Coy left, D Coy in Reserve.	
	21		Several men ill with entry agent slightly gas storingh had another Battalion ordered to wire new communication trench DOUCHY shelled heavily at 11.30 P.M	
	22		DOUCHY and AYETTE shelled with 5.9's at 3 a.m but no damage done. 2/Lt R GOODIER and Cpl. 8. H. 9. killed with 5.9's at 11.30 P.M. The battalion was relieved by the 29th Brigade at 12.30 A.M and we came in for a turn in reserve	
	23		Our guns put down a very heavy barrage for the raid by the Retaliation Very heavy rain in the morning. We had 13 Officers 15 Sgts to 43 corporals and 253 owners of the 2nd Battalion American Regiment attached to us for 48 hours instruction 313	

WAR DIARY
or
INTELLIGENCE SUMMARY.
(Erase heading not required.)

Army Form C. 2118.

Instructions regarding War Diaries and Intelligence Summaries are contained in F. S. Regs., Part II. and the Staff Manual respectively. Title pages will be prepared in manuscript.

Place	Date	Hour	Summary of Events and Information	Remarks and references to Appendices
AYETTE	24		The Division on our right made a raid at 1.45 a.m. Battalion officers replying in maintaining harassing fire and NCO's Box 24" billet with 5.9" at intervals during the day.	
MONCHY	25		The troops came returned to their rest at 4 P.M. Battalion relieved 10th Kings Regt. and in relief marched back to MONCHY LE M.	
	26		M. & L.I. made the battalion having no Lewis gun officers Battalion bathed and cleaning up. Very heavy rain most of the afternoon	
	27		most of the battalions trimmers plucked out having the night, meal or not off all day.	
	28		wounds. Till my but for three companies practiced attack in the open.	
	29		Companies practiced attack in the open Battalion relieved 2nd	
	30		South Staffords in support trench. B Coy right D Coy left in front PURPLE LINE, C Coy left + right in support Purple line.	
ADINFER WOOD	31		Battalion working under R.E from 3-7 P.M.	

WAR DIARY
or
INTELLIGENCE SUMMARY
(Erase heading not required.)

Army Form C. 2118

Place	Date	Hour	Summary of Events and Information	Remarks and references to Appendices
			Casualties	
			1 O.R. killed 2/Lt J.J. Evans Wounded 1 O.R. 1 O.R. U.S.A.	
			Ration strength 694 O.R.	
			25 Officers	
			Trench strength 584 O.R.	
			22 Officers	
				M.C. Smith Lt Col
				Comdg 17th R Brigade

6th Brigade.

2nd Division.

1/17th BATTALION

ROYAL FUSILIERS

AUGUST 1918.

WAR DIARY / INTELLIGENCE SUMMARY

Army Form C. 2118.

1/L.R. Fusiliers

August 1918

Place	Date	Hour	Summary of Events and Information	Remarks and references to Appendices
ADINFER WOOD	1		Battalion in support. Working parties under supervision of the R.E. &c.	
	2		O.C. Dragon inspected the most front lines at POMMIER. Sent out by travellers half platoons. Occupied in firing a belt or two and digging new pits.	
	3		On morning under R.E. supervision, dug out new emplacements in the front line. A Coy on right. Relieved the 2nd South Staffords in front line in the right sub sector. B Coys left, C Coy on right to be withdrawn	
AVETTE	4		D Coy centre, B Coys left, C Coy in support. Relief complete by 11.35 p.m. Quiet and uneventful night. No more than a few orders to concentrate on the wire in the 5th battalion known to be sent. The emplacements were not	
	5		right company front, and still the other emplacements on the left. Our R.A.F. officers covering up to the 31th party to recover pits in the wood. Down the Juncheon had not in a son the Juncheon hurry the formation at 5 p.m. K Coy 17 3rd 6th arrived my tanks hurry the formation attacked to the battalion front there 319 Regt. A.E.F. came up to be attacked to each company and the of Hits, on platoon being attacked to each company and always allived emphasis being sent back to POMMIER. The battalion consisted in moving on the new crops, and of instructions was told for the movements to stand them on arrival. There but them in in the front line at no possible during the day and.	
	6		night.	

WAR DIARY
or
INTELLIGENCE SUMMARY.
(Erase heading not required.)

Army Form C. 2118.

Place	Date	Hour	Summary of Events and Information	Remarks and references to Appendices
AYETTE	7		The enemy put down a very heavy artillery concentration on the valley north of DOUCHY. They used 5.9's & 4.2's & medium T.M. during shoot. A man organised shoot on the enemy front line by the Brigade on our left at 4.35 P.M. The Divisional were relieved by the Brigade the AYETTE - DOUCHY Road. 2/Lt W.S. HUGHES. M.C. M.M. joined the Battalion and was posted to A Coy. Lt F.C. SMITH joined the Battalion as signalling officer.	
	8		Enemy snipers were found active throughout the day on our battery positions. D Coy sent out a fighting patrol of 2 officers and 40 OR's to reconn. if the enemy were holding the posts just north of the COURCELLES ROAD. The patrol did not meet with any opposition and found the enemy clear of the area between the AYETTE - COURCELLES and AYETTE MOYENVILLE Roads.	
	9		A certain number of the enemy were seen in the vicinity of MOYBLAIN TRENCH. Our planes went out & bombed COURCELLES in daylight and were not heavily fired on. The Battalion plus the company of The Americans was relieved by the 1st Kings, the Americans marched back to LA BEZIQUE FARM the Battalion in relief marched to MONCHY. The relief was complete at 9.5.5 P.M.	

WAR DIARY
or
INTELLIGENCE SUMMARY.

Army Form C. 2118.

(Erase heading not required.)

Instructions regarding War Diaries and Intelligence Summaries are contained in F. S. Regs., Part II. and the Staff Manual respectively. Title pages will be prepared in manuscript.

Place	Date	Hour	Summary of Events and Information	Remarks and references to Appendices
MONCHY	10		The Battalion was billeted. We used a short rifle range that had been constructed E of MONCHY.	
	11		Two companies went on the range and the others did a very hot day. Tactical exercises.	
	12		The Battalion continued to use the range during the day. The enemy shelled our billets in the town somewhat at night. Football continued as usual & killed battalion soccer championship not football was continued. Enemy shelled battalion area at night.	
	13		The Battalion moved up at 8 PM to relieve the 2nd South Staffords, as they could not march to HUMBERCAMP, in the front line area being taken over by the Americans. In the front Purple Line C by on right Aa on left, in support line B by in right Dd on left. Reports came through that the enemy were retiring opposite SERRE and we got when orders to join in case of a general German retirement. The S.O.S. went up on our front and on that of the 99th Brigade, but the guns would not fire as the 1st Kings had patrols right out.	
ADINFER WOOD	14		Went through the orders with regard to our advance until all the company commanders were thoroughly acquainted with them.	
	15		The Americans are to first proceed no nearer COUR CEILLES TO WOOD and push on towards CERTSLIES? and the present front line	

Army Form C. 2118

WAR DIARY
or
INTELLIGENCE SUMMARY.
(Erase heading not required.)

Instructions regarding War Diaries and Intelligence Summaries are contained in F. S. Regs., Part II. and the Staff Manual respectively. Title pages will be prepared in manuscript.

Place	Date	Hour	Summary of Events and Information	Remarks and references to Appendices
ADINFER WOOD	16		The Battalion did not do any work worth mentioning. The 2nd South Staffords came up and relieved the 1st Royal Berks and 23rd Royal Fusiliers on the 99th Brigade front.	
	17		The battalion were employed in carrying in ammunition and making fire steps for ammunition dumps.	
	18		At 2 P.M. we got an order that we were to relieve the 2nd Battalion of the 319th American Regiment in the front line 2 nights out, not on the 19/20th. No moving arrangements had already been made for the relief to-morrow night. There is every sign of an offensive taking place on this front in the near future, ammunition in very large quantities is coming up. A big tank was sight first outside D Coy centre, C Coy left with B Coy in support. Relief complete at 11.5–5 PM	
AYETTE	19		A Coy reported that they had not thought their post to be an outpost line at all owned and he was ordered to change them and report new positions. The O.C. 23rd Royal Innuskilens came to arrange about taking over our front line on the night of the 20/21st – at that they were to attack from our front line a Brigade of the 6th Brigade came in to arrange about taking over our left. Company H.Q. go on a Brigade H.Q. We were ordered to reconnoitre suitable positions for putting the Battalion into in case of being shelling. We also reconnoitred alternative positions to form a

Army Form C. 2118.

WAR DIARY
or
INTELLIGENCE SUMMARY.
(Erase heading not required.)

Place	Date	Hour	Summary of Events and Information	Remarks and references to Appendices
AYETTE	19		to reoccupied in case of being greatly shelling. Colonel Brodie VC MC came to arrange about taking over & request no for on the MOYENVILLE Road inclusive to-night, and we made arrangements to interchange C Coy in outpost. 4 prisoners captured by the Staffords last night reported that the enemy intended retaking his outpost line. Apart no and we were ordered to re-inforce the outpost to have to-night the 8 WC CHANCELLOR MC gamed in turns from Officer to flew of the attack to the IV and VIth Corps come in. The attack is being done by one Divisions, the first Objective being from MOYENVILLE to ACHET-LE-GRAND. The 99th Brigade are taking the first objective and then the 3rd Division is going through them and we are in support to the 3rd Division. The were shelled the purple Event line most of the afternoon evidently trying to knock out guns for horse in 4.5.5 am to 9 am.	
	20		The 23rd Division did not arrive up to relieve me till 1 AM and at that time AYETTE and DOUCHY were being very heavily and shelled not the relief took place under very great difficulties. At 4 am the whole of Bn HQrs troth shelled them in the dug-outs round an area, no there were a very large number of gas all round. No the barrage seemed fromities at 4.3.5 am	
	21			

WAR DIARY
or
INTELLIGENCE SUMMARY.
(Erase heading not required.)

Army Form C. 2118.

Place	Date	Hour	Summary of Events and Information	Remarks and references to Appendices
AYETTE	21		and seemed a very good one indeed. We are told that the 99th Brigade had got their objective with practically no loss. We were notified at 11 am that it was not probable that we would be called upon. It was a very hot day indeed and gradually a huge number of men belonging to A and D Coys began to suffer from the unusual gas. Both companies were moved every night out of the affected area to a flank. By nightfull we had had the following gas casualties 2/Lts WATERS, JAMES, AUSTEN and SAUNDERS and 88 OR's.	
	22		The gas casualties continued to come down and by 3 pm Capts PANTING, 2/Lts CULE and MORRIS had also gone down and the number of men had increased to 138. At 6.30 pm we got a warning order that the attack would be continued on the 23rd, and that after the 3rd Division had taken COMIECOURT, the 2nd Division would go through them and take ERVILLERS, BEHAGNIES, and SAPIGNIES. The 6th Brigade plus the 1st Royal Berks to attack ERVILLERS. It was to be moved out by the 2nd South Staffords on its right, 1st Kings Regt on the left, the 1st Royal Berks in support to the Staffords and 17th Royal Fusiliers in support to the Kings. We had to be in position by 3 am at 11.30 pm the Brigadier met all commanding officers at the 17th RF's HQrs	

WAR DIARY
or
INTELLIGENCE SUMMARY.

Army Form C. 2118.

Place	Date	Hour	Summary of Events and Information	Remarks and references to Appendices
AYETTE	22		and went over the scheme. After that a company commanders conference was held and further orders received. C Coy under Capt Johnson to be on the left, B Coy under Capt Smart on the right, and A Coy under 2/Lt NORRINGTON in support. The main role of the Battalion will be to support the Kings and cover for them	
	23		The Battalion moved off at 6.15 A.M. and moved along the northern outskirts of AYETTE to its forming up position just west of MOYBLAIN TRENCH in A.8.a & c. The Battalion was in position by 7.30 A.M. At 10.15 A.M. the Battalion moved off taking 500 yds in rear of the Kings' and got up to their position West of the ARRAS–ALBERT Railway without any casualties at 10.55 A.M. As soon as our barrage came down the Battalion moved forward and Battalion H.Qrs. were established on the West side of the Railway embankment at approx. A.16.6.5. The enemy barrage seemed to come down on the ridge just East of the Railway and on the whole we were pretty heavy. The village of COURCELLES was also heavily shelled and this caused a great deal of trouble to "A" Coy carrying parties. At 11.40 A.M. we were in touch with "C" & "B" Coys, both of them had taken up their appointed positions and had got in touch with O.C. 1st KINGS and had started their consolidation in A.17 & d. After 2.0 P.M. the Coys were busily occupied in carrying "C" Coy during its advance captured five Germans, just left of the 1st KINGS attack. Casualties for that day were 1 Killed – 28 wounded.	

Army Form C. 2118.

WAR DIARY
or
INTELLIGENCE SUMMARY.
(Erase heading not required.)

Instructions regarding War Diaries and Intelligence Summaries are contained in F. S. Regs., Part II. and the Staff Manual respectively. Title pages will be prepared in manuscript.

Place	Date	Hour	Summary of Events and Information	Remarks and references to Appendices
COURCELLES	24		There was a fair amount of shelling during the night. At 1.40 P.M. the G.O.C. came into our orders that the Battalion to take part in an attack being done by the 99th Bde. Also the 1st KINGS on the village of MORY and on MORY COPSE. The 17th Royal Fusiliers were to follow the 99th Bde. and if the attack on MORY COPSE was successful, they were to move in a South-easterly direction and gain possession of the high ground in B26 & 27, especial attention being paid to JULIA TRENCH which was reported to be occupied by the Enemy. The attack was due to begin at 2:30 P.M. There was no time to get out any orders and the scheme of attack was briefly explained to Coy. Commanders and then the Battalion moved off to ERVILLERS. When the Battalion arrived on the ERVILLERS—MORY Road it was discovered that the 99th Bde. had not moved off and so the Battalion halted for half an hour. We then got into touch with the 1st ROYAL BERKS. and they notified us when they were moving. We moved off again at 3.50 P.M. and moved just North of the village of ERVILLERS. We attempted to form a Battalion H.qrs. in ERVILLERS but the village was shelled too heavily and we established our H.qrs. North of the Village at B.13.f.3.1. Col. KING reported that he had attained his objective and the Battalion moved forward at 5.5 P.M. Capt. GIBSON of "C" Coy reported that his Coy was finally enfiladed by Machine Gun fire from MORY and from the west of MORY and that he was digging in along the ERVILLERS—MORY Road at B26a 95-95 and westwards along that Road. I think	

(A7093) Wt W12590/M1793 75,40 6. 1/17. D. D. & L., Ltd. Forms/C.2118/14.

WAR DIARY or INTELLIGENCE SUMMARY

Army Form C. 2118.

Place	Date	Hour	Summary of Events and Information	Remarks and references to Appendices
COURCELLES	24		forward to the SPUR east of ERVILLERS and came under Machine Gun fire from MORY and then tried to get round the northern part of ERVILLERS but was informed by the S/STAFFORDS that it was impossible to get forward there. I then met the G.O.C. who ordered me to establish an outpost line astride the MORY ROAD. "B" Coy the right sector, took up a line from B20c 2-8 – B20a 9-9. "C" Coy the left sector, took up a line from B14c 90-00 – B14d 90-10. "A" Coy in support in sunken road B14a 0-7 – B14c 4-9. This outpost line was established by 8.0 PM. The Battalion was very heavily shelled with a mixture of H.E. and gas, from 10 PM onwards. 2 killed – 18 wounded.	
ERVILLERS	25		The Battalion was relieved by "A" and "B" Coys. of the 5th K.O.Y.L.I. The relief took place under difficult circumstances as the enemy were shelling very heavily. Relief was complete at 4.25 AM. and the Battalion in relief marched back to the AERODROME, east of AYETTE (A7d 4-3)	
AYETTE	26		The Battalion spent the day constructing shelters on their area (West of the AERODROME ½ just north of the COURCELLES ROAD. 2Lt J. BROWNLEE and a draft of 31 other ranks joined the Battalion. 2Lt J. BROWNLEE was posted to B Coy; Between 5.5 AM and 6.0 AM. a bomb exploded amidst a fire in the Battalion area, 8 men were wounded.	
	27		The Battalion bathed at AYETTE. The mens' kit and all trench stores were inspected.	

Army Form C. 2118.

WAR DIARY
or
INTELLIGENCE SUMMARY.
(Erase heading not required.)

Place	Date	Hour	Summary of Events and Information	Remarks and references to Appendices
AYETTE	28		The Battalion carried on with the usual training under Company arrangements (Arms Drill, Platoon Drill, P.T. & B.F. &) 2 Lt D. ETHERIDGE and a party of 74 other ranks joined the Battalion. 2 Lt ETHERIDGE was posted to "D" Coy.	
	29		The Battalion carried on with the usual training	
	30		The Battalion carried on with the usual training during the morning. A Brigade exercise with the special object of transmitting information was carried out in the afternoon in conjunction with the 1st KINGS and the S/STAFFORDS under the direction of the G.O.C.	
	31		The Battalion carried on with the usual training during the morning, all Nos 1 and 2 of the LEWIS GUNNERS fired on the K.R.R's range at A.13.c.1-8 during the afternoon. A draft of 32 other ranks joined the Bn.	

Casualties a/Capt H A PANTING M.C. 2/Lt F G WATERS, 2/Lt R E AUSTEN 2/Lt G SANDERS
2/Lt J W JAMES, 2/Lt S CULE, 2/Lt J J CARSON, 2/Lt W B MORRIS all gas casualties
KILLED 4 O Rs WOUNDED 228

CAPTURED ENEMY MATERIAL Light MGs 16 Heavy MGs 18. Trench Mortars 2
Guns 77 m m 6 Anti-Tank Rifles 2.

Ration Strength 25 officers 551 O Rs
Trench Strength 22 441 "

W C Smith Lt-Col
Comdg 17th R Fusiliers

6th Brigade
2nd Division.

1/17th BATTALION

ROYAL FUSILIERS

SEPTEMBER 1918.

WAR DIARY

SEPTEMBER 1918

INTELLIGENCE SUMMARY. 11th ROYAL FUSILIERS

Army Form C. 2118.

Place	Date	Hour	Summary of Events and Information	Remarks and references to Appendices
AYETTE	SEPT. 1		The Battalion bathed. Word was received from the G.O.C. that the Battalion was to be prepared to move forward at any moment. Lt. Col. SMITH-Leay so disposed him self and the command of the Battalion to Maj. FITZWARREN-SMITH.	
	2		The Battalion moved forward at 5.55 AM proceeding to BEHAGNIES, Battalion H.Qrs. was established at H2 a 5.8. At 1.30 PM the Battalion was ordered to proceed to, and occupy the trench 2000 yds. West of VAULX-VRAUCOURT at B29 d. Battalion H.Qrs. being established at B29 d 75-80. At 6.30 PM the G.O.C. called and gave orders to the effect that the Battalion was to relieve the 5th K.O.Y.L.I's who occupied the line East of VAULX-VRAUCOURT running approximately from C27 d 9.3 through I3 b 3.0 to I3 c 90.15. The 6th Infantry Brigade would continue the attack the following morning, the 5th's open their being on the right and left respectively. The final objective would be the high ground S. West of MORCHIES (I5 a b 5 to I11 a 0.6) and the final objective the high ground East of MORCHIES running through J1 a 4.3, J1 a 0.0, I12 d 0.3, I12 a 6.0 and I12 c 5.5. The disposition of the 6th Infantry Brigade were: the 17th ROYAL FUSILIERS on the left, the S/STAFFORDS on the right, and the 1st KINGS in reserve. Maj. Morrett went forward with O.C. S/STAFFORDS to get in touch with the Battalion Commander of 5th K.O.Y.L.I's and arrange the relief. He returned at 8.50 PM and a Coy Commanders conference was held. "A" Coy on the right, "B" Coy on the left and	35-4

Army Form C. 2118.

WAR DIARY
or
INTELLIGENCE SUMMARY.

(Erase heading not required.)

Instructions regarding War Diaries and Intelligence Summaries are contained in F. S. Regs., Part II. and the Staff Manual respectively. Title pages will be prepared in manuscript.

Place	Date	Hour	Summary of Events and Information	Remarks and references to Appendices
AYETTE	2 (contd)		"E" Coy in reserve. The G.O.C. called again at 11.20 P.M. and gave his final orders mentioning that it was reported that the enemy had retired from MORCHIES and that the Brigade would push forward to the east of BEAUMETZ as far as the road running through J.14.f.	
VAULX-VRAUCOURT	3		The Battalion moved off at 12.45 AM and the relief of the 5th KOYLI'S was completed at 3.30 AM. Battalion H.qrs. was established at VAULX, C26d.3-7 At 5.20 AM the attack was launched, "A" Coy on the right (Capt. ASHWELL) "B" Coy on the left (Capt. SWORD) and "C" Coy in reserve (2nd Lt HARRIS) The first objective was gained without opposition, reports to this effect reaching Battalion H.qrs. at 7.0 AM. As soon as the barrage covered the advance of MORCHIES and BEAUMETZ were taken without any serious opposition, a few H.E. and gas shells fell in the new east of MORCHIES and in the neighbourhood of BEAUMETZ. At 8.0 AM Battalion H.qrs. advanced to 14d.3-5 and orders were issued to Coy commanders to consolidate in depth at the road running north-east through J.14.f. Verbal message received at 11.30 AM that the objective was gained. At 11.30 AM the GOC saw Battalion Commander and instructed them to continue the advance from J.14.f at 1.0 PM. The 99th Bde would be	

Army Form C. 2118

WAR DIARY
or
INTELLIGENCE SUMMARY.
(Erase heading not required.)

Instructions regarding War Diaries and Intelligence Summaries are contained in F.S. Regs., Part II. and the Staff Manual respectively. Title pages will be prepared in manuscript.

Place	Date	Hour	Summary of Events and Information	Remarks and references to Appendices
VAULX	3 (contd)		withdrawn and the 6th Brigade would take over the whole Divisional front. The 17th ROYAL FUSILIERS would then be on the left, the S. STAFFORDS on the right and the 1st KING'S in reserve. The Battalion's northern boundary would be a line running east from J4 d.00 along J3d to K7 d.27 and the southern, a line running from J6 a.00 through J17 central thence to the SUGAR FACTORY at J18 d.3.2 and thence to the objective which was the high ground east of DEMICOURT, approx J.18 d.52 — K7 central. The boundary dividing two sub forced objectives was a line running from J10 c.05 to K.C.0.0 thence East. Afterwards the objective was altered to run in a curve from BOURSIES to the high ground on K7 central to J18 d.5.2 in order that the left flank might be in touch with the GUARDS. The Battalion would have 3 Whippet tanks to help them and Cavalry patrols would be pushed out in front to LARGO and Maj SMITH and the Adjutant at 12:0 noon orders were issued to receive and deliver final instructions to forward Coy Commanders. At 12:30 PM Bn Hqrs. advanced to BEAUMETZ at J14 f 7.0 on the DOIGNIES ROAD. On reaching J14 f, where the Battalion had recently reported that they were in position, no trace of the Battalion could be found. Maj SMITH and the Adjutant reconnoitered and at 1.45 PM found the Battalion in the Sunken Road S.W. of BEAUMETZ running through J20a with the reserve Coy in trenches in J19 a + d. A report had been previously sent to the Brigade that touch had been lost with the Battalion. O.C. Coys were hastily interviewed and the situation explained. The Coys were formed and the advance continued at 2.30 P.M. At 2.0 P.M. Maj SMITH was hit on the right hip by a snow ball, the convos a very bad however but he carried on	

(A7092). Wt. W2899/M1293. 75,000. 4/17. D.D. & L., Ltd. Forms/C.2118/14.

Army Form C. 2118.

WAR DIARY
or
INTELLIGENCE SUMMARY.
(Erase heading not required.)

Instructions regarding War Diaries and Intelligence Summaries are contained in F.S. Regs., Part II. and the Staff Manual respectively. Title pages will be prepared in manuscript.

Place	Date	Hour	Summary of Events and Information	Remarks and references to Appendices
VAULX	3 (contd)		DOIGNIES was taken with very little opposition but the advance was held up on the ridge running through J.17 central by oblique and enfilade M.G. fire from the vicinity of BOURSIES. B Coy called for 2 Platoons from the reserve Coy on account of casualties sustained. Battalion Hqrs was established at trench east of DOIGNIES, J.17a 2.8. At 5.30 PM own artillery brought fire to bear on the enemy MG positions and at 6.20 PM the advance was continued on DEMICOURT. The village was taken but considerable difficulty was experienced on account of very heavy shelling. Coys reported opposite grand at 6.55 PM. The Coys reorganized and consolidated along STURGEON SUPPORT, GRAYLING TRENCH, TROUT POST and the DEMICOURT/HERMIES ROAD to just north of the SUGAR FACTORY (J.6c&d, J.12b, K.7a+c, J.12d and J.1P 2+d) posts were thrown out 300 yards in front. The reserve Coy (2 Platoons) occupied JUNIPER TRENCH in J.17a astride the DOIGNIES/DEMICOURT ROAD. Touch was maintained with the S/STAFFORDS on the right but we lost touch with the GUARDS on the left. B Coy pushed north, took BOURSIES thus regaining touch with the GUARDS. The C.O immediately took steps to have the ground to the east of DOIGNIES reconnoitred and alternative positions selected in case the line thereabouts Lt Col SMITH returned at 8.30 PM and took over the command of the Battalion.	
DOIGNIES	4		At 6.0 AM the 1st Kings' passed through our front line with the object of pushing forward up to the CANAL DU NORD, the 17th ROYAL FUSILIERS remaining in their existing position. Our left Coy was bombed during the day with hand grenades, casualties being sustained. At 1.30 PM word was received that the	

WAR DIARY or INTELLIGENCE SUMMARY

Army Form C. 2118.

(Erase heading not required.)

Place	Date	Hour	Summary of Events and Information	Remarks and references to Appendices
DAISNIES	4 (contd)		Battalion moved to be relieved by the 1st K.R.R.s sometime during the night and the Battalion moved back to BEAUMETZ	
	5		Coys reported relief complete at 2.30 a.m. The Battalion moved to BEAUMETZ Battalion Hqrs being established at J.13 central. 2 Lt W.F. HUGHES attended 3rd Bn. 2 Lt J. BROWNLEE to duty. Casualties 2nd/4th Sept. – 2 Lt W.F. HUGHES attended 3rd Bn., 2 Lt J. BROWNLEE to duty, attached personnel 6th Bn. Sct – OR's Killed 8, Wounded 42, Missing 1. The General Greened and visited the Battalion area at 11.30 a.m. R.R.F. PANTING rejoined the Battalion.	
BEAUMETZ	6		At 2.0 a.m. the Battalion area was heavily shelled with 5.9s H.V. shells. The village was shelled intermittently during the day in consequence of which the Battalion had orders to move north of the BAPAUME/CAMBRAI ROAD in the vicinity of CHAUFOURS WOOD. Bn Hqrs were established at J.12a 15.30.	
	7		The Battalion area was again shelled during the morning orders were received to move further west to I.17a between MURCHIES and BEUGNY. Bn Hqrs were established at I.17a 6.8.	
MURCHIES	8		The Battalion carried out musketry & Lewis gun training during the morning. 2 Lts A.E. MAY, J.B.L. PLANT, J.A.C. GAVET and J.S. McMENAMIN joined the Battalion. 2 Lts MAY & PLANT being posted to "B" Coy. the rest to "D" Coy.	
	9		The Battalion carried out with the usual training during the morning	
	10		The Battalion carried out with the usual training during the morning	

Army Form C.2118

WAR DIARY
or
INTELLIGENCE SUMMARY.
(Erase heading not required.)

Place	Date	Hour	Summary of Events and Information	Remarks and references to Appendices
MOEUVRES	11		The Battalion carried on with the usual training the morning and out arrangements.	
	12		The Battalion carried on with the usual training during the morning. A warning order was received during the morning stating that the 6th Brigade might be relieving the 5th. It was cancelled about 10.0 P.M. for the time being, but the Brigade mentioned that the Battalion would probably relieve the 2/4th Royal Fusiliers in the morning.	
	13		Word was received that the Brigade would relieve the 5th Rifle Brigade on the left, 1st Kings on the right and the 1/4th Royal Fusiliers in newly won HERNIES. At 9.30 A.M. Lt Col SMITH and the Adjutant rode over to HERNIES in order to arrange for the relief of the 2/4th Royal Fusiliers. At 2.30 P.M. a Coy Commanders conference was held, "B" Coy with 2 Platoons & "A" Coy on the right in the QUARRY (approx J29 a 5.7) "C" Coy with 2 Platoons on the left as JUNIPER TRENCH (J24 a 7.2). The Battalion moved off at 5.45 P.M. and the relief was reported complete at 8.45 P.M. Battalion HQrs was established in HERNIES at J29 c 70.95. Owing to lack of accommodation for "A"+"C" Coy movement JUNIPER TRENCH and 3 Platoons of "B" Coy were placed in Battalion HQrs. Next morning it was the intention of the Battalion HQrs would actually be taken over by the Brigade.	

Army Form C. 2118.

WAR DIARY
or
INTELLIGENCE SUMMARY.

(Erase heading not required.)

Instructions regarding War Diaries and Intelligence Summaries are contained in F. S. Regs., Part II. and the Staff Manual respectively. Title pages will be prepared in manuscript.

Place	Date	Hour	Summary of Events and Information	Remarks and references to Appendices
HERMIES	14		The surroundings of HERMIES were reconnoitred with a view to finding suitable Hqrs for the Battalion. Word was received that the 1st KINGS and S.STAFFORDS would be moving forward. The Battalion Hqrs and B Coy moved forward at 7.30PM and took up the S.STAFFORDS Hqrs at J18 d 3.8. A draft of 41 OR joined the Battalion.	
DEMICOURT	15		Word was received that the Division would be relieved with 16.4 by the 3rd Division. The Battalion area was shelled during the night. At 10.0 PM Operation Orders were received. The Battalion would be relieved by the 7th SHROPSHIRE LIGHT INFANTRY after the 17th ROYAL FUSILIERS would move back to BEE WOOD near BEHAGNIES (B25 c 79) returning the night 16/17th at MORCHIES.	
	16		The Commanding Officer of the 7th SHROPSHIRE L.I. arrived at 10.0 AM and orders to make arrangements for the relief. The relief was not completed at 10.10 a.m. The Battalion moved back spending the night at MORCHIES Battalion Hqrs was established at I 11 d 55-80. A draft of 4 OR joined the Battalion.	
MORCHIES	17		There was a very severe thunderstorm at 10 AM great inconvenience was caused on account of the poor state of the shelters. At 3.0 PM the Battalion moved off and arrived at the area allotted near BEE WOOD, BEHAGNIES at about 5.30PM. Battalion Hqrs was established at B 25 c 75-95. A draft of 23 O.Ranks joined the Battalion.	

Army Form C. 2118

WAR DIARY
or
INTELLIGENCE SUMMARY.
(Erase heading not required.)

Place	Date	Hour	Summary of Events and Information	Remarks and references to Appendices
BEHAGNIES	18		The men's kits and trench stores inspected and anything short was carried out during the morning. The remainder of the day was spent in cleaning and improving of bivos. 2nd Lt C.N. JARRETT joined the Battalion and was posted to "A" Coy.	
	19		The Battalion carried on with the usual training during the morning under Coy. arrangements. During the afternoon all officers & NCOs received instruction from the O.C. 15th TANK Bn. (32) for a scheme to be carried out in the morning. Lt J. M. D. BRADLEY joined the Battalion and was posted to "A" Coy.	
	20		The Battalion trained in the Bn. Bath House. Scheme with 15th TANK Bn. cancelled. Companies carried on with usual training during the morning. The Commanding officer and Adjutant reconnoitred the ground EAST of LANGICOURT and on towards LOUVERAL when the Bn. would operate if called upon for counterattack. The B.O.C. & 2nd Bde. held a conference of commanders/officers at 9.0 pm. Outline sketch of proposed attack was explained.	
	21		The C.O. held a company commanders conference at 6.30 a.m. re explosion proposed scheme of attack. The utmost secrecy was impressed. Companies carried on with training toying special attention to practising "The Coy. attack." Smoke bombs were used.	
	22		No parades. The Padre held voluntary services at 8.0 a.m. and 12 noon.	
	23.		Morning parades started with Battalion Drill. The Commanding officer took the morning parade. The rest of the morning companies carried on with the usual training	

WAR DIARY
or
INTELLIGENCE SUMMARY.

Army Form C. 2118.

Place	Date	Hour	Summary of Events and Information	Remarks and references to Appendices
BEHAGNIES	23		The Commanding Officer visited the 2nd Divisional Reception Camps at POMMIER.	
	24		Companies practised 'the attack' from 6.0am to 10.0am. At 10.30am the Battalion paraded for a route march under the 2nd i/c (moment). Route to BAPAUME and back along the ARRAS BAPAUME Road. The object of the march was to harden the men's feet for the coming attack. At 5.30pm G.O.C. 2nd Division presented medal ribbons to the Brigade. 4 O/Rs and 100 O.R's (whole). There were 7 recipients from the Battalion.	
	25		Companies carried on with the usual training. A warning order was received that we should move up with the trenches EAST of BOISNES about 4.30pm next day. In the evening the final for the Inter-Coy Polo Cup was played. C Coy represented the Battalion and beat B Coy 2nd South Staffs (1s by 2—1 after a few faults).	
	26		Coy: prepared for movement up the line. The 100 nucleus and (3rds) proceeds to POMMIER. Stores and surplus kit were moved to reserved huts in B 19.A. and a group of 6 men were left. At 10.0 am the Commanding Officer attended a conference at G.H.Q./Bde. 14/n.w. Final movement orders were issued. The Battalion moved off at 5.0 pm. The Transport moved to a position between BEAUMETZ and ST AQUIRE. M/in SMITH, the Adjutant and A/e.C (by commanding the Orderly Room) remained in the old position. The different companies moved extremely difficult owing to the congested amount of traffic on the roads and trenches and all the confusion of the crossing of the roads.	

WAR DIARY
or
INTELLIGENCE SUMMARY
(Erase heading not required.)

Army Form C. 2118

Place	Date	Hour	Summary of Events and Information	Remarks and references to Appendices
FLESQUIERES	27		Battalion moved in to assembly area East of RUYAULCOURT at 9.45 p.m. The ammunition and rations for the following day were issued. The battalion had a hot meal. The troops were very cheerful. At 5.20 a.m. A company was commanded by LIEUT. BRADLEY, B Coy by CAPT G.S. MURRAY, C Coy by 2/LT T.W. BENNETT, D Coy by LIEUT H.A. PANTING. M.O. J.L. ℅ the Brigade was on level 16, 1 hour. The bombardment was very intense. The enemy replied very slightly. The order of march was 2nd Scottish Rifles, 1st Cameronians, 17th Royal Fusiliers, 11th T.M. Battery, then 1/9th R.E.13. The battalion was ready under to move at 15 minutes notice at 6.20 am. Orders to move came at 6.40 am and the battalion followed the South Staffords, the Kings Regt next and to rear Order of march for the battalion B.C. A.D. B.H.Q. 9.3. The battalion moved out by the village of DEMICOURT and then on by a causeway to TRESCAULT to LA LOCK and then moved past BIR HAUL to getting the Lark Posts were troubles were experienced and many had to be left behind. The battalion assembled on the East of BIR HAUL on the canal, the whole thing was being begun on the rear at	

WAR DIARY
or
INTELLIGENCE SUMMARY

(Erase heading not required.)

Army Form C. 2118.

Place	Date	Hour	Summary of Events and Information	Remarks and references to Appendices
			of the both. The battalion were in position to fire & drive off the marching the advance and sending forward scouts to get thro direct huts in the wood. They engaged H.Q.R.s 3 & R's and recovering 2/Lt. F.W. CROMWELL & 11 O.R. who retired wounded for the battalion to move to the support line in K.13.c & d. The brigade intending to be in the support line and at the same time the 5th K.R.R. were already attempting to still holding not on BRAINCOURT NEGLE in the source and as soon as I first learned this we avoided to approach. The battalion moved forward in file marching in half-company from. 8 was to manoeuvre from [?] to new if even possible. Owing the manoeuvring the battalion the trenches being full of the Germans D companies & T. & & were established at K.17.b.15-40 C. & move and K.13.d, K.17.a.B and K.13. A in K.11.c. C and D Coys were in the [?] with the 2nd [?] Regt and ordered to support them in case the Brigade was ordered to attack. Brig. A was in touch with the 1st K.Rif.R. and could support them on D.P. if battalion ordered and learning the enemy ordered from ORIVAL WOOD and the OC battalion signalled to brigade that the OC 1st Rifles and after discussing the advice would retire.	

Orders came in that the Brigade would form up through the Brigades Division and attack ORIVAL WOOD and then attack CANTAING TRENCH and CANTAING SUPPORT between MINE WOOD and L3.d.6.3. 8 minutes the between battalions LEECH ALLEY in 29.t and L3.d.Smith Street attacking on the right, 1st Kings on the left, with the 17th Royal Fusiliers in support. After all objectives were gained troops were to push forward to some MINE WOOD. Zero hour 6 P.M. Two battery commanders were ordered to report to Leading Battalion commander. 17 Divisional H.Q. were ordered to be in the PREMY CHAPEL – GRAIN COURT Road at approx L.9.C. The Brigade were under front of heavy artillery fire and hostile machine gun fire in front of ORIVAL WOOD. Some minutes later the attack, and in front of the direction of ROUALIN WOOD. These machine guns were from the direction of 7.30 P.M. and holding up left of 17th Royal Fusiliers were not suffered in L.3.d. and The Brigade line ran from L.3.d.30.05 along a trench running south into L.1.H.b. The Kings had advanced up there to find an enemy strong point of the 17th Royal Fusiliers were adjoining the Kings and held up by the light would eventually to from a defensive flank at the light which could encounter with after dark. Bn HQs were at L.8.c.90.05 and a German gun pit, the whole Brigade were more heavily shelled up to 9 P.M.

Place	Date	Hour	Summary of Events and Information	Remarks and references to Appendices
NOYELLES	28		At 2 am orders were received that the attack would be continued. The 99th Brigade attaching on the right, the 6th Brigade on the left. Dividing lines between Brigades Road running L.5.d.5.1 to L.1.b central thence to B.2.a.3.2. Objectives LA THE TRENCH - CANTAING TRENCH - CANTAING SUPPORT. NINE WOOD - NOYELLES Crossings over Canal ST QUENTIN and high ground east of the CANAL in B.1 and B.2 finishing points between butts lines B.8 & 75 L.9 central L.15.a 2.0 L5.1.3. To L.6.a.9.6. Zero hour 5.15 am. The Brigade met with very little resistance and by 3.30 am NOYELLES had been captured and the river ESCAUT crossed. Considerable resistance was met with at the small crossings over the advance of the whole Division was held up by M.H.Gs in are established at L.5.c.15.24. At 11am the 8 O C interviewed the C.O. with a view to attacking MARCOING TRENCH and the high ground in B.1 and B.2 & method advised & ways to get up companies were the C.O. refused to get out going home. They never met the getting under the ricks of the canal and bringing up of D Company on the enemy side of the canal not attaching it itself. D company were ordered to carry out the initial attack with one platoon of B coy

WAR DIARY or INTELLIGENCE SUMMARY

Army Form C. 2118

2/Lt FAWATERS and others to reconnoitre the river with a view to finding out if it was practicable to get a raft across. This officer swam the canal with a rope and attached it on the far side and then returned & reported on construction by the patrols sappers. The VI Corps reported that the 57th Division had crossed the canal in F.29.d 7.2 and L. The I.O.C. reported the 17th Royal Irish Rifles to cross the canal by means of a raft swimming under the canal at F.29.d 7.2 and stated that the 63rd Division were marching on the left and the 99th Brigade on the right. Only D Coy were to cross the canal until after PONTOONS had been ordered up but to whom that task had fallen was not known. On enquiring the MARCOIGN line the GHQ was to be down the tunnel leading from L.6.a 60.65 to G.2.d 75.65. The Bridges might being first Bde were to cross the canal by the Lock Bridge and as before the front had not fallen back to the canal at F.29.d 75.19. C Coy was to form defensive flank freeing and the A Coy to hold the tunnel crossing running on the W front. From 3pm - 5pm two Lewis gun + 13 men + 16 machine guns would barrage the high ground between PARIS COPSE and PINCE WOOD 3" S.T.Ms was to put down a barrage from zero to zero + on the tunnel immediately E of the canal

WAR DIARY
or
INTELLIGENCE SUMMARY

Army Form C. 2118.

Instructions regarding War Diaries and Intelligence Summaries are contained in F. S. Regs., Part II. and the Staff Manual respectively. Title pages will be prepared in manuscript.

Place	Date	Hour	Summary of Events and Information	Remarks and references to Appendices
			Advanced B⁰ Report centre will be at F.29.d.65.30. Zero hour 7 P.M. Company began to cross the canal at 5.15 P.M. but the artillery put a creeping barrage to the line Chaussee-emplies the eastern end of the canal & the bridge across the canal. At 6.20 P.M. B + D Coys were notified that the 77 I.Bergalais was not attacking, as orders were out to form a defensive flank as soon as the S. Tibo was taken and we were to hasten orders not for the Italians but to attack that our centre had hand over the Italian link to attack without us, and the scene stabilised. Quite a light during the first half hour of the attack. The first effort on Louvers the enemy had 2 machine guns that were afterwards out of men is the engineers were regularised by the army. eng. Incd. hit that path which were made impossible & heavy enemy barrage on the machine guns. The attack was not successful except that a company of bombers went up to time the enemy in S. Killing of the dist. line but remained comparatively quiet from 10.45 onwards. The casualties ...	

D. B. & L., London, E.C.
(A10266). Wt W5300/P713 750,000 2/18 Sch. 62 Forms/C2118/16.

WAR DIARY
or
INTELLIGENCE SUMMARY

(Erase heading not required.)

Army Form C. 2118.

Place	Date	Hour	Summary of Events and Information	Remarks and references to Appendices
	29		at 3am the 87th Infantry attacked the Ridge but having got to [illegible] the 57th Div were in range of and hypres which they had to cross a certain amount of confusion ensued and they were fill back to the west side of the Canal Expt 9 SPECIAL M.M with the 100 tanks of 8 Coy 9.5 n.a.D met by LAM and M.G fire M.C returned the situation the machine gun fire was now [illegible] at all & a [illegible] and casualties were very heavy. A [illegible] of the [illegible] certain numbers of troops were seen west of the canal starting to advance but the 97th Brigade who were attacking at some distance and had to keep in open at a 30 [illegible] in the first few troops of the [illegible] that the 87th Brigade informed of the situation and at 7am the CO went up to clear up the situation and found the lead troops of the troops and others at the canal by the lack bridge. The [illegible] at [illegible] 0.4.1.3 in the machine line few fire etc. The Canal at [illegible] 0.4.1.3 decided to cross. The situation was discussed with the Kings and the necessary company commanders of the Ruttadur sent out and [illegible] that an enemy of the to advance at 10.15 am a report came in that the enemy attacked the Canal where had advanced	

Army Form C. 2118.

WAR DIARY
or
INTELLIGENCE SUMMARY.
(Erase heading not required.)

Instructions regarding War Diaries and Intelligence Summaries are contained in F. S. Regs., Part II. and the Staff Manual respectively. Title pages will be prepared in manuscript.

Place	Date	Hour	Summary of Events and Information	Remarks and references to Appendices
	29		from 7 to 8 C out of and by 9 am the battalion took up a line between PARIS COPSE and RANGE WOOD. A/T [?] informed the Coml. [Commanding Officer?] and was sent them on to G.I.H.Q.B. The battalion had advanced beyond the line that the [?] support to take up and the Comdt. [?] adjutant (Capt. Cuban LEA) went forward to see them back and a [?] forth and knew gave were being burnt not by the Germans. Captain SPENCER and Lt. White moving forward with the SMITH as Iwrf [?] had come up in [?] [?] placed with regiment came up. As [?] have have with the battalion then came after the battalion had incident they repeat at 6 pm the [?] received [?] messaging in 6.2.b.I.SK. 3.05 sent up [?] the 29th 1913 all forward my group of the [?] [?] [?] now wished that the 5 at brigade De Brigade sent and an order that the 6 [?] at 8 am [?] the would attack through the 29th Division to attack it at 9 pm that the brit [?] would Brigade sent in an order at 9 pm that the brit [?] attack was be relieved by the 1st Royal [?] for [?] and [?]	

Army Form C. 2118.

WAR DIARY
or
INTELLIGENCE SUMMARY.
(Erase heading not required.)

Instructions regarding War Diaries and Intelligence Summaries are contained in F. S. Regs., Part II. and the Staff Manual respectively. Title pages will be prepared in manuscript.

Place	Date	Hour	Summary of Events and Information	Remarks and references to Appendices
	30		completed at 11.45 P.M. The battalion concentrated in the area F29d and L6a. H.Q. moved back to NOYELLES.	
			Casualties. KILLED.	
			2/Lieut. W.F. HUGHES M.C. M.M. died of wounds 7/9/18.	
			W.F. WILLIAMS killed in action 27/9/18	
			Lieut. J. McD. BRADLEY died of wounds 30/9/18	
			36 other Ranks	
			WOUNDED.	
			Lieut. (A/Capt.) H.A. PANTING M.C. Wounded. 29/9/18	
			" (A/Capt.) J. SPENCER M.M. " "	
			" H.R. ETHERIDGE M.M. " "	
			" E.G. WATERS " "	
			" J.S. McMENAMIN " "	
			" O.L. BRIDGES " (acc) "	
			" T.O. LAWRENCE M.M. Wounded "	
			" F.W. BECKWITH " 27/9/18	
			190 O.R. an M.R singes	

Sheet 1.

17th RF

RECORD OF OPERATIONS - 2nd/4th SEPT.,1918.

Map Ref.57c

1st Sept. AYETTE. Word was received that the Battalion was to be prepared to move forward at any moment. Lt.Col.SMITH being indisposed handed over the command of the Battalion to Major FITZWARINE SMITH.

2nd Sept. AYETTE. The Battalion moved forward at 5-55 a.m. proceeding to BEHAGNIES. Battalion Hqrs. was established at H.2.a.5.8 At 1-30 p.m. the Battalion was ordered to proceed to and occupy the trench 2000 yards West of VAULX at B.29.d., Battalion Hqrs. being established at B.29.d.75.80. At 6-20 p.m. the G.O.C. called and gave orders to the effect that the Battalion would relieve the 5th K.O.Y.L.I.s who occupied the line East of VAULX running approximately from C.27.d.9.3. through I.3.b.3.0. to I.3.c.90.15. The 6th Infantry Brigade would continue the attack the following morning, the 5th and 99th Brigades being on the right and left respectively. The first objective would be the high ground West and S.West of MORCHIES (I.5.a.0.5. to I.11.a.0.6.) and the final objective the high ground East of MORCHIES running through J.1.a.4.3. J.1.a.0.0., I.12.b.0.3., I.12.a.6.0., and I.12.c.5.8. The dispositions of the 6th Infantry Brigade were the 17th ROYAL FUSILIERS on the left, the S.STAFFORDS on the right and the 1st KING'S in reserve.
 Major SMITH went forward with O.C.S.STAFFORDS to get in touch with the Battalion Commander of 5th K.O.Y.L.I's. and arrange the relief. He returned at 8-50 p.m. and a Company Commanders conference was held. "A"Coy. on the right, "B"Coy. on the left and "C"Coy. in reserve.
 The G.O.C. called again at 11-20 p.m. and gave his final orders mentioning that it was reported that the enemy had retired from MORCHIES and that the Brigade would push forward to the east of BEAUMETZ as far as the road running through J.14.b.

3rd Sept. VAULX. The Battalion moved off at 12-45 a.m. and the relief of the 5th K.O.Y.L.I's. was completed at 3-30 a.m. Battalion Hqrs. was established at VAULX-VRAUCOURT,C.26.d.3.7.
 At 5-20 a.m. the attack was launched, "A"Coy. on the right (Capt.ASHWELL), "B"Coy. on the left (Capt.SWORD) and "C"Coy. in reserve (2nd Lt.HARRIS), the first objective was gained without opposition, reports to this effect reaching Battalion Hqrs. at 7 a.m. As soon as the barrage ceased the advance continued, MORCHIES and BEAUMETZ were taken without any serious opposition, a few H.E. and Gas shells fell on the area east of MORCHIES and in the neighbourhood of BEAUMETZ.
 At 8 a.m. Battalion Hqrs. advanced to I.4.d.3.5. and orders were issued to Coy. Commanders to consolidate in depth at the road running north-east through J.14.b. Verbal message received at 11-30 a.m. that the objective was gained.
 At 11-30 a.m. the G.O.C. saw Battalion Commanders and instructed them to continue the advance from J.14.b. at 1 p.m. The 99th Bde. would be withdrawn and the 6th Bde. would take over the whole front, the 17th ROYAL FUSILIERS would be on the left, the S.STAFFORDS on the right and the 1st KING'S in reserve. The Battalion's northern boundary would be a line running east from J.4.d.0.0. along grid. to K.7.b.2.7. and the southern, a line running from J.16.a.0.0. through J.17.central, thence to the SUGAR FACTORY at J.18.d.3.2. inclusive. The objective was the high ground east of DEMICOURT, approx. J.18.d.5.2. - K.7.central.
 The Company dividing line was fixed approx. a line running from J.10.c.0.5. to K.7.c.0.0., thence east. Afterwards the objective was altered to run in a curve from BOURSIES to the high ground in K.7.central to J.18.d.5.2. in order that the left flank might be in touch with the GUARDS. The Battalion would have 3 Whippet tanks to help them and Cavalry patrols would be pushed out in front.
 At 12 noon orders were issued to Coys and Major SMITH and the Adjutant rode forward to interview Coy.Commanders and deliver final instructions.

Sheet 2.

RECORD OF OPERATIONS - 2nd/4th SEPT.,1918 (contd.)

At 12-30 p.m. Battalion Hqrs. advanced to BEAUMETZ at J.14.b.7.0. on the DOIGNIES Road.

On reaching J.14.b., where the Battalion had verbally reported that they were in position, no trace of the Battalion could be found. Major SMITH and the Adjutant, reconnoitred and at 1-45 p.m. found the Battalion in the Sunken Road S.W. of BEAUMETZ running through J.20.a. with the reserve Coy. in trenches in J.19.a. and b/d. A report had been previously sent to the Brigade that we had lost touch with the Battalion. Coy. Commanders were hastily interviewed and the situation explained. The Coys. were formed up and the advance continued at 2-30 p.m. At 2 p.m. Major SMITH was hit on the right hip by a nose cap, this caused a very bad bruise but he carried on.

DOIGNIES was taken with very little opposition but the advance was held up on the ridge running through J.17.Central by oblique and enfilade M.G.fire from the vicinity of BOURSIES, "B" Coy. called for 2 Platoons from the reserve Coy. on account of casualties sustained.

Battalion Hqrs. was established in trench east of DOIGNIES, J.17.a.2.8. At 5-30 p.m. our artillery brought fire to bear on the enemy's M.G.positions and at 6-20 p.m. the advance was continued on DEMICOURT. The village was taken but considerable difficulty was experienced on account of very heavy shelling. Coys. reported objective gained at 6-55 p.m. The Coys. reorganized and consolidated along STURGEON SUPPORT, GRAYLING TRENCH, TROUT POST, and the DEMICOURT-HERMIES road to just south of the SUGAR FACTORY (J.6.c.and d, J.12.b, K.7.a and c, J.12.d, and J.18.b and d) posts were thrown out 300 yards in front. The reserve Coy.(2 Platoons) occupied JUNIPER TRENCH in J.17.a. astride the DOIGNIES - DEMICOURT Road.

Touch was maintained with the S.STAFFORDS on the right but we lost touch with the GUARDS on the left. "B"Coy. pushed north, took BOURSIES thus regaining touch with the GUARDS. The C.O.immediately took steps to have the ground to the east of DOIGNIES reconnoitred and alternative positions selected in case the line became untenable.

Lt.Col.SMITH returned at 8-30 p.m. and took over the command of the Battalion.

4th Sept. DOIGNIES. At 6 a.m. the 1st KING'S passed through our front line with the object of pushing forward as far as the Canal DU NORD, the 17th ROYAL FUSILIERS remaining in their existing positions. Our left Coy. was bombed during the day with hand grenades, casualties being sustained. At 1-30 p.m. word was received that the Battalion would be relieved by the 1st K.R.Rs. sometime during the night and the Battalion move back to BEAUMETZ.

5th Sept. DOIGNIES. Coys reported relief complete at 2-30 a.m. The Battalion moved to BEAUMETZ, Battalion Hqrs. being established at J.13.central.

CASUALTIES.
On 3rd Sept. 2nd Lieut.W.F.HUGHES M.C.,M.M. wounded.
2nd Lieut.J.BROWNLEE M.C. wounded to duty, ultimately evacuated 6th Sept.
Killed 8 O.Rs.   Wounded 42 O.Rs.   Missing 1 O.R.

W.C.Smith

8/9/18.
Lieut.Col.
Commanding 17th Royal Fusiliers.

6th Brigade.
2nd Division.

1/17th BATTALION

ROYAL FUSILIERS

OCTOBER 1918.

Army Form C. 2118.

WDE 36

WAR DIARY
or
INTELLIGENCE SUMMARY.

17th R. Div.

(Erase heading not required.)

36 W.

Army Form C. 2118.

WAR DIARY
or
INTELLIGENCE SUMMARY.
(Erase heading not required.)

Instructions regarding War Diaries and Intelligence Summaries are contained in F.S. Regs., Part II. and the Staff Manual respectively. Title pages will be prepared in manuscript.

Place	Date	Hour	Summary of Events and Information	Remarks and references to Appendices
FLETRANT	7		The Command the WORD [illegible]...	
FOREXVILLE	8		At 11.30 [?] the [illegible] at 8.15 am the GOC [illegible] ... that the [illegible] ... 99th [Brigade?] ... and the [illegible] ... and that the [illegible] to retire [illegible] to the 99th Brigade to [illegible] our L'OEUVRE. General McNAMARA ordered two companies to take up position on the L'EPINE-RUMILLY Road, and 2 companies were ordered to move. The remainder of the [illegible] moved up into the village of [illegible] approach. A big gun was ordered to move up to move to [illegible] by BCV and 6 [illegible] arrived. Amid [illegible] Dumphy told them he was forward at 11.20. 10 minutes later. Amid Dumphy [illegible] attacked SERAIN VILLERS again. At 1 PM the 3rd Division [illegible] Marched forward. At 3 PM the 99th Brigade attacked FOREN-VILLE and the FOREXVILLE-CAMBRAI Road but the attack failed owing to machine gun fire from the country between SERAIN VILLERS and NIERGNIES. The GOC out in orders that the NIERGNIES and from SERAIN VILLERS [illegible]	

WAR DIARY or INTELLIGENCE SUMMARY

Army Form C. 2118.

Place	Date	Hour	Summary of Events and Information	Remarks and references to Appendices
FOREMVILLE	8		In the event of the 3 PM attack of the 49th Bde's failing further attack was to be made at 6 PM. The Corps commander directed given orders that FOREMVILLE was to be captured on 9th to allow the grounds summer to attack overnight. They might also have an 9th. The 3rd Division were unable to make another attack on 9th. VILLERS at 6 PM. At 4 PM the DC having heard that the 3 PM attack had failed, ordered the 147th Bde to attack FOREMVILLE at 6 PM. The CO ordered C and A companies to move forward at the neighbourhood of the 23rd Royal Fusiliers H.Q. at G.16.b.7.3. to learn formed at NAMARA and the CO then went forward to G.16.d.7.3. to hear the latest news about the entrances from the CO's of the 23rd Royal all companies were on their move ordered to push on at G.16.c.7.3 at once. The 1st Royal Bucks were ordered to furnish guides to the three companies, 1st moving up to the Red Lion and then there emerged off line. A short conference between the CO and the company commanders took place in a ditch out at G.16.c.9.3 at which the following arrangements were arrived. D coy battalion were to attack FOREMVILLE & capture east of Toffleek's line. East of the villages the 3rd Division to attack on the right, and one company of the 23rd Royal Fusiliers were to form a defensive flank on the left. The	

D. D. & L., London, E.C.
(A10266) Wt W5300/P713 750,000 2/18 Sch. 52 Forms/C2118/16.

WAR DIARY
INTELLIGENCE SUMMARY.
(Erase heading not required.)

Army Form C. 2118.

Place	Date	Hour	Summary of Events and Information	Remarks and references to Appendices
FOREN VILLE	3		Battalion were to form up just west of the Red Line at H13.b.7.3 and the Coy of HTC No. 28 Coy the extreme right. On the left, A Coy in support and C Coy in reserve. With the support of the village tanks were to be detailed moving on the right of and the 3rd Division on the right line the 23rd KFA with the 3rd Division on the right from H36.7.1. Then E2 to FORENVILLE. The final objective was the road H13n 10.00 bathing H9 being at G.18.7.3 on the east bank to the road H13n 10.00 bathing H9 being at G.18.7.3 on the east bank to the and L'DEVURE. Plans to Brigade at Moet and L'DEVURE. Capt HEWETT, the acting adjutant went to see that the Battalion was in position. He said all the companies were in position at 5.15 PM and the company being about 300 yds from the FOREN VILLE - CAMBRAI Road at 6 PM. At 7.35 PM a message came in from 2/Lt NORMINGTON commanding B Coy that 6.57 PM he was informed that the village had been captured and the final line was being consolidated, but that no reports had come into Battalion HQ up to that time owing to touch of touch being lost with the two platoons of B Coy to the right of bomb the movements to meet them. The CO learned this had come up from the 23rd K 0-0 line SAA and Top of Tanks to front line. 3.0 & 5.0 ammunition 2172 was brought up to the front line. The CO waited for a performance to be sent out. Then received	

WAR DIARY
or
INTELLIGENCE SUMMARY.
(Erase heading not required.)

Army Form C. 2118.

Place	Date	Hour	Summary of Events and Information	Remarks and references to Appendices
FRESNEVILLE			to work in mopping up the area. This OC ordered B of the 25th to Right run fire to be placed after the enemy at the Right garrison and this morning movement at Capt GIBSON O.C. reported 12 tanks had been ordered with 9th for an advance about 10 prisoners had been taken. 5 guns and 2 bog battery [illegible] machine guns and ammunition. The ammunition of the battalion had been slight. at 6.15 P.M. The enemy were reported to be counter-attacking the Cav an our left and the 99th Brigade were ordered to be sent to support them. at 1.30 am orders came through that the Brigade was [illegible] to start the attack at 5.20 am. The barrage for the new attack was 300 yards West of the FOREN VABIS - CAMIRAI Rd. It came down 300 yards West of the FOREN VABIS Rd. The line was ordered to withdraw from FOREN VABIS to 4.45 am and later to line 300 yds West of the [illegible] There met the [illegible] Dragoons [illegible] and afterwards given to start forward past Thoms? The Division were ordered to advance on in the FRESNIERES now. The 99th R.B. [illegible] were ordered to move to hook 70 on the Italian Regt. To move [illegible] with an [illegible] to the battalion [illegible] lorries at 6.40 am. A [illegible] moved on arrival to the battalion [illegible]	
LODIN ?				

WAR DIARY
or
INTELLIGENCE SUMMARY.

(Erase heading not required.)

Army Form C. 2118.

Place	Date	Hour	Summary of Events and Information	Remarks and references to Appendices
LOCK 7	9		At NINE WOOD. The Battalion arrived at Lock 7 at 10 am. 9th & 2 oc. 9th. Brigade were in the area to Lock 7 to find the battalion for the reconstruction. The lot marched to the 99th Brigade H.Q. & of the Division where were and is engaged to the billets on 9th work.	
	10		The battalion that not are employed on various activities for the 99th Brigade.	
	11		Two 100 nominal roll detailed for much clearing up of POMMIERS. The battalion started training in various subjects in the battalion front. took out the two Companies in the Battalion front. A conference of all the Company Officers in the 2 Divisions was held at 2 PM at which various points to conversion were discussed. The afternoon were bivouac & others came up, that the Brigade would move to NIERGNIES the nominal 7th to Lock 7 at 3 PM.	
	12			
	13		The Battalion moved off at 0740 and arrived at NIERGNIES at about 1300. Battalion Hqrs were established in the Chateau (57B A30 c 54-33)	
NIERGNIES	14		(The Battalion carried on with training (P.T, B.F, musketry and extended order drill) during the morning. The afternoon was spent in improving billets and bringing dead horses. The Divisional General called and	

WAR DIARY or INTELLIGENCE SUMMARY

Army Form C. 2118.

Place	Date	Hour	Summary of Events and Information	Remarks and references to Appendices
NIERGNIES	14 contd.		undefended villas. A 50 yards range was improvised, two companies and the Lewis gunners fired.	
	15		The Battalion carried out a Brigade attack on FORENVILLE (57B H & C) followed by a short march in marching order.	
	16		The Battalion carried on with the usual training two companies firing on the range.	
	17		The Battalion carried on with the usual training, two companies fired on the range. Dead horses were frozen in the vicinity of the village.	
	18		The Battalion concentrated on the collection of salvage, every available man being employed both during the morning and afternoon. The accident occurred at 15.15, whilst an enemy unexploded aeroplane bomb was exploded at 57B, A 30 c 7.4. Crenelles; wounded 12.	
	19		There was a route march of about 10 miles in the morning, the band attended, artillery & M.G. formations were practised.	
	20		The Battalion carried on with training during the morning. 2.Lt W.E.M. COOK joined the Battalion, he was posted to A Coy.	

Army Form C. 2118.

WAR DIARY
or
INTELLIGENCE SUMMARY.
(Erase heading not required.)

Instructions regarding War Diaries and Intelligence Summaries are contained in F. S. Regs., Part II. and the Staff Manual respectively. Title pages will be prepared in manuscript.

Place	Date OCT.	Hour	Summary of Events and Information	Remarks and references to Appendices
NIERGNIES	21		The Battalion carried on with the usual training two companies firing on the range. Word was received that the Battalion would probably be moving forward to ST. HILAIRE on the morrow.	
"	22		The Battalion moved off at 1310 arriving at ST. HILAIRE (57B c 6 d 27) at 2015. Battalion HQrs were established at 57B C 6 d 27.	
ST HILAIRE	23		The G.O.C 57th called and inspected billets. Word was received during the morning that the Battalion would shortly proceed to ST. PYTHON. This was confirmed and the Bn moved off at 1530 and arrived at ST. PYTHON 1815. Bn HQrs were established at 57 A V 3067. A warning order was received that the Bn. would at the morrow move into O5B on the morrow and that the Bde. would shortly proceed to VERTAIN.	
ST PYTHON	24		Orders to move were received. The Bn. moved at 0830 and arrived at VERTAIN 1010. Bn. HQrs were established at 51A W 5A FS X C N L F.S. SWORD. 2 Lt CARSON and 2 Lt MAY rejoined the Bn. Capt SNORDEN rejoined the Bn. from leave. A draft of 20 O.Rs joined the Bn.	
VERTAIN	25		The Bn carried on with musketry training under Bn arrangements. Capt A.H. AYSCOUGH M.C rejoined the Bn. and took over command of D.Cy. also 2 Lt E. GILLETT who was posted to B Cy.	

WAR DIARY
or
INTELLIGENCE SUMMARY

Army Form C. 2118

Place	Date	Hour	Summary of Events and Information	Remarks and references to Appendices
VERTAIN	26		The C.O. proceeded to England on leave and Major S.T.M. HOLE M.C. took over command of the Battalion. The Battalion carried on with Musketry training and practised the "Attack" by Companies. On platoon of 'A' Coy practises Smoke tactics under the C.O. The Divisional Band gave a performance in the Square. 2/Lieut R.A. COOK joined the Battalion and was posted to "G" Coy.	
	27		The Battalion carried on with usual training including Musketry and Platoon in the Attack. S.B.R's were inspected by the Brigade Gas Officer. One platoon of 'A' Coy under 2/Lieut W.S.M. COOK paraded under the Commanding Officer for instruction in Smoke Tactics. All Battalion officers underwent revolver practice.	
	28		A warning order was received that the Brigade would relieve the 8th Brigade, 3rd Division in the line on the night 29/30 Oct. The Battalion carried out Musketry training and Attack practice.	
	29		Companies were at the disposal of Company Commanders for preparation. Orders were received that the Battalion would relieve 2nd ROYAL SCOTS	

Army Form C. 2118.

WAR DIARY
or
INTELLIGENCE SUMMARY.
(Erase heading not required.)

Place	Date	Hour	Summary of Events and Information	Remarks and references to Appendices
VERTAIN	29		In the line. The C.O., Adjutant, Coy. Commanders & others at 9am to reconnoitre. Bn returned at noon. The Battalion left METS at 14.05 hrs to proceed to the line, the transport & riosters and details remaining until further orders were received. Relief of 2 Royal Scots completed at 6.30 pm. Line ran in NE-SW direction opposite MILLERS Fm. the 3rd Coy on Rt. (opposite wood where was a stone x-roads), only posts line held with B Coy Hotchkiss & Lewis guns. D Coy Left Bn in support. Was shelled during day but no casualties. Advanced posts were pushed out at dawn under Lt. BACON and COOK. Two Patrols were pushed out at dawn under Lt. BACON and COOK. Enemy were found to be occupying Orchard in R4d and LA FOLIE FARM.	
	30			
	31		GOC 61st Bde wishes the line and arranged that a small raid should be carried out on night of 31/1 Nov LA FOLIE FARM. Enemy were quiet during day, but much harassing fire at night.	

Army Form C. 2118.

WAR DIARY
or
INTELLIGENCE SUMMARY.
(Erase heading not required.)

Instructions regarding War Diaries and Intelligence Summaries are contained in F. S. Regs., Part II. and the Staff Manual respectively. Title pages will be prepared in manuscript.

Place	Date	Hour	Summary of Events and Information	Remarks and references to Appendices
			CASUALTIES.	
			MC	
			2/Lieut. H. DETHERIDGE MM died of wounds 3/10/18	
			" M.A.GAULT do. 10/10/18	
			18 Other ranks killed	
			2/Lieut J.L. WHITE Wounded 5/10/18	
			" A.G. POWELL " 5/10/18	
			44 Other ranks Wounded	
			NIL MISSING	
			HONOURS & AWARDS.	
			M.C. Captain. H.F. ASHWELL	
			2/Lieut. H.D ETHERIDGE.	
			D.C.M. 1219 C.S.M. ATKINS A.D.	
			M.M. 809 A/C. COTTOCK A.E. (Bar)	Peter Strength 25. 506
			1190 A/CSM KERRY W.S.	Trench. 20. 384
			354 C.S.M. BUSSETT C.	
			6267 A/L. Cpl. McLEVY J.	
			75155 " GARNER F.H.J.	
			73175 L/C HARVEY H.E.	
			69619 L/C LAIDLAW T.	

J. Powell
Bn Major R.F. Fus

6th Brigade.

2nd Division.

1/17th BATTALION

ROYAL FUSILIERS

NOVEMBER 1918.

Army Form C. 2118

WAR DIARY
or
INTELLIGENCE SUMMARY.
(Erase heading not required.)

17th ROYAL FUSILIERS

Place	Date	Hour	Summary of Events and Information	Remarks and references to Appendices
RUESNES	November 1		A raid was carried out against LA FOLIE FARM at midnight 31/1 Nov. Raiding Party 25 O.R. under Lieut ROLF. Party divided into three, two sections to hold the flanks, the remainder attacked the centre. Cooperated with a barrage of 18 pdrs from 2 batteries for 13 mins. The farm was found to be occupied. 9 prisoners were taken, including 1 officer, they belonged to the 67 Regt, Nassauten. A patrol was sent out at dawn from the left of our line. LA FOLIE FARM was found to be unoccupied at daylight. Orders were received at 6.0 p.m. by my and patrol out to hold the base of VILLERS POL – 26 GUESNOY Rd. Major HOLE established an advanced HqRs at LA RELIEVE FARM. Three fighting patrols left our line under 2 Lieuts HOLLAND, MAY and WAY with the object of gaining touch with the enemy at the ORCHARD Rd. LA FOLIE FARM and VIEUX MOULIN. All objectives were found simply held and patrols were unable to push forward. Casualties 2 officers & one minor & stray shell. Wounded were collected at 6.a.m. without inc. Lieutly pick when 2 casualties we killed and wounded.	
	2		Quiet day. Advance parties of 5 K.O.Y.L.I. reconnoitred the line. We were relieved by 5 K.O.Y.L.I. the same evening. Relief commenced at 7.30 p.m. and was completed by 10.40 p.m. The Battalion moved back to billets at SOLESMES. One wounded servant/our Tea was served to the Bn at ESCARMAIN on the way over 1.	
SOLESMES	3.		Bn present in billets at 3.40 am. The battalions were parading and the Battalion formed also by 10 a.m. Major J.T. POWELL 522.1 took over temporary command of the Battalion were Major SSA HOLENCI & paid to 10 a.m. Warning orders received that the Bn would proceed to ESCARMAIN to be 10 morrow.	
ESCARMAIN	4		The Bn moved to ESCARMAIN starting at 6.40 a.m. March via VERTAIN. Rams much bothered by traffic. Billeted by 11.30 a.m. Warning proceed to VILLERS POL which was ordered at 12 p.m. Hqrs in Chateau.	
	5		Remained at ESCARMAIN.	
	6		Remained at ESCARMAIN. Aeroplanes reconnoitred G.O.C. 2nd Div anspects today weather being wet.	

Army Form C. 2118

WAR DIARY
or
INTELLIGENCE SUMMARY.
(Erase heading not required.)

Instructions regarding War Diaries and Intelligence Summaries are contained in F. S. Regs., Part II. and the Staff Manual respectively. Title pages will be prepared in manuscript.

Place	Date	Hour	Summary of Events and Information	Remarks and references to Appendices
VILLERS POL	Nov 7		The Battalion evacuated billets at ESCARPAIN at 10.40 and marched to VILLERS POL (route as arranged). Transport proceeded via Le QUESNOY. The road was broken towards the end of the march but the Bn. was in billets by 1.15pm. The Band accompanied the Bn.. All surplus Stores and Packs were dumped at ESCARPAIN under a guard. Billets in VILLERS POL were about the average.	
WARGNIES le PETIT	8		Bn evacuated Billets at VILLERS POL at 10.00 and marched to WARGNIES-le-PETIT. Arrived at 11.15 No billets had been allotted. The C.O. and 2/Lt found billets for A C & D Coys near 11pm. B Coy & Transport was accomodated at NW end of PREUX-au-SART. Had a rather poor quill very unsatisfactory. Coys day billets but A Coy bivouaced crowded	
	9	11am	A Coy moved to PREUX au SART. Bn worked in clearing roads in the vicinity of PREUX au SART and WARGNIES LE PETIT.	
PREUX au SART	10		The Battalion were employed on road clearing between PREUX au SART and ANFROIPRET	
	11		The Battalion carried on with the usual training under Coy arrangements, at NOON a Battalion parade was held and was informed officially that hostilities would cease at 1100. Orders were received that hostilities would cease at 1100.	
	12		The Battalion was engaged in road cleaning and buying local horses in the neighbourhood of PREUX au SART	
	13		At 7am a march of about 10 miles was carried out, route via ANFROIPRET and ST. WAAST	
	14		The Battalion paraded in kit and ceremonial drill practice	
	15		The Battalion spent the morning cleaning and inspecting equipment, clothing	

Army Form C. 2118.

WAR DIARY
or
INTELLIGENCE SUMMARY.
(Erase heading not required.)

Place	Date	Hour	Summary of Events and Information	Remarks and references to Appendices
PREUX AU SART	15 contd		Orders were issued out giving Coy. arrangements. A warning order was received to the effect that the Battalion would move to BERMERIES on the morrow, this was subsequently amended to LA SAULE.	
	16		The Battalion moved at 09.30, the front attacked LA SAULE was reached at 11.00. Battalion H.d Qrs was established at 3 J 20·35 (VALENCIENNES 1/50000) Orders were received to the effect that the Battalion would move to MAUBEUGE on the morrow.	
LA SAULE.	17.		At 00.30 the orders regarding the move to MAUBEUGE were cancelled. The Battalion carried on with Physical Training under Coy arrangements. The remainder of the day was spent in cleaning and improving billets. Orders were received that the Battalion would proceed to MAUBEUGE on the morrow.	
	18		The Battalion moved at 09.30, the Band being in attendance. The route taken was via BAVAI and LA LONGLEVILLE. The roads were somewhat congested but little delay was experienced on account of the excellence of the Traffic control. MAUBEUGE was reached at about 14.00. The men immediately received hot meat. Battalion Hd Qrs was established in the Barracks at 3 L 71·33 (VALENCIENNES 1/50000). The G.O.C. Division congratulated the Battalion on their smart appearance and the excellence of the march discipline. Orders were received that the Battalion would remain in MAUBEUGE for the morrow.	
MAUBEUGE	19		The Commanding Officer inspected billets. The remainder of the day was devoted to football and other recreation. Orders were received that the Bn would proceed to ESTINNE-AU-MONT on the morrow.	
	20		The Battalion moved at 07.45 and arrived at ESTINNE AU-MONT at 12.30. Excellent billets were available. Food rations, and the people were	

WAR DIARY
or
INTELLIGENCE SUMMARY.

(Erase heading not required.)

Army Form C. 2118.

Place	Date	Hour	Summary of Events and Information	Remarks and references to Appendices
MAUBEUGE	20		all was done to make the Battalion comfortable	
ESTINNES -AU-MONT	21		Billets were embraced at the brewery, the Battalion billeted	
	22		The Battalion were employed cleaning weapons in the vicinity of ESTINNES AU MONT.	
(BELGIUM)	23		The Battalion carried on with the usual training until 1130 when a Battalion parade was held, at which ceremonial drill was practised. Nn9L on receipt that the Battalion would proceed to ANDERLUES on the morrow. A further march was employed in the afternoon as part of the 6th Inf brigade route. 1st R.F. 4 yards, 2nd R.F. 2nd & 1st R.B.	
	24		The Battalion moved at 08.24 and proceeded to ANDERLUES about 1130. Notice was received that the Battalion would move to CHARLEROI on the morrow.	
ANDERLUES	25		LA NEUVE VILLE near MONTIGNIES SUR SAMBRE. The Battalion moved at 10.05 and arrived at Mt MONTIGNIES sur SAMBRE at 02.00. Excellent billets were available for all ranks and the Battalion received a very hearty welcome from the people of CHARLEROI	
LA NEUVE VILLE MONTIGNIES	26		Arrangements were made with the proprietor of the Colliery at NEUVE-VILLE to see the Colliery Staff. The Battalion to know more but inspection has been	
	27		Copies were at the disposal of their commanders for P.T., Bayonet fighting, Guards	

Army Form C. 2118.

WAR DIARY
or
INTELLIGENCE SUMMARY.

(Erase heading not required.)

Place	Date	Hour	Summary of Events and Information	Remarks and references to Appendices
MONTIGNIES LA NEUVE VILLE	27		Duties and a lecture on march discipline. Arrangements were made for a party of 10 Officers and 40 ORs to visit the battlefield of WATERLOO, two motor lorries were placed at the disposal of the Battalion. Word was received that the Battalion would move to VITRIVAL on the morrow.	
	28		The Battalion moved at 0810 and arrived at VITRIVAL at 1220. Word was received that the Battalion would proceed to WEPION on the morrow.	
VITRIVAL	29		The Battalion moved at 0820 and arrived at WEPION at 1230. Battalion Hd Qrs were established at the CHATEAU BAYOT, situated just Est [East] of the village.	
WEPION	30		Companies were at the disposal of commanders for cleaning up and general duties.	

CASUALTIES.   Killed 3 ORs.   Wounded 19 Offrs. Missing 1 OR.

AWARDS   Capt. D.G. GIBSON M.C.   Bar to M.C.

MILITARY MEDAL.
81828 L/Sgt. A. BIRCH. D.C.M.
48510 Pte. F. IRVINE
594188 Sgt. A. MACDONALD
1723 Pte. A.W. SINNICKS
53301 L/c. E. HELCOOT
1463 L/c. T. ROSE
66344 Pte. J. JARMAN

Army Form C. 2118.

WAR DIARY
or
INTELLIGENCE SUMMARY.
(Erase heading not required.)

Place	Date	Hour	Summary of Events and Information	Remarks and references to Appendices
WEPION	30		AWARDS MILITARY MEDAL 1920. L/C. H.H. HEARNE 12685 L/C W. SMITH 5964 PTE J.S. DAWSON 77739 PTE H.J. MIBBS 61710 PTE S. HUBBARD 93460 SGT T.W. ELLIOTT 51054 CPL H. BOWLES 75127 PTE A.E. BOWLER 77609 PTE A.T. SMEATHERS Ration Strength. 30 Officers 495 Other Ranks. Trench Strength 28 Officers 379 Other Ranks. 30th November 1918 J.P. Roach Major Comdg 17 Royal Fusiliers	

6th Brigade.

2nd Division.

1/17th BATTALION

ROYAL FUSILIERS

DECEMBER 1918.

WAR DIARY
or
INTELLIGENCE SUMMARY.

17th ROYAL FUSILIERS

Place	Date DEC	Hour	Summary of Events and Information	Remarks and references to Appendices
WEPION	1		No training was carried out. A Armistice service was held at 1130 which was well attended.	
	2		The Battalion carried on with the usual training	
	3		A Battalion parade was held and ceremonial was carried out in view of the fact that the Battalion moved to BONNEVILLE the next day. Orders were received to the effect that the Battalion moved to BONNEVILLE at 1250.	
	4		The Battalion moved at 0810 arriving at BONNEVILLE at 1250. There were no incidents shown during the march. Orders were received that the Battalion would move to HUY on the morrow.	
BONNEVILLE	5		The Battalion moved at 0830 arriving at HUY at 1230. The return was very muddy on account of systems working to its capacity and at that scale to alternate. The G.O.C. Division met the Battalion at ANDENNE. Lt Col W.O. SMITH M.C. returned from leave and took over command of the Battalion. A Draft of 2 OR Joined the Battalion. Orders were received that the Battalion would proceed to ELLEMELLE on the morrow.	
HUY	6		The Battalion moved at 0825 arriving at ELLEMELLE at 1240. Major J.J. POWELL left the Battalion on other to join the 2nd OXFORD & BUCKS LIGHT INFTY. Orders were received that the Battalion would move to AWAILLE on the morrow.	
ELLEMELLE	7		The Battalion moved at 0815 arriving at AWAILLE at 0140. Orders were received that the Battalion would proceed to LA REID on the morrow.	
AWAILLE	8		The Battalion moved at 0905 and arrived at BASSE DESNIE (near LA REID) at 1200. Orders were received to the effect that the Battalion	

WAR DIARY
or
INTELLIGENCE SUMMARY.

(Erase heading not required.)

Army Form C. 2118

Place	Date Dec	Hour	Summary of Events and Information	Remarks and references to Appendices
AWAILLE	8		Move by M.T. from ORCHAMPS AREA on the morning of the 8th. Arrived at night and billeted in AWAILLE & MÉAN AREA.	
BASSE-DESNIE	9	0200	The Battalion moved off 08.35 a.m. on the 9th & arrived at BÜRNENVILLE and ME12 at 0200. The Bn. HQ was spread out & to accept an early lunch. Battalion moved off to take over billets from Infantry.	
BÜRNENVILLE	10		There was a Bn. parade & pay-out on 10th. W/T. was received by the Battalion which moved to the ELSENBORN TRUPPEN LAGER on 11 month 11.	
	11	0730	The Battalion moved at 0730 and arrived at ELSENBORN LAGER at	
		0155	W/T was received that the Battalion would move to INGENBROICH on the morning.	
ELSENBORN LAGER	12	1250	The Battalion moved at 0815 and arrived at INGENBROICH BEI MONTJOIE at 1250. Orders were received that the Battalion would move to DROVE area on the morrow.	
INGENBROICH	13		The Battalion moved at 0845 and arrived at DROVE 0300. The march was very interesting on account of the snow which fell during the whole day. W/T was received to the effect that the Battalion would move to DÜREN on the morrow.	
DROVE	14			
DÜREN	15		The Battalion moved at 0906 and arrived at DÜREN at 1100. Companies at the disposal of the Inf.Bde. commander for clearing up &c	

WAR DIARY
or
INTELLIGENCE SUMMARY.

Army Form C. 2118

Place	Date	Hour	Summary of Events and Information	Remarks and references to Appendices
DÜREN	Dec 15		Church of England services were held at 1100 and 1800. Officers J.F.H.J.T and E.W. DIXON joined the Battalion and were posted to A and B Coys respectively. A Rugby match was played with the Royal Rifle Corps.	
	16		Coys were at the disposal of Company Commanders for Leave, etc.	
	17		Coys were at the disposal of Coy Commanders for Arms Drill, P.T. and steady drill. 2 Lt G.R. BARR (West Riffs) joined the Battalion and was posted to D Coy.	
	18		Coys were at the disposal of Coy Commanders for Arms Drill, P.T. & steady drill. All NCOs received instruction in Guard Mounting under the R.S.M.	
	19		Coys were at the disposal of Coy Commanders for Arms Drill, P.T. & Guard Duties. All N.C.Os received instruction in Guard Mounting under the R.S.M.	
	20		The Battalion inspected billets in the 64th area and moved at 11.0 to the Kaiserliche Peachstrasse. 2 Lt H.E. MOXON and 150 O.R. joined the Battalion C. Coy. A draft of 42 O.R. joined the Battalion.	
	21		The Commanding Officer inspected the Battalion by Companies. The Battalion Battel.	
	22		The G.O.C. 64th Inf Bde Inspected billets. Church of England services were held at 0900, 1100 and 1800.	

WAR DIARY
or
INTELLIGENCE SUMMARY

Army Form C. 2118

Place	Date 1918 DEC	Hour	Summary of Events and Information	Remarks and references to Appendices
DÜREN	23		Men were at the disposal of Coy Commanders for P.T. Games, arms and steady drill. A meeting of the Platoon and Company Commanders and Offrs i/c was held.	
	24		Coys were at the disposal of their Commanders for P.T. Games, Arms and Steady drill and Saluting. A football match was played with the 1st Bn. Kings. Regt. 2 goals to 2 in favor of the Bn.	
	25		Voluntary services were held which were well attended. The inter-Company thrown not tournament tomorrow on account of the difficulty of obtaining a suitable ball.	
	26		No parades were held. Football match was played A & B Coy and B & C Coy. The men had a very good Christmas dinner which were thoroughly appreciated.	
	27		Men were at the disposal of Coy Commanders for P.T. Games, arms and steady drill. A football match was played Officers & Sergeants. Result. Officers 4 goals, Sgts 2 goals.	
	28		The Commanding Officer inspected Companies in full marching order. A Rugby football match was played against the 1st Kings Regt. 1st Kings 21 points 17th R.Fus. nil. A draft of 41 ORs joined the Bn.	
	29		Church of England, Presbyterian services were held which were well attended.	
	30		There was a Route march in full marching order. Pte. NIDERAU and STUCKHEIM the Band attended. 2Lieut J.W. JAMES and G. F. HILTON joined the Battalion and	

Army Form C. 2118

WAR DIARY
or
INTELLIGENCE SUMMARY.
(Erase heading not required.)

Place	Date	Hour	Summary of Events and Information	Remarks and references to Appendices
DÜREN	1918 DEC 30		were posted to C and B Coys respectively. Lieut. S.L. MYRE MC USA joined the Battalion for temporary duty VICE Lieut. C.S. CANTOUGH MC USA.	
	31		Companies were at the disposal of their commands for General Monthly Duties, P.T., and Arms Drill. Education in elementary subjects commenced. A football match was played against 2nd Armoured Mgrs during the afternoon. Ration Strength. 35 Officers 493 Other Ranks. MENTIONS. Lt Col. W.C. SMITH M.C. Capt & Qmr J.H.W. GRAY Capt A.L. FELTON No 1910 Pte T.H. PHILLIPS.	

W.C. Smith Lieut. Col.
Commanding 17th Royal Fusiliers

2ND DIVISION
6TH INFY BDE

6 MACHINE GUN COMPANY
JAN - DEC 1916

6th Brigade.
2nd Division.

6th BRIGADE MACHINE GUN COMPANY ::: JANUARY 1916.

WAR DIARY

6th Bde Machine Gun Coy. Army Form C. 2118.

or

INTELLIGENCE SUMMARY.

(Erase heading not required.)

Instructions regarding War Diaries and Intelligence Summaries are contained in F.S. Regs., Part II and the Staff Manual respectively. Title pages will be prepared in manuscript.

Hour, Date, Place	Summary of Events and Information	Remarks and references to Appendices
January 4th 1916	The Company was formed consisting of personnel from 1st St George's, 2nd St George's, 1st Royal Fusiliers and 1st King's Royal Rifle Corps. The following Officers also came Capt. B.M. Bourne, 1st Royal Fusiliers, 2nd Lieuts Elcock and Carlton St George, Dobson and Dodd, 1st Royal Fusiliers, Paddison 1st K.R.R.C. The Company was billeted at LE CORNET BOURDOIS	
January 16th 1916	Company moved from LE CORNET BOURDOIS to billets at LE QUESNOY.	
January 18th 1916	2nd Lt. Singalan, 2nd St George's joined. 8 guns of Company firing 8 guns of 35th Bde. M.G. Coy 1 and 3 sections went into the Givenchy sector B2 and B3.	
January 19th 1916	Nos 2 and 4 sections relieved Nos 1 and 3 sections. Guns more or less in the same position.	

Army Form C. 2118.

WAR DIARY
or
INTELLIGENCE SUMMARY.

(Erase heading not required.)

Instructions regarding War Diaries and Intelligence Summaries are contained in F.S. Regs., Part II. and the Staff Manual respectively. Title pages will be prepared in manuscript.

Hour, Date, Place	Summary of Events and Information	Remarks and references to Appendices
January 21st 1916	N°s 1 and 3 Sections relieved N°s 2 and 4.	
January 23rd 1916	N°s 2 and 4 Sections relieved N°s 1 and 3.	
January 25th 1916	N°s 1 and 3 Sections relieved N°s 2 and 4.	
January 27th 1916	N°s 2 and 4 Sections relieved N°s 1 and 3.	
January 29th 1916	N°s 1 and 3 Sections relieved N°s 2 and 4.	
January 31st 1916	N°s 2 and 4 Sections relieved N°s 1 and 3.	Brisbane Capt Cmdg 4 coy

6th Brigade.

2nd Division.

6th BRIGADE MACHINE GUN COMPANY ::: FEBRUARY 1916.

Army Form C. 2118

WAR DIARY
or
INTELLIGENCE SUMMARY of 6th Brigade Machine Gun Coy

(Erase heading not required.)

Place	Date	Hour	Summary of Events and Information	Remarks and references to Appendices
	5/2/16		The Company was relieved by the M.M.G. attached 99th Brigade. Four guns were left in the trenches by 99th Inf. Brigade. On relief the Company marched to billets at FERME-DU-ROI	
	8/2/16		The Company moved billets from FERME DU ROI to GORRE	
	11/2/16		Nine guns of Company relieved nine guns of 5th Infantry Brigade in sections C, D and E, FESTUBERT. Nos 1 and 3 Sections went in the trenches.	
	13/2/16		Nos 2 and 4 Sections relieved Nos 1 and 3	
	15/2/16		Nos 1 and 3 Sections relieved Nos 2 and 4	
	17/2/16		Nos 2 and 4 Sections relieved Nos 1 and 3.	
	19/2/16		The Company was relieved by Coys guns of 115th Infantry Brigade.	

Army Form C. 2118

WAR DIARY of 6th Brigade
or
INTELLIGENCE SUMMARY
Machine Gun C[ompany]

(Erase heading not required.)

Instructions regarding War Diaries and Intelligence Summaries are contained in F.S. Regs., Part II. and the Staff Manual respectively. Title Pages will be prepared in manuscript.

Place	Date	Hour	Summary of Events and Information	Remarks and references to Appendices
	20/2/16		The Company moves billets to CENSE DU VALLÉE	
	25/2/16		The Company moves billets to FOSSE 10.	
	26/2/16		The Company took over trenches from 32nd Regiment 18th Division French Army. Six guns in the front line and 2 (two) guns in support. Nos 1 and 3 Sections in the trenches	
	4/1/16		Nos 2 and 4 Sections reserves Nos 1 and 3 some in	Milburn Capt OC 6M/Gun Coy H.G.Coy

1875 Wt. W.593/826 1,000,000 4/15 J.B.C. & A. A.D.S.S./Forms/C. 2118.

6th Brigade.

2nd Division.

6th BRIGADE MACHINE GUN COMPANY ::: M A R C H 1916.

Army Form C. 2118.

WAR DIARY
or
INTELLIGENCE SUMMARY

(*Erase heading not required.*)

1st Brigade
Machine Gun Coy.

Instructions regarding War Diaries and Intelligence Summaries are contained in F. S. Regs., Part II. and the Staff Manual respectively. Title Pages will be prepared in manuscript.

Place	Date	Hour	Summary of Events and Information	Remarks and references to Appendices
In the field	1/3/16		No 1 and 2 Sections relieved No 3 and 4	
	2/3/16		No 1 and 2 Sections relieved No 3 and 4	
	5/3/16		No 3 and 5 Sections relieved No 3 and 4	
	7/3/16		No 2 and 4 Sections relieved No 1 and 3	
			2/Lt R.A. Golden joins the Company	
	9/3/16		No 1 and 3 Sections relieved No 2 and 4	
	11/3/16		No 2 and 4 Sections relieved No 1 and 3	
	13/3/16		No 1 and 3 Sections relieved No 2 and 4	
	15/3/16		No 1 Lieut Stevens returned No 3 and 2	
			1st Company warned for duty 339 Squadron and moved	
	16/3/16		The Company moved back to billets in Oudar	

Shilbune
Capt.

6th Brigade.
2nd Division.

6th BRIGADE MACHINE GUN COMPANY:: APRIL 1916.

Army Form C. 2118.

WAR DIARY
or
INTELLIGENCE SUMMARY
(Erase heading not required.)

Instructions regarding War Diaries and Intelligence Summaries are contained in F. S. Regs., Part II. and the Staff Manual respectively. Title Pages will be prepared in manuscript.

MACHINE GUN COMPANY
No ....
Date ...Apl. 1916
6th INFANTRY BRIGADE

Place	Date	Hour	Summary of Events and Information	Remarks and references to Appendices
In the field	2.4.16		The Company moves billets to HERSIN taking over from 5th Bn. M.G. Coy	
	7.4.16		11. O.R. reinforcements arrived.	
	12.4.16		The Company moved billets to BRUAY.	
	13.4.16		The Company moved billets to BOMY. 1st Army Training Area.	
	17.4.16		The Company moved billets to BRUAY.	
	18.4.16		The Company relieved the 68th M.G. Coy in the CALONNE sector. Nos 1 and 3 sections in the trenches. Reserve sections billeted at FOSSE. 10.	
	19.4.16		2nd Lt. CAMPBELL joins the Company.	
	20.4.16		2nd Lt. PEARSON wounded (at duty) 1. O.R. killed. Nos 2 and 4 Sections relieve Nos 1 and 3.	
	22.4.16		Nos 1 and 3 Sections relieve Nos 2 and 4.	
	23.4.16		4 Guns moved from front line to support.	
	24.4.16		Nos 2 and 4 Sections relieve Nos 1 and 3.	
	26.4.16		Nos 1 and 3 Sections relieve Nos 2 and 4.	

Army Form C. 2118.

WAR DIARY
or
INTELLIGENCE SUMMARY
(Erase heading not required.)

April 1916

Instructions regarding War Diaries and Intelligence Summaries are contained in F. S. Regs., Part II. and the Staff Manual respectively. Title Pages will be prepared in manuscript.

Place	Date	Hour	Summary of Events and Information	Remarks and references to Appendices
In the field	28.4.16		N°s 2 and 4 Sections relieves N°s 1 and 3	
	30.4.16		N°s 1 and 3 Sections relieves N°s 2 and 4	

6th Brigade.
2nd Division.

6th NRIGADE MACHINEE GUN COMPANY ::: M A Y 1916.

Army Form C. 2118.

WAR DIARY
or
INTELLIGENCE SUMMARY
(Erase heading not required.)

6th. Bde. Machine Gun Company.

Instructions regarding War Diaries and Intelligence Summaries are contained in F.S. Regs., Part II. and the Staff Manual respectively. Title Pages will be prepared in manuscript.

Place	Date	Hour	Summary of Events and Information	Remarks and references to Appendices
In the Field.	MAY 1st.			
"	2nd.		2/Lieut. F.A.L.Sloot.Joined the Company.	
"	4th.		Nos. 2 & 4 sections relieved Nos. Q-F-E-1&3.	
"	6th.		Nos. 1 & 3 " " Nos. 2 & 4.	
"	8th.		Nos. 2&4 " " Nos. 1 & 3.	
"	10th.		Nos. 1 & 3 " " Nos. 2 & 4.	
"	12th.		Nos. 2 & 4 " " Nos. 1 & 3.	
"	13th.		3.O.R.Reinforcements arrived.	
"	14th.		Nos. 2 & 4 Sections relieved Nos. 1 & 3.	
"	16th.		Nos. 1 & 3 " " Nos. 2 & 4.	
"	18th.		Company was relieved by the 1st. Bde. Machine Gun Company	
"	21st.		Company moved billets to BRUAY Under one hours notice to move.	
"	22nd.		Company moved by moter lorries to MESNIL BOUCHE	
"	26th.		Company relieved the 141st.& 142nd. & 4th. Bdes.Machine Gun Companies.in the VIMY RIDGE sector. 5Guns in the front line and 6 in reserve. Nos. 2 & 4 Sections the line & trenches.	

Army Form C. 2118.

WAR DIARY
or
INTELLIGENCE SUMMARY
(Erase heading not required.)

Instructions regarding War Diaries and Intelligence Summaries are contained in F. S. Regs., Part II. and the Staff Manual respectively. Title Pages will be prepared in manuscript.

Place	Date	Hour	Summary of Events and Information	Remarks and references to Appendices
In the FIELD.	MAY 27th.		Nos. 1 & 3 Sections moved billets from MESNIL BOUCHE to VILLERS-AU-BOIS.	
"	28th.		Nos. 1 & 3 Sections relieved Nos. 2 & 4.	
"	30th.		Nos. 2 & 4 " " Nos. 1 & 3.	

31/5/16.

[signature]
Lieut. for Capt.
Commdg. 6th. Bde. Machine Gun Company.

6th Brigade.
2nd Division.

6th BRIGADE MACHINE GUN COMPANY ::: JUNE 1916.

Army Form C. 2118.

WAR DIARY
or
INTELLIGENCE SUMMARY

(Erase heading not required.)

6th.Bde.Machine Gun Company.

Instructions regarding War Diaries and Intelligence Summaries are contained in F.S. Regs., Part II. and the Staff Manual respectively. Title Pages will be prepared in manuscript.

Place	Date	Hour	Summary of Events and Information	Remarks and references to Appendices
In the Field	June 2nd.		Nos.1 & 3 Sections Relieved Nos.2 & 4 2 O.R. Reinforcements arrived. 1 & 3	
"	5th.		Nos. 2&4 Sections relieved Nos. 1-F-3.	
"	6th.		Capt.B.Milburn wounded (at duty)	
"	7th.		Nos.1 & 3 Sections relieved Nos.2 & 4.	
"	9th.		The guns of the Company were relieved by the guns of 99th.Bde.Machine Gun Coy.from the Front Line. Eight guns were left in reserve in BAJOLLE AND MAISTRIE LINES.No.2 & 4 Sections in the Trenches.	
"	11th.		Nos.1 & 3 Sections relieved Nos.2 & 4.	
"	13th.		Nos.2 & 4 Sections relieved Nos.1 & 3.	
"	15th.		Nos.1&3 Sections relieved Nos.2 & 4. 1 O.R. Reinforcement arrived.	
"	17th.		The guns of the Company relieved the guns of the 5th.Bde.Machine Gun Coy. 2 guns in the Front Line 4 guns in Immediate Support,and 2guns in reserve BERTHONVAL(MY-RIDGE Sector. Nos.2 & 4 Sections In the Trenches.	
"	19th.		Nos.1 & 3 relieved Nos. W 2T& 4 .	
"	21st.		Nos.2 & 4 Sections relieved Nos.1 & 3.	
"	23rd.		Nos.1 &3 Sections relieved Nos.2 & 4.	
"	25th.		Nos.2 & 4 Sections relieved Nos.1 & 3.	

Army Form C. 2118.

WAR DIARY
or
INTELLIGENCE SUMMARY

(Erase heading not required.)

6th. Bde. Machine Gun Coy.

Instructions regarding War Diaries and Intelligence Summaries are contained in F. S. Regs., Part II. and the Staff Manual respectively. Title Pages will be prepared in manuscript.

Place	Date	Hour	Summary of Events and Information	Remarks and references to Appendices
In the Field.	June 27th.		Nos. 1 & 3 Sections relieved Nos. 2 & 4.	
"	28th.		Nos. 2 & 4 Sections relieved Nos. 1 & 3.	

[signature] Lieut. for Capt
Commdg. 6th. Bde. Machine Gun Coy.

2449 Wt. W14957/M90 750,000 1/16 J.B.C. & A. Forms/C.2118/12.

6th Inf.Bde.
2nd Div.

WAR DIARY

6th MACHINE GUN COMPANY.

J U L Y

1 9 1 6

6th Inf.Bde.
2nd Div.

WAR
DIARY

6th MACHINE GUN COMPANY.

J U L Y

1 9 1 6

6th Brigade Machine Gun Coy

Army Form C. 2118.

WAR DIARY
or
INTELLIGENCE SUMMARY
(Erase heading not required.)

6 M G Coy

Place	Date	Hour	Summary of Events and Information	Remarks and references to Appendices
Bully Grenay	July 1		Lieut B.W. Crick joined the Company.	
	4th		No 1 and 3 Sections returned to the unit.	
			The Company was relieved by the 99th Bn M.G.Ct from the front line. 6 guns in reserve in the Bully Grenay and Maroc lines. Nos 2 & 4 Sections in the trenches.	
	6th		Nos 1 and 3 returns. Nos 2 & 4 Sections.	
	8th		Nos 2 & 4 Sections relieved by 1 and 3.	
	11th		The Company relieved on 5th Bn M.G.Coy. No 1 and 3 sections in the trenches. Sector No 1 and 3. Remainder in CARENCY.	
	12th		2 Runs R Brown wounded as 2nd O.R.	
	14th		Sergt Curley died of wounds. No 2 Section returns No 1 & 3 in trenches No 2 - 4 in reserve	

Army Form C. 2118.

6th Bn. Machine Gun Co.
6" M.G.C

WAR DIARY
or
INTELLIGENCE SUMMARY
(Erase heading not required.)

Instructions regarding War Diaries and Intelligence Summaries are contained in F.S. Regs., Part II. and the Staff Manual respectively. Title Pages will be prepared in manuscript.

Place	Date	Hour	Summary of Events and Information	Remarks and references to Appendices
In the Field	July 15		2 Lieut J. H. Shuggar left the Coy.	
"	17th		The Coy was relieved by the 141st Bde M.G.C. Coy moves to Chateau de la Haie.	
"	18th		The Coy moves ____ to MAGNICOURT.	
"	19th	10 pm	The Coy moves to entrain at BRYAS.	
"	20th		The Coy detrains at LONGEAU and marches to VILLE SUR ANCRE.	
"	23rd	2pm	The Coy moves to Bois des Tailles. 2 Lieut G.S. Coulson joins the Company.	
"	25th		The Coy moves to CARNOY.	
"	27th		Lieut M. J. Kavanagh moves up to take action (at Duty) 1 O.R. wounded. 1st Coy moves up to take action at DELVILLE WOOD. Casualties of the Coy were: 1 killed 11 wounded + 4 missing (one party)	

Army Form C. 2118.

WAR DIARY
or
INTELLIGENCE SUMMARY
(Erase heading not required.)

6th Bde Machine Gun Coy

Instructions regarding War Diaries and Intelligence Summaries are contained in F. S. Regs., Part II. and the Staff Manual respectively. Title Pages will be prepared in manuscript.

Place	Date	Hour	Summary of Events and Information	Remarks and references to Appendices
In the field	July 29th		2nd Lieut. C.B. Crompton reported wounds and missing. Casualties among other ranks 4 killed and 11 wounded, 8 wounded, 2 shell shock and 4 missing.	
"	29th		Capt. B. Ingleson reported wounded. Casualties among other ranks 14 killed, 1 missing and 8 wounded; 3 missing accounted for.	
"	30		Casualties among other ranks 1 killed, 3 wounded, 1 missing and 1 wounded at duty.	
"	31		22 OR Reinforcement arrived.	

M.T. Kavanagh Lieut. for Capt
Comdg. 6th Bde Machine Gun Coy

6th Brigade
2nd Division.

6th Brigade MACHINE GUN COMPANY

AUGUST 1 9 1 6

WAR DIARY
INTELLIGENCE SUMMARY

(Erase heading not required.)

Vol 3. 6th Machine Gun Coy

Place	Date	Hour	Summary of Events and Information	Remarks and references to Appendices
FIELD	1/8/16		The Company was relieved by the 26 Company from Delville Wood	
	4/8/16	20	Shrapnel reinforcements arrived	
	6/8/16		The Company relieved the 5th Company from WATERLOT FARM and BERNAFAY WOOD. N° 3 & 4 sections in old trenches	
	7/8/16		N°s 1 & 2 Sections relieved N°3 & 4.	
	9/8/16		The Company was relieved by the 14th Company.	
	10/8/16		The Company moves from reserve to HAPPY VALLEY.	

Army Form C. 2118.

6th Machine Gun Coy

WAR DIARY
or
INTELLIGENCE SUMMARY

(Erase heading not required.)

Place	Date	Hour	Summary of Events and Information	Remarks and references to Appendices
FIELD	12/9/16		The Company moved into billets at MEAULTE. 2nd Lieuts. Lois, Glover and Medhurst joined.	
FIELD	13/9/16		The Company marched from MEAULTE to MERICOURT and entrained. 6th Company detrained at SALEAX and moved by horse lorries to billets at BELLOY-SUR-SOMME. 2nd Lieut. K. S. Agnew joined.	
	14/9/16		2nd Lt. J. C. Baylies joined the Company.	
	15/9/16		The Company moved billets at 1.15 pm to VIGNACOURT. 6. O.R. reinforcements joined.	
	17/9/16		The Company moved billets at 2 pm to RIBEAUCOURT.	
	18/9/16		The Company moved to AUTHIE (BOIS DE WARNIMONT)	

Army Form C. 2118.

WAR DIARY
or
INTELLIGENCE SUMMARY

6th Machine Gun Coy

(Erase heading not required.)

Place	Date	Hour	Summary of Events and Information	Remarks and references to Appendices
FIELD	20/8/16		The Coy Company moved into the line in the SERRE Sector, relieving the 1st Guards Machine Gun Company. 12 Guns in the line. N°s 3 & 4 Sections in the trenches. Capt W.G. Hewett commanding Company.	
	22/8/16		N°s 1 & 2 Sections relieved N°s 3 & 4.	
	23/8/16		N°s 3 & 4 Sections relieved N°s 1 & 2.	
	26/8/16		2nd Lieut W.W. Coleman joins the Company.	
	28/8/16		N°s 1 & 2 Sections relieves N°s 3 & 4.	
	31/8/16		N°s 3 & 4 Sections relieves N°s 1 & 2.	

Copy No.....

FIRE ORDERS.

by Lieut. M. KAVANAGH, Commanding 6th. Machine Gun Coy.

August 7th - 8th. 1916.

1. One hour before Zero No. 7 will engage Machine Gun House at battle sight range and continue firing until Zero.5.

2. No. 7 will fire during the night of the 7th/8th on the GUILLEMONT - GINCHY road in T.19.b. and will return to the above target after dealing with Machine Gun House. It will cease fire on this target at Zero 15. Range 900 yards.

3. No. 4. Gun will fire during the night 7th/8th and up till Zero 10, on the cross roads in GINCHY at T.13.d.8.5. at 1575 yards, giving a traverse of 250 yards right and left.

4. No. 4.B will fire during the night of 7th/8th on GINCHY - WEDGE WOOD ROAD from cross roads at T.20.c.2.4. to road junction at T.26.c.1.9. at 2000 yards. It will continue fire till Zero 30 when it will lift to 2800 yards.

5. No. 3.B will fire during night 7th/8th on the same target as No. 4.B from cross roads at T.13.d.8.7. to cross roads at T.20.c.2.4. It will continue fire till Zero.30 when it will lift to 2800 yards.

6. If it is considered suitable No. 2 B will fire at approaches to GINCHY in T.14. at 2700 yards. It can continue to fire till one hour after Zero.

These orders must be carried out as far as the fire of the enemy artillery permits. They are liable to be changed in so far as they are affected by the advance of our own men.

Communication between guns must be maintained as far as possible, and reports should be sent to me at Battalion Headquarters near S.24.b.5.5.

(Sd.) M. Kavanagh

7.8.16.
Lieutenant,
Commanding 6th Machine Gun Company.

6th Brigade.

2nd Division.

6th BRIGADE MACHINE GUN COMPANY ::: SEPTEMBER 1916.

Army Form C. 2118.

Vol I
C.M. Machine Gun Corps

WAR DIARY
or
INTELLIGENCE SUMMARY
(Erase heading not required.)

Instructions regarding War Diaries and Intelligence Summaries are contained in F. S. Regs., Part II. and the Staff Manual respectively. Title Pages will be prepared in manuscript.

Place	Date	Hour	Summary of Events and Information	Remarks and references to Appendices
Anti Field	29/9/16			
Same Sector	3/9/16		Nos. 1+2 Sections relieved Nos. 3+4 Sections to reserve.	
	6/9/16		" 3+4 " " 1+2 " "	
	7/9/16		" 1+2 " " 3+4 " "	
	11/9/16		Reinforcements. 6 Other Ranks Arrived (Cinematograph No Corps)	
	12/9/16		Lieut. M.J. Kavanagh (commanding left for M.G. Corps H.Q. G.O.R. transferred to Corriers. No. 3+4. Sections relieved Nos. 1+2. 2nd Lieut. J.M. NOLAN (Reinforcement) arrived Casualties 1 O.R. Killed	
	13/9/16			

2449 Wt. W14957/M90 750,000 1/16 J.B.C. & A. Forms/C.2118/12.

Army Form C. 2118.

WAR DIARY
or
INTELLIGENCE SUMMARY
(Erase heading not required.)

Place	Date	Hour	Summary of Events and Information	Remarks and references to Appendices
Little Field Somectin	16/9/16		Nos 1 + 2 Sections relieved Nos 3 + 4 Sections.	
	19/9/16		Captn. J.P. Roberts, 2nd in Command Joined.	
	20/9/16		Guns 8, 9, 10 + 11 Relieved by 117th M.G. Coy. in Serre Sector. Nos 1 to 7 Guns relieved by No. 4 Section C+ M.G. Coy.	
Courcelles au Bois	21/9/16		Coy. moved to Bus-les-Artois by Rail, arriving at 1 P.m. Billets in WOOD - Huts & Bivouacs	
	22/9/16		2nd Lieut. G.L. Garlick proceeded to M.G. Corps, Grantham. 2nd Lieut. Glover returned from Hospital.	
	23/9/16		No-3 Section relieved No. 4 Section in Trenches - Serre Sector.	

WAR DIARY
or
INTELLIGENCE SUMMARY

(Erase heading not required.)

Army Form C. 2118.

Place	Date	Hour	Summary of Events and Information	Remarks and references to Appendices
Bus les Artois	23/9/16	8am	Working party 1 Officer and 2 x Cos + 30 NCOs (R.9, 2.2.) (Sheet 57D. 1/40000) for Neuborg.	
	24/9/16		2nd Lieut. W. Glennie joined from M. I. Course. 4 O.R. proceeded to Havre Army Rest Camp at Shellf for about 3 days Captain A.G. Newett granted leave from 27.9.16 to 2/10/16	
	25/9/16		Captain J.P. Roberts takes over Command. Lieut Birch & H. Otter (Rects) proceeded to Camiers for W.G. Course.	
	26/9		No 2 Section relieves W. 8 Section in Trenches. Weather fine. Units 2 hours notice to move. Lieut G. McPhee reports for transport duties	

Army Form C. 2118.

WAR DIARY
or
INTELLIGENCE SUMMARY
(Erase heading not required.)

Place	Date	Hour	Summary of Events and Information	Remarks and references to Appendices
Thus an Artois	29/9/16	8.30 am	Orders received to proceed to Norman Training Establishment. No 1 Section relieved No 2 Section in Trenches. Marches Wet.	

6th Brigade.

2nd Division.

6th BRIGADE MACHINE GUN COMPANY ::: OCTOBER 1916.

Army Form C. 2118.

WAR DIARY
or
INTELLIGENCE SUMMARY
(Erase heading not required.)

8th Machine Gun Coy/8th Corps

Place	Date	Hour	Summary of Events and Information	Remarks and references to Appendices
HEBUTERNE SECTOR BUS-LES-ARTOIS	1/10/16	7am	RELIEF. Four guns of No 4 Section under 2/Lt W. Nolan, 8th Machine Gun Coy/8th Corps. Four guns of 117th M.G. Coy in Supplements V1. Y2. Y6. and V.7. HEBUTERNE Right Section. Guides furnished by 117th M.G. Coy. BREAKFASTS 6 A.M.	
			1 O.R. sent to ETAPLES being under age.	
			1 NCO. proceeded to HAVRE for Transport Course.	
			2 OR " " Second Army REST CAMP, MONT	
			WINTER TIME comes into force	
	2/10	1 AM	No. 3 Section relieves No. 1 Section in Trenches.	
		8.15 pm	Lieut. H. J. KAVAN & Corpl Churwood Military Cross	
	3/10		Captain W.G. Hewitt returned from leave.	
			6 O.R. Reinforcements arrived.	
			Everything under Don't Notice to move - troops forbidden to leave Billets area	
	4/10	11.30 am	Four guns of No. 4 Section relieved by the guns of the 2nd M.G. Coy in Supplements V1. V2. Y6 & V.7. HEBUTERNE Sector.	✓

Army Form C. 2118.

WAR DIARY
or
INTELLIGENCE SUMMARY
(Erase heading not required.)

Instructions regarding War Diaries and Intelligence Summaries are contained in F. S. Regs., Part II. and the Staff Manual respectively. Title Pages will be prepared in manuscript.

Place	Date	Hour	Summary of Events and Information	Remarks and references to Appendices
HEBUTERNE Section	5/9/16	2pm	Seven Sections of 6th M.G.Coy in SERRE Sector relieved by 99th M.G. Coy. Coy. moved to Hutments at BERTRANCOURT on Reliefs.	
	6/9/16	7:30	Working Party 55 NCOs & Men	
		7pm	No 3 Section (7 Guns) relieved by 99th M.G. Coy.	
	7/9/16	7:30	Working Party 55 NCOs & Men	
		7:30am	Working Party 55 NCOs & Men	
			Company moved to BUCHUILLERS at moment's notice.	
			1 MGO & 2 OR left for Fourth Army Rest Camp AULT.	
BUCHUILLERS	8/9/16	9am	Special Training	
"	9/9/16	"	1 O.R. Reinforcement arrived. Special Training Area 19	
"	10/9/16	"	" "	
"	11/9/16	"	Special Training	

Army Form C. 2118.

WAR DIARY
or
INTELLIGENCE SUMMARY
(Erase heading not required.)

Instructions regarding War Diaries and Intelligence Summaries are contained in F. S. Regs., Part II. and the Staff Manual respectively. Title Pages will be prepared in manuscript.

"3"

Place	Date	Hour	Summary of Events and Information	Remarks and references to Appendices
PUCHVILLERS	12/9/16	9.15 am	Special Training - tactical exs. for N.C.O.s	
"	13/9/16		1 O.R. Reinforcement arrived	
"	"		1 O.R. wounded (bruised)	
"	"	10.30 am	Special Training of Reserves	
"	14/9/16	9 am	Coy. Training	
"	15/9/16	9 am	" "	
"	"		2 O.R. posted to Troops Army Rest Camp, Pern. T.	
"	"		Bigard rustic short notice to move	
"	16/9/16		8 O.R. (2 from each Battalion in Brigade) report as Wheeler Passes	
"	17/9/16		Divisional training	
"	18/9/16	9.30 am	Bn. moved to BERTRANCOURT arriving 1.30 p.m. by March Route Billets in Hut Camps	

2449 Wt. W14957/M90 750,000 1/16 J.B.C. & A. Forms/C.2118/12.

Army Form C. 2118.

WAR DIARY
or
INTELLIGENCE SUMMARY
(Erase heading not required.)

Instructions regarding War Diaries and Intelligence Summaries are contained in F. S. Regs., Part II. and the Staff Manual respectively. Title Pages will be prepared in manuscript.

Place	Date	Hour	Summary of Events and Information	Remarks and references to Appendices
PROVENES	18/9/16		Capt R.F. DODD rejoined from employment on Staff of 57 Infy Bgde.	
	19/9/16	11am	Lieut. W.S. Todd slightly injured whilst horse-riding and fell "Dog" reported to hospital	
BERTRAN- COURT	19/9/16	9am	Working Party of 1 N.C.O. + 15 men to report duty at Town Major for Road cleaning.	
			Weather very wet. Drill parades cancelled	
	20/9/16		4 O.R. Reinforcements (Privates from N.G. Base) arrived.	
			Working party increased to 2 N.C.O. + 30 Men (Road Cleaning)	
"	21/9/16		Return of 2 N.C.O. + 30 Men handed over to R.S.O. Staff work.	
			Sergt. J. Harris (M.G.O.) reported to Lieut-Colonel HENDERSON,146.	
			Confidential orders moved from BERTRANCOURT to billets at MAILLY-MAILLET	
"	22/9/16	12 noon 9am	received 2 Sections of Vickers Guns of 97th M.G. Coy, the 2 Section acting as carrying party.	

2449 Wt. W14957/M90 750,000 1/16 J.B.C. & A. Forms/C.2118/12.

Army Form C. 2118.

WAR DIARY
or
INTELLIGENCE SUMMARY
(Erase heading not required.)

Instructions regarding War Diaries and Intelligence Summaries are contained in F.S. Regs., Part II. and the Staff Manual respectively. Title Pages will be prepared in manuscript.

Place	Date	Hour	Summary of Events and Information	Remarks and references to Appendices
MAILLY MAILLET	24/10/16		No. 4 section relieves No. 1 Sec. in Trenches.	
			1 O.R. accidentally injured by fall from truck.	
	25/10/16		Casualties	
			1 O.R. wounded (Remaining at Duty) - Trenches	
	"	10 pm	Hostile Shelling of Billets - 1 O.R. wounded & taken to Hospital	
			Lootte Shelling of Billets.	
	26/10/16	6 pm	No. 2 Sec. relieves No. 4 Sec. in Trenches	
		6 am	Heavy hostile shelling of billets lasting one hour	
	28/10/16	Noon	Our Batteries retaliate	
		4.30 pm	No. 1 Sec. relieves No. 2 in Trenches	
BERTVISART	29/10	10 am	Pack animal parade. Brig. Genl. Bryan's heads/ ro at Beauxort about 10.30 am	

2449 Wt. W14957/Mgo 750,000 1/16 J.B.C. & A. Forms/C.2118/12.

Army Form C. 2118

WAR DIARY
or
INTELLIGENCE SUMMARY
(Erase heading not required.)

Instructions regarding War Diaries and Intelligence Summaries are contained in F. S. Regs., Part II. and the Staff Manual respectively. Title Pages will be prepared in manuscript.

Place	Date	Hour	Summary of Events and Information	Remarks and references to Appendices
Mailly MAILLET	29/9/16	10 p.m.	Orders received for relief by 99th M.G. Coy, to include all available trench mortar equip. line.	
	30/9/16	12 noon	Orders for move to BERTRANCOURT to take one billet & 99 M.G. Coy cancelled - Coy to remain in present billets. 99 M.G. Coy to relieve 112th Inf. Coy. Annalié	
			3 O.R. wounded in front line trench by a rifle fire. 1 O.R. remaining at duty.	
	31/10/16		1 Officer Reinforcement - proceed	

6th Brigade.

2nd Division

6th BRIGADE MACHINE GUN COMPANY :: NOVEMBER 1916.

WAR DIARY
or
INTELLIGENCE SUMMARY

Army Form C.2118.

6TH M.G. COMPANY

Vol XI

Instructions regarding War Diaries and Intelligence Summaries are contained in F.S. Regs., Part II. and the Staff Manual respectively. Title Pages will be prepared in manuscript.

(Erase heading not required.)

Place	Date	Hour	Summary of Events and Information	Remarks and references to Appendices
MAILLY MAILLET	1/7/16		Working party of 1 NCO. & 20 men for Royal Engineers	
	2nd		Working party of 2 NCO's & 18 men for Land Drains	
	3rd		Working party of 2 NCO's & 20 men for Land Drains	
	4th		Working party NCO's & 15 men for trench cleaning	
	5th		Working party 2 NCOs & 15 men for trench cleaning	
	6th		One section (No 2) relieve the 99th Coy. in the SERRE sector. Placement take over in R.I. Rt. 52, 53, 54. Relief complete by 10.30am	
	7th		Hostile artillery was very active in our sector of the line.	
	8th		Lieut Dodd struck off strength. Baths were allotted to the Company from 10am to 12 noon.	
	9th		No 3 Section relieved No 2 Section in the line. Hostile artillery very active in vicinity of H.Elts	
	10th		Company received orders regarding forthcoming attack. No 1 Section occupy Dugout now MONK STREET. Relief complete 1.30am	
	11th		To inform relieved No 3 Section in the line. Relief complete 8.30am No 2 Section moved into line at 5pm and occupy R.O. in MONK STREET.	
	12.		All Section Supplies handed by 12/7/16	

Army Form C. 2118.

WAR DIARY
or
INTELLIGENCE SUMMARY

(Erase heading not required.)

Instructions regarding War Diaries and Intelligence Summaries are contained in F. S. Regs., Part II. and the Staff Manual respectively. Title Pages will be prepared in manuscript.

Place	Date	Hour	Summary of Events and Information	Remarks and references to Appendices
SERRE SECTOR	12/7/16			
	13/7/16	4.45	Distribution:— Guns going over, MONK TRENCH. Guns covering emplacements in LEGEND & VALLARD & TAUPIN PLACES. Guns moved into position to supporting 2 South Staffs & supporting Brigades. Gun distribution:— 1 Section L. 2 in centre, guns 2 over with 4th and 8th waves of infantry. At zero 6 guns moved forward with infantry. Remaining 3 guns in S.3, S.2. B.R. cover to advance B guns unopposed. D.O. MONK TRENCH. 2 gun teams of [?] crossing between their line and covered the infantry who were unable to advance. One gun was blown up, the other gun having itself unable to [?] was withdrawn. The gun was damaged by shell fire during the operation, all available teh[?] were used. The 2 gun crew of the 2nd South Staff reached their line & thence fire onto the enemy who was enfilading the infantry. The 2 gun teams continued firing Carvelio [?] and was to be withdrawn after to infantry have been forced back. The 2 guns with [?] supporting units wing [?] 17 Howitzers kept [?] high number of Packhouse and sent Dobson round up they got across to the	

2449 Wt. W14957/M90 750,000 1/16 J.B.C. & A. Forms/C.2118/12.

WAR DIARY
or
INTELLIGENCE SUMMARY

Army Form C. 2118.

German line had suffered heavily & had to be reinforced before reaching their objective. One gun was knocked out and all the team C.2.O.s become casualties. The remaining guns covered the party who were forced to retire eventually & the gun was withdrawn to our own front line. One gun was discharged on the way, when the guns were being withdrawn, an officer left Flanders and formed with the reserve guns, a line & Mont TRENCH. to the guns in S.3. S.4. R.2. R.3 the remainder in the reserve line for the infantry to reorganise. The heavy gun team lay about 60hr on the 13th the guns were ordered to fall back to LEGEND Trench relieved by the gun teams which had been reorganised in TAYPIA. The relieved gunners moved back to TAYPIA and were reorganised.

On the 14th length of 15th Trench difficulty was experienced in moving Jungleston to positions as the enemy kept up a continual barrage on the trench and positions.

On the 14th again a team was sent under Lieut M Nolan to the support of the Leinsters trench. The gun was ordered to move forward to the Quadrilateral and

Army Form C. 2118.

WAR DIARY
or
INTELLIGENCE SUMMARY
(Erase heading not required.)

Instructions regarding War Diaries and Intelligence Summaries are contained in F. S. Regs., Part II. and the Staff Manual respectively. Title Pages will be prepared in manuscript.

Place	Date	Hour	Summary of Events and Information	Remarks and references to Appendices
SERRE SECTOR.	14/7/16		Here occupy a defensive position. Orders were received that the Coy should be relieved on the night of 15th. This did not take place & the Coys were brought up on the 14th & on the morning of the 14th. On 15th Reinforcement of 13 O.Rs arrived. Casualties sustained:– 2 O.Rs Killed. 1 Officer Wounded (Lieut R.Buchanan) 26 O.Rs Wounded. 2 O.Rs Missing	
MAILLY MAILLET	16/7/16			
LOUVENCOURT	"		The Company were taken from MAILLY-MAILLET in lorries to LOUVENCOURT.	
Authieule	19		Moved from Louvencourt to Authieule. Movement completed 3.30 pm Lieut Dobson to Well (Worth) & Lieut Shee proceeded on leave.	No.11409 No.16095
Autheux	21		Moved from Authieule to Autheux. Movement completed by 2 pm. H/Cpl Shirley proceeded on leave.	No.16093
Le Fosté	22		Moved from Autheux to Le Fosté. Movement completed by 12.30pm. Pte. Liddle, Hewitt, Evans & O'Connell reported to Company from Hospital.	No.1138 No.11151 No.11050 No.16112

Army Form C. 2118.

WAR DIARY
or
INTELLIGENCE SUMMARY

(Erase heading not required.)

Instructions regarding War Diaries and Intelligence Summaries are contained in F. S. Regs., Part II. and the Staff Manual respectively. Title Pages will be prepared in manuscript.

Place	Date	Hour	Summary of Events and Information	Remarks and references to Appendices
NOYELLE EN CHAUSSEE	24/11/16		March from LE HAMEL to NOYELLE-EN-CHAUSSEE. Movement complete by 11 am.	
FOREST L'ABBAYE	25/11/16	11am	March from Noyelle-en-Chausee to FOREST L'ABBAYE. Movement complete by 11.30. Lt Lyttle and Lt Pantry proceeded on leave. Winter conditions very unfavourable. No civilian laundries available in obtaining any kind of convenience for drying clothes. Nº 16050 Nº 9089	
FOREST L'ABBAYE	26/11/16		Lieut Steven, Lieut Hills, Lieut Bailey, Lieut Hart proceeded to GHQ Nº 15003 Nº 17085 School of Instruction for Officers. Reinforcement of Lieut McCormack and 20 ORs arrive. Lt Hope, Lt Walter alloted to Nº 16099 hospital.	
CAPENNES	27.		March from Forest L'Abbaye to CAPENNES. Lieut Buck and Lt Lewis proceed on leave.	
	28.		Training began. Lt Lilly, Lt Sanders proceed on leave.	
	29.		Reinforcement of one Officer, 2/Lieut W. J. Arnell, 6th Northumberland, proceeded on leave.	
	30			

6th Brigade
2nd Division.

6th BRIGADE MACHINE GUN COMPANY :.:: DECEMBER 1916.

WAR DIARY or INTELLIGENCE SUMMARY

Army Form C. 2118

6th MACHINE GUN COMPANY

Place	Date	Hour	Summary of Events and Information	Remarks and references to Appendices
Gapennes	Dec 1st		17709 Pte Baker arrived on leave. 17909 & 7 Cpl Hawes go returned from one month's leave. Critical training commenced at 1 st West elementary training Mechanism, Stripping, Elementary Gun Drill, Indication, Recognition, Edgar Clothonet. Normal training. Immediate action. Daily cleaning. Belt filling. Supply & Care. Physical training, use of Grenade. Anti Etc.	
	3		11708 Pte Abgett arrived on leave. Cpl A P Dixon arrived on leave.	
	5		17100 Sgt R Neway granted a temp Commission proceeded to M G Base Depot. Pte H Sollers 17708 & 25777 Pte Cunning arrived on leave. 16063 Cpl Gilbert & 16095 Cpl W Staley returned from leave.	
	6		17708 Pte Middleton proceed on leave.	
	7		16065 Pte Gatford } Signallers from hospital	
			16005 Pte Holford }	
			21359 Pte Lamond }	
			Reviewed training commands.	
	9		Lecture Range Discipline. Point, Blank, Danger & after dangers. Fire Orders, use. use in silence. Range T.O.S. distances. Range Cards. in attack, in Elevation. Scan Action. Belt filling. Village fighting. Cover and concealment. Capture a General. The Company marches to ARGENVILLERS at 9am. & took	

Army Form C. 2118.

1/342A
31/1/916

WAR DIARY
or
INTELLIGENCE SUMMARY
(Erase heading not required.)

Instructions regarding War Diaries and Intelligence Summaries are contained in F.S. Regs., Part II. and the Staff Manual respectively. Title Pages will be prepared in manuscript.

Place	Date	Hour	Summary of Events and Information	Remarks and references to Appendices
GIVENCHY	Dec 20		16064 Pte Webb proceeded on leave	
	21.		16063 Pte Rogers and 17108 L/Cpl Webber returned from leave	
	22.		16038 Sgt James proceeded on leave. 17097 Sgt Brown proceeded to Coy.	
	23.		Coy-Sgt-Mjr Colley proceeded to Company Cpl McRae returned on leave and took over command.	
	24.		25774 Pte McElroy proceeded on leave	
	25.		Xmas day was observed as a holiday and a special dinner was provided for the troops.	
	26.			
	27.		16089 Sgt Jones proceeded on leave	
	29.		2/Lieut J.B. Glover returned from leave. 11409 Pte Webb returned from leave	
	30.		17103 Pte McIlwaine proceeded on leave. 16416 Pte H Heyes returned from leave	
	31.		6954 Pte Saunders & 25772 Pte J.V. Chapman proceeded on leave. The Coy team were beaten in a V Coy race and received in V Coy race	

WAR DIARY
or
INTELLIGENCE SUMMARY
(Erase heading not required.)

Army Form C. 2118
1/342 A
31/1/7/6

Place	Date	Hour	Summary of Events and Information	Remarks and references to Appendices
	Dec 1916 9		4th Bn appointed Place in Brigade for G.O.C's inspection Capt J.P Roberts proceeded on leave. Lieut E.M Rickers	
	10		Capt Burns returned from leave	
	11		16076 Pte Bird reported at the Coy. 17406 Pte Riley proceeded on leave	
	12		16053 Pte E Crisps and 19019 Pte Barkley returned from leave	
	13		16049 Pte P Riley proceeded on leave	
	14		Lieut Burns & Clarke proceeded on leave. 17076 Pte Liffe proceeded on one month's leave. 9th Coy relieving 8th Coy at Divisional 18. ORs were sent to make 9th 4th Coy up to strength. 17107 Pte Pain & 16060 Pte E.Hogue ?? returning from leave	
	15		2nd Officers (Lieuts Syl.b, & 60 ORs proceeded to 4th Army (Lieut Burns) for shooting in farms on Range	
	16		15775 Pte Whale proceeded on Leave, 18233 Pte H Hicks returned from leave	
	17		15771 Pte Carrington proceeded on leave. 17746 Pte Boyd returned from leave	
	18		19099 Pte Walsh was sent to M G Base Depot being under age 17095 C.Q.M.S Singleton proceeded to the HQ to take over C.S.M over Comms. Q.M.S proceeded to ABBEVILLE	
	19		Colonel Stewart M.C proceeded on leave. Lieut J.P Dobson late H/ast H.C Offre & 25777 Pte Kenway returning from leave	

Army Form C. 2118

1/34.2.A.
3/12/16

WAR DIARY
or
INTELLIGENCE SUMMARY
(Erase heading not required.)

Place	Date	Hour	Summary of Events and Information	Remarks and references to Appendices
CAPENNES	Dec 20		3rd Week Special Leave. Netheravon, Stripping, Gas Bags, Commuted Drill, Bathfilling, Stoppages, Fumes, Before, During & After firing, Range taking, Infantry Drill, Village fighting, Range work, Packing Mules, Tactical Schemes - Attack & Defence in Trench Warfare, Construction of Emplacements, Bombing. Football during the afternoons.	

2ND DIVISION
6TH INFY BDE

6TH MACHINE GUN COMPANY

JAN - DEC 1917.

6th Brigade.
2nd Division.

6th MACHINE GUN COMPANY

JANUARY 1917.

Army Form C. 2118

WAR DIARY
or
INTELLIGENCE SUMMARY.
(Erase heading not required.)

Instructions regarding War Diaries and Intelligence Summaries are contained in F. S. Regs., Part II and the Staff Manual respectively. Title pages will be prepared in manuscript.

MACHINE GUN COMPANY
6th INFANTRY BRIGADE

6 M G Coy
Vol /3

Place	Date	Hour	Summary of Events and Information	Remarks and references to Appendices
CAPENNES	January 1914		No 16049 Pte S Cooper No 15703 Pte C Evans attended to Hospital	
	2		No 1419 Pte H Hudson and Lieut L J Cloud proceeded on leave. No 15049 Pte G Michell and No 12521 Pte T Gilman proceeded to Cyou Reinforce No 16060 Pte E Maguidge reported from Cyour Mrs Nanwas HQrs. Returned to HQ	
"	4		Company took part in Divisional Show No 16069 Sgt H Page transferred to England	
"	5		No 12715 Pte W Wheeler and No 16083 Sgt H Lewis returned from leave. That HR Garnett and No 1731 Pte R Morgan Arrived on leave	
"	7		Lieut W J Hewitt MC rejoined from leave	
"	8		No 1115 Pte R Shaw and No 16061 Pte W Hedges reurned to Hospital No 15765 L/Cpl Howden W Smith & Employment a Reinforce	
GRIMONT	9	12 noon	Company moved from Capennes to Grimont at Reinforcement of men and some other ranks returned from leave.	
			Company moved from Grimont and took over Brittle-in Foreminer	
Rutheullers	11		Company moved from Rutheullers and took over Buzton Ferny	
Avelny	12		Sgt F G Neville Arrived in leave	
"	13		Lieut L J Cloud, No 16069 -524 C Jones, No 16134 Pte P Henry Clement Corporal, No 6669 Pte C R Thompson from Clearing Pom a Reinforce a Reinforce No 15049 Pte G Wignell Arrived to join the 5th M G Coy	
	14		No 1722 Pte N Metcalfe returned from leave	

Army Form C. 2118.

WAR DIARY
or
INTELLIGENCE SUMMARY.

(Erase heading not required.)

Place	Date	Hour	Summary of Events and Information	Remarks and references to Appendices
August	15		No 1145 Pte A Hewitt wounded on Patrol sent to M.R. M.C. & ADS wounded by Shell fire	
	16		Lieut J Carter & wounded on Patrol No 25750 L/Cpl Dennis No 25767 L/Cpl Bacon, No 25762 L/Cpl Oldham No 25762 L/Cpl Pring No 17719 Pte Henderson returned from Leave No 17116 Pte Sharp returned from Casting Course No 25750 Pte A Loveth admitted to Hospital	
	17		No 17098 R.S. Pye relieved from leave No 25759 Pte Henry proceeded on Leave	
	18		No 5583u Pte Holdham admitted to Hospital	
	19		No 558bu Pte Holdham admitted to Hospital	
2 Sections In Line 2 Sections Wallace Huts	20		Cpl Bell relieved the 5th Pln in the CORCELETTE SECT. No 3 and No 4 Sections took over positions in the line. No 1 and No 2 Sections moved to Wallace Huts	
	21		No 41907 Pte J Reynolds, No 9501 Pte Pugh, No 1253 Pte G Forshay admitted to Hospital. No 17106 Pte E Knight proceeded on Leave No 17199 Pte C Morgan returned from Leave	
	22		No 43094 Pte Sloman, No 50807 Pte L E Taylor No 17045 Pte L E Taylor and No 16047 Pte Cooper admitted to Hospital No 17115 Pte H Sims reported to Bn from Hospital No 16089 Pte W Hughes proceeded to a Leb. Officer Cadet Corps	

WAR DIARY
or
INTELLIGENCE SUMMARY.

(Erase heading not required.)

Army Form C. 211

Instructions regarding War Diaries and Intelligence Summaries are contained in F. S. Regs., Part II. and the Staff Manual respectively. Title pages will be prepared in manuscript.

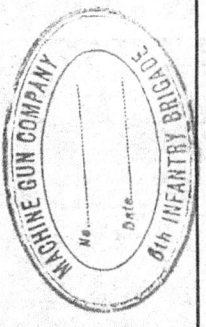

Place	Date	Hour	Summary of Events and Information	Remarks and references to Appendices
2 Section in line 2 Section in WALLACE HUTS	23		Major N.G. Howett M.C. and Lieut D.C. Cloud were on attachment to Hosp. temporarily sick. Capt J.P. Roberts took over Command of the Coy.	
	24		No 1 and No 2 Section relieve No 3 and No 4 Now Situation as for (Courcelette sector)	
	25		No 15750 Sgt C Bource and No 5760 Sgt Smith Chapman proceeded to the Coy as a Reinforcement. Reinforcement of 10 O.R. joined the Coy.	
	27		No 646 Sgt H. Macdonald admitted Hospital. No 1606 Pte Sturridge rejoined the Coy from Hospital	
Bouzincourt	28		No 1 Sec relieved by 5th Bde Company take over billets in Bouzincourt. Relief completed by 12 midnight	
	29		Capt W.H. Cartier returned from leave	
	30			
	31		8 O.R.'s 2 and 3 Staff Sturbery attached took back to join their Unit	

6th Brigade.

2nd Division.

6th MACHINE GUN COMPANY ::: FEBRUARY 1917.

WAR DIARY
or
INTELLIGENCE SUMMARY

Army Form C. 2118

6th M.G. Company

January 1917

Place	Date	Hour	Summary of Events and Information	Remarks and references to Appendices
Bazincourt	1/2/17		Major W.E. Lewis M.G. resumes to Company from hospital. Lieut. A.P. Dobson M.G. admitted to hospital 16 cars.	
	5		Company moves from Bazincourt and support lines to the Brigade at Usna Hill.	
	7		Ant Air Craft night firing commenced. One section of 2 guns was actively engaged then the day until 13/2/17 for the purpose of combating hostile aircraft which was very active in this vicinity. This experience proved very successful.	
			Lieuts J.P. Nolan & 2 N.C.O.s proceeded to attend a M.G. Course held at Camiers	
	9		Lieut H.R. Artis admitted to Hospital sick	
	10		Reinforcement of 6 O.R. arrived	
	12		Lieut A.P. Dobson M.G. returns to Company from Hospital	
	13		Reinforcement of 3 O.R. arrived. 2 O.R. attached to the Company	
	14		In accordance with Brigade offensive action by 6 Div the 2 Gun from No 1 Section under Lieut H.R. Chapman moved into forward destroyed from to Lv No 1 Section under 2/Lt. McCarron moved into position in the neighbourhood of Destroyed Farm	
L.N.C	15		5 Guns, No 2 Section and (No 4 Section less 2 guns) moved into position. Lt Smith under Lieut Camp Chase	

WAR DIARY
or
INTELLIGENCE SUMMARY.

(Erase heading not required.)

Army Form C. 211

Place	Date	Hour	Summary of Events and Information	Remarks and references to Appendices
Trenches	15/11		2 Guns No 1 Section under Lieut. A.P. Dolson M.C. moved up to Redoubt O₁ O₂.	
			3 Guns (No 1 Section) under Capt Lewes moved to Redoubt position on the Albert-Bapaume Road. Centres of Courcelette and Martinpuich 1 of reverence in going up. The rest of the 6th MG Coy in Reserve position rest quarters carried out by 6th Inf Bde.	
			5 Guns in and around Lt Smyth's # emplacement below an below Sugpost and around Sunken ROAD in M8 Central.	
			2 Guns in Destremont FARM firing an enfilade on M8 and al.	
			2 Guns SW of Destremont Trench fired on P 4 s.	
			2 Guns in Destremont O₁ O₂ enfilades Gallwitz Trench.	
			3 Guns in Dugout in Circle road Courcelette and Martinpuich	
			2 Guns in Destremont Trench sweeps valley M9 Central	
			In addition to above are action of 5th Can. M.G Coy morning the following position have been arranged as follows	
			The fire of Bouncer Redoubt M7 Central, already known to those of own to the 5th Australian M.G Coy fired on as continuation of below Sugpost and on ground from M7 a.d. w- M7 c.5.3	
			Two sections were standing by to fire on any targets	

WAR DIARY or INTELLIGENCE SUMMARY

Place	Date	Hour	Summary of Events and Information	Remarks and references to Appendices
L.W.B	1/7		Targets that might offer in the sector either close to or effectively engaged by the guns in Candles & Barrage was two formed in front & on to right front. **Barrage Fire.** All guns of course opened fire at zero keeping a rigid rate of fire until zero + 30 after which shelling was more or less from commanders own orders to open or cease fire as soon as S.O.S. was given. **Ammunition** in boxes & the gun were taken up to the farms & Kruisstraat machine and at Le Sars and at Destroyed Farm. **Communication** Telephones were used between A.D's & the S.A.A's Battalion HQ's. These worked satisfactorily but as the wires were so frequently used, most of the work was done by runners. **Rationing** There seemed difficulty about rationing as limbers could be brought near where animal could be brought up to its position on the right sector. All to the farm where it may hundred yds west of the position in the right sector. Close down to the road and were kept away from the regular emplacement. The position chosen gave a maximum	

A5834 Wt.W4973/M687 750,000 8/16 D.D.&L.Ltd. Forms/C.2118/13.

WAR DIARY
or
INTELLIGENCE SUMMARY.

(Erase heading not required.)

Army Form C. 2118

Place	Date	Hour	Summary of Events and Information	Remarks and references to Appendices
LINE	17.		maximum fire effect on his right & left and on many cases enforced shell late into trenches though to our knowledge not part of the day they were not located. From locations then unknown to the enemy arms were kept flaming there. The selection of a hall emplacement away from the trigger and in some cases two M.G. emplacements gave us peculation. Casualties 2 O.R. wounded.	
	18/9		Relieved 99 M.G.Coy in support of gallantry position. Right Sector Pts 5.R. VALLEY RESERVE Left Sector O1, O2, O3 on the 32 aero was reader. Source position & gun positions on R12 C.O.5.3 R12 C.N.6 were without archers & Pt d.9.5 Pt a.4.5 under Lieut Lokes Relief completed by 3am	
	21.		Two gun methoden from R12 C.O.5.3 M.R.C.M.6 The gun moves to No 8 Post under Lieut Norell guns in Pt d.9.5 M.O.4.5 moved to 1 Dolan relieved by Lieut Steer. Casualties Lieut arguses 1Pt G.Coy relieved in above position by 24M Coy Lilly arguses by 1300.	
	23		Company on relief move to write trailer at ALBERT	

Army Form C. 211

WAR DIARY
or
INTELLIGENCE SUMMARY.

(Erase heading not required.)

Instructions regarding War Diaries and Intelligence Summaries are contained in F. S. Regs., Part II. and the Staff Manual respectively. Title pages will be prepared in manuscript.

MACHINE GUN COMPANY
8th INFANTRY BRIGADE

Place	Date	Hour	Summary of Events and Information	Remarks and references to Appendices
ALBERT	23		Whit Sunday service to Company today	
	24		Usual cleaning up of Dugouts	
	25		& Preparation to relieve 17th Corps Pioneers	
	26		Special care of names & were Brunewig to unsnarg to	
	27		attain men in knowledge of Lewis Gunnery	

"SECRET"

6th Inf Bde

Herewith report on employment of machine guns in conjunction with proposed operations.

(a) 1) ESTREMONT TRENCH was reconnoitred.
This was found to have several short stretches completed, from which machine gun fire could be brought to bear on the following points.

(i) From M 20 a 8.3. The valley running through M 9 central can be effectively engaged. Range from 2100 yards upwards, the bullets passing over our front line at approximately 130 feet.

(ii) From M 20 b 1.4. LITTLE WOOD, n Mqd & M10c, and the trench in front can be engaged.
Range 1900 / 2200. Bullets passing front line at 110 feet / 245.

(iii) PYS can be sprinkled from M 20. b. 3.4 Range 2500. Bullets passing over M.14 a 6.8. at 300 feet.

(b) DESTREMONT FARM proved suitable for 2 machine guns.

(i) To enfilade trench from trench junction M 8 d.5.6. Range 1600 yards. bullets passing over front line at about 80 feet. The men in the front line should be warned.

(ii) To sweep reverse slope from junction of COULEE and GRUNDY to junction of COULEE and SUNKEN ROAD in M 8 a central Range 2300 - Bullets at 260 feet

(c) The ground in and around LE SARS is suitable for enfilading BELOW, & BELOW SUPPORT, (SUNKEN ROAD) in M 8 a.
The junction of GALLOWITZ and BELOW can also be engaged. RANGE 1800 yards, bullets at 120 feet above front posts.
BELOW extension in M 7 a could be reached if required; range 2600 yards, bullets passing at 360 feet.
Actual positions have not yet been reconnoitred as the village is not in our area and a relief was in progress.

(d) From the guns at present in defensive positions, the following targets can be engaged.
(1) From R 3, the junction in N 9 c 7½. 4½. Range 2600, bullets at 400 feet.
(2) From either of the O positions, GALLOWITZ and the NEW GALLOWITZ can be sprayed. Range 2600 yards (approx.) Bullets at 250 feet. (approx)
(3) The battery reserve gun - to trench running from GUARD Trench up to GALLOWITZ Trench. Range 1700 yards approx, bullets at 50 feet.

There is dug-out accomodation in DESTREMONT trench & DESTREMONT FARM.
It is uncertain what accomodation there may be at LE SARS.

It should be understood that the positions of some of the guns are approximate, as it may be necessary to move them backwards or forwards in order to make the f bullets fall with a maximum effect on certain slopes.

With the cooperation of the guns in the present defensive positions, the whole front from PYS to DYKE ROAD will be thoroughly swept by enfilade machine gun fire.

Thus it is suggested that fire should not be opened until the assault has taken place, as the maximum effect will be obtained when the enemy prepare to counter attack.

It should be noticed that no fire of a directly overhead nature is being brought to bear, thus obviating any possibility of firing on our own troops.

It would be of great assistance if the assaulting troops could send a "light signal" on the objective being taken, so that an ~~on the any sign of a counter attack~~ immediate machine gun barrage can be opened.

This would be much more satisfactory than working on time.

W.G. Lewell Maj
Comg No 6 Coy MGC

4/2/17

14 Inf Bde

Ref your Instructions
The guns that are to be used in conjunction
with the operations are
at VESARS. 5
COSTREMOIT FARM 2
"   TRENCH 4
VALLEY RESERVE   : M 19 b . 10 . 3
R1   M 20 a . 7 . 5
S1   : M 14 c . 8 . 2
O1 }   R 24 d . 0 . 8
O2 }

<u>1</u> O1 & O2 are outside brigade area —
The remaining guns outside brigade area are
S2   R. 17 b 9½ 5½
R3   R 24 a central
R4 & R5   R 23 b 2. 5
O3+O4   O4 & O5   R 23 d 9 8

<u>2</u> I presume in this para — you refer to guns outside our
sector —
O1 & O2 have been allotted to help our task —
Ref. & R 24 d 98

<u>3</u> I am manning O1 and O2 on relief of 5th Bde

<u>4</u> R2 at M 13 d 8½. 1½ — R3 at R 24 a central — R4 &
R5 at R 23 b 2 5 — O4 & O5 at R 23 d 9 8 — S2 at R 17 b
will require only to be manned by   9½ - 5½
the 5th Bde — They are not being used for our task
but will be wanted to help the
99 Bde by their fire —

P.T.O

5. If this is not clear — Please wire for me to come to you in the morning —

W.S. Hewett Maj
Cmdg 6th ₁/13ᵃ M-G Cᵒ

10/2/17

O.C. 6th M.G. Coy. 10/2/17   URGENT   SECRET

For the operations I understand you will have

    5 guns in LE SARS
    2 "   " DESTREMONT FARM
    4 "   " DESTREMONT Trench.
    1 "   " VALLEY RESERVE ⎫
    1 "   " R1 position   ⎬ Give map
    1 "   " S1   "   ⎬ References
    2 "   " O positions.   ⎭ of these.

1. Of these latter as well as guns in other present defensive positions ~~will be sent~~ how many will be out of our Brigade Area? (The dividing line between the two Brigades will be No 11 Post, down NEW STREET to No 7 Post in YELLOW LINE (about R.19.6.4.2) to WEST MIRAUMONT Dugouts) –

2. How many of these guns will cover our own particular task? Give their numbers & map references.

3. Have you made any arrangements with 99th Bde for keeping them in their present positions (such as are required).

4. You said you wanted reliefs for S2, 4, 5. R2 & 3. O3 & 4. Say where these are, and whether they will cover the particular task allotted to this Brigade.

5. ~~Reply by bearer.~~

E.L. Wright Capt BM
6th Inf Bde

6th Inf Bde

With Ref your G.S. 60/18 para 1:—

The remaining defensive positions R2 - R3 - R4 -
R5 - O3 - O4 - S2 are not being occupied
by 11-99th Bde. These will have to
be manned by 5th Army Bde M.G. Coy.

W G Weaver Maj
Cmdg 6th M.G. Co.

Hewitt
Roberts
3 Subalterns

MESSAGES AND SIGNALS.

Sender's Number.	Day of Month.	In reply to Number.	AAA
N.7	15		

The M.G. of 6th Coy are situated as follows
1 Section forward
1 gun in Strong point at R11 d 3 4½
1 gun in Strong point at R11 d 9 7
1 gun about GR11 b 9 . 4
1 gun about R 12 b 1 . 9
These positions are approximate
1 Section on the left.
1 gun at R 4 R 23 b 2 d [KENORA]
1 gun at R 3 about R 24 a 5 8
2 guns at O 1 & R 24 a 0 0
1 gun at O 2 R 24 a 0 0

MESSAGE

Prefix .... Code .... m.	Words	Charge	This messag...		
Office of Origin and Service Instructions.					
	Sent		...........Service.		
....	At..............m.			From	
....	To				
....	By	(Signature of "Franking Officer.")	By		

TO {

Sender's Number.	Day of Month.	In reply to Number.	A A A

1 section on right
1 gun at R2 — near M 19 b 4½ 9½
1 gun at Valley Reserve M 19 b 5 0
1 gun at R1 M 20 a 6 6
1 gun at S1 near M 13 d 10 6

Reserve section
1 gun was at S2 — this is being
brought down as it is said to
be damaged.
3 guns at Company Head Quarters

From
Place
Time

Prefix .... Code			
Office of Origin and Service Instructions.	Sent		
	At .... m.		
	To		
	By	(Signature of "Franking Officer.")	By ....

TO				

Sender's Number.	Day of Month.	In reply to Number.	AAA
Point on wheel guns are laid			
S1 R1	} E Command Dyke Road		
Valley Reserve			
R2 R3 } M 76			
01.02 R12 a 10.10 and M1			
R4 M 5 C Central			
Four forward guns are in case of counter attack.			
			W.G. Hamilton

From
Place
Time

The above may be forwarded as now corrected.   (Z)

Censor.   Signature of Addressor or person authorised to telegraph in his name.

* This line should be erased if not required.

MGS

1 gun at M15b25 to shoot on to M2d central
3 guns in Gunpits   Enfilades sunken Road & BELOW
                                                    & BELOW.

1 gun at M15b5.1   enfilading BELOW extension
1 gun at M15c86   trained on but not firing at
                                M8d61 -
1 gun M15d0.7   ditto on M14b5.9.
2 guns M20d75   shooting on M9 central
1 gun M15d79   shooting far end of SUNKEN Road

2 guns in reserve -
a Rapid rate from zero to zero + 30.
Desultory fire until SOS & then rapid -

Headquarters,

   2nd Division.

       Reference conversation this afternoon.

      I enclose here map showing proposed position and tasks of the Guns of the 6th Machine Gun Company, and 1 Section 5th Machine Gun Company, for the coming operations :-

5 guns in LE SARS, numbered 1, 2, 3, 4 and 5 on the map,
               to enfilade BELOW and BELOW SUPPORT TRENCHES.

2 guns in DESTREMONT FARM, numbered 6 and 7, to fire on
               trenches in M.8.b. and d.

2 guns S.W. of DESTREMONT FARM, numbered 10 and 11,
               to fire on PYS.

2 guns in DESTREMONT TRENCH, numbered 8 and 9, one to
               sweep the VALLEY, M.9.central, the other to fire on LITTLE WOOD.

3 guns in Reserve, one in LE SARS and 2 in DESTREMONT
               FARM.

      In addition to the above, the following present defensive positions will be occupied :-

        S.1.   )
        R.1.   )   By Section of
        R.2.   )   5th Machine Gun Company.
VALLEY RESERVE.)

     O.1 and O.2.

      Please return map.

                                Brigadier General,

12.2.17.   Commanding, 6th Infantry Brigade.

6th Brigade.

2nd Division.

6th MACHINE GUN COMPANY ::: MARCH 1917.

Army Form C. 2118.

WAR DIARY
or
INTELLIGENCE SUMMARY.
(Erase heading not required.)

March 1917 Vol 15

Place	Date	Hour	Summary of Events and Information	Remarks and references to Appendices
ALBERT	5		The Company moved from Albert and the support area to USNA HILL & Euro were eryssed first night & day on Duke Rd Right dortis under relief by 5th MG Coy on the ground. Reinforcements of 3 ORs arrived. 6 subaltern & 6 MG Coy were ordered to operate with the 90th Inf Bde in the offensive action the following particulars were issued. Dispositions of Guns. 2 Guns in Pts about M. 6.2.9. Per Gun to fire on Sim Kerr Pts in G.33.c. and the Rt to Left of the zero + X to Loybart Trench Traversing their G.33.c.9.0 to G.33.8.7.7. and firing on Pulmor behind Per Gun to fire on Ravine in G.33.c Gens Zero+X to Left on Loybart Trench Traversing G.33.6. 2 Guns in Bowser Redoubt about M.1.a.3.9. Per Gun on Ravine in G.33.c Off. Zero+X to Left to Loybart Through on G.33.6. on Quan to fire at Cuba Road in G.33.a. Off. Zero+X 10 Left on to Loybart Trenche on G.33.d.2 Guns in Courlite Trench about M.7.b.1. Per Gun to fire at G.33.a.5.5. to M.3.1.8.7. Off. Zero+X to Lt. to Loybart Trench in G.33.w.c.	
USNA HILL	8		Ammunition 10 Boxes per Gun Reserve 1000 r.ds per Gun S.A.A Targets Full instructions have been issued to each Officer who will be personally responsible for the correct carrying of same orders. All guns to be in new position one hour before zero Opening Fire All guns will open rapid fire at zero on bright stars above O. Zero+ x and Left to become targets & continue rapid fire until zero+20 Off. Zero+20 only desultory fire once a minute until	

WAR DIARY or INTELLIGENCE SUMMARY

Army Form C. 2118

Place	Date	Hour	Summary of Events and Information	Remarks and references to Appendices
In the line Coy	8		In case of S.O.S. signal will be issued Green Green Green Green for our Longuest Trench (300 Target) Compensation To Capt Dawson Order Trench 177 & 2 Cpls Each Officer will over orderly men on 3 day. One orderly from 6119 Coy to report to 99" Inf Bde on 3 day. Orders to be brought to M.G.C. 2. at Roy each night.	
	9		On accidents work above Quevellers Road No Sections & Lieuts in No 2 sector moved up to Sector. Removing 2 Guns & guns of No. 1 Section moved up to Sector. Capt Peters in charge of No 1 Coy as operating on the offensive.	
	10		Attack on Grevillers Trench by 99" Inf Bde. C/119 & 9 Sections covered attack 3 Guns under Capt Chapman occupied position to enfilade Rayner & Sunray Trench Capt C/33 Remouse of 3 guns enfilading from neighbourhood of R33 to Coulee Trench	
	11		1. 6/119 Capelaine 99. 34 Coy in Courcelette Sector was Relieved on conclusion. 5 Guns in Quarry Trench 6 Guns in Goose with 72 Trench. Relief completed by 9 a.m. 1/9/17 Capt Chapman Relieved by Lieut N.C.Cormack	

WAR DIARY
or
INTELLIGENCE SUMMARY.

Army Form C. 2118.

Place	Date	Hour	Summary of Events and Information	Remarks and references to Appendices
	12/3		Evacuation of Lewhart Line by the enemy. 16 guns under Lieut Curtis attached to Right Battalion 1st Kings. 3 guns under Lieut McCormack attached to Left Battn.	
	13		The guns followed the advance of Infantry & garrisons strong points. The following (ie Brigade Commander's attack) to take all garrison power touch was established with 18 Australian Div (5th M.G.Coy) on the right and 18th Div 54th M.G.Coy on the left.	
	14		No 4 Section under Lt. Nolan moved into Clase Lighton to Barastres en Gap. Three guns were responsible for protection of left flank of the Brigade. Lieut Butler relieved by Lieut Sanders on gun site G.9.d.9.6. Lieut Snoxell No 2 Section relieved Lieut McCormack in strong point G.30.d.2.6., G.28.1.4. & G.9.d.9.6.	
	15 16		Lieut Nolan moved into reserve into Barnes. Gos.C. with 2 guns (1st Section) Lieut McCormack & 2 O.R's proceeded to Carrieu on 17 G. Course	
	17		Enemy evacuated Bihucourt Line. No 3 Section under Lieut Glover attacked to 1st Kings Batt moved into G.26.6.9.9.	
	18		No 4 Section attached to 1st Kings Batt moved into S.13.g.9.5 ones & farmer East of the outpost line running 800x in front of Shygnies L.P.SIGNIES. Lieut Clapham moved into Clase Lighton. Reserve Coy H.Q. on Gos. 2.8.0. Lieut Snoxell moved into Reserve and Gun his in Gos.a. Lieut of transport moved up war gun fits in Gos.a. Lieut Clapham moved into Syb.gues (attacks to 2 so Sypps)	
	19		Infantry advance guard moved on Mory. No 4 Section under Lt Nolan moved with war guard and occupied position. 2 guns under Lt Nolan at B.H. at 2.8. 2 guns under Lieut Sanders in B.23. Central. No 1 Section under	

WAR DIARY or INTELLIGENCE SUMMARY

Army Form C. 2118

Place	Date	Hour	Summary of Events and Information	Remarks and references to Appendices
	19		Lieut Clapham moved into Close Support in B16.a. Casualty of 1 officer wounded. No 2 Section under Lieut Showell and No 3 Section under Lieut Clauson moved into Reserve in H8.C. Transport moved up into H8.c. 2 Section (Nos 2 & No 3) withdrew and were into DYKE VALLEY Transport went back to USNA HK. 2 Section (No1 & No4) relieved by 52nd M.G.Coy in position previously in own about Mory.	
	20		ROLE of 6th M.G.Coy in Recent Operation. 1 Section was generally in the front line of defence & 1 section was in close support. The remaining sections were some way back, joining & were ever to relieve the sections in front. Transport. Transport was done almost entirely by pack animal. These were used for conveying the guns in the forward area & for carrying guns into the favorable during the advance. By this use of pack animals the manual labour was reduced to a minimum. Pack animals were ready alongside to man guns of the strongpoint forward and kept in ready near the Reserve Section in the gun fighting of 12/13th guns were brought into action from limbers Guns Tripods The guns were kept free from dirt by keeping them wrapped in blankets. No difficulty was experienced with the tripods so it was carried every near to most of the positions by pack animal.	

Army Form C. 2118.

WAR DIARY
or
INTELLIGENCE SUMMARY.
(Erase heading not required.)

MACHINE GUN COMPANY
No. 3
Date 3/2/17
6th INFANTRY BRIGADE

Instructions regarding War Diaries and Intelligence Summaries are contained in F. S. Regs., Part II. and the Staff Manual respectively. Title pages will be prepared in manuscript.

Place	Date	Hour	Summary of Events and Information	Remarks and references to Appendices
			Ammunition	
			6 b y Boxes per gun normal amount carried. S.A.A. was obtained from nearest dumps the necessity of having ours was noted with filling was emphasised.	
			Communication	
			Rumour has to be relied upon do a great extent. It was found impractical to run our own telephone communication. Had to be made of Bn arrangements. The orderlies all given to keep in touch with Coy HQs.	
			Rations	
			During the time the Coy was in the line it was rations daily to limber were brought to Coy HQs, then when the ration was sent on from animal to carrier teams.	
	20		2 Sectns (Nos 1 & Nos 4) moved into DYKE VALLEY.	
USNA HILL	21		Coy moved into USNA HILL	
Warloy Billon	22		Coy moved into billets at Warloy. Billon. (1 Of. rnd rnks 31.)	
La Vicogne	26		Coy moved from Warloy. Billon to La Vicogne.	
Occoches	27		Coy moved from La Vicogne to Occoches.	
Nurcq	29		Coy moved from Occoches to Nurcq	
Moncky Cayeux	30		Coy moved from Nurcq to Moncky Cayeux	
	31		Lieut. A.P. Dobson. M.C. goins on to Coy of 2nd Hindustanifornce Coy as reinforcement.	

"A" Form. Army Form C. 2121
MESSAGES AND SIGNALS.

SECRET

TO: 6th Inf Bde

Sender's Number.	Day of Month	In reply to Number	AAA
S 111	6		

The two machine guns found by your MG Coy at W.18.b.6.3 will be moved back to their old position at X.14.b as soon as possible aaa They will be so placed as to cover with their fire the Ammunition Dumps at X.14.d, X.20.b and X.13.a.0.5 aaa Your MG Officer must ensure that communications are re-established between the guns and Searchlight aaa The two guns at POZIERES will remain in position aaa All guns are to be in position by day and night aaa Please report when this move is complete aaa Accomodation for MG section at X.14.b must be arranged with Searchlight Section aaa Acknowledge

From: 2nd Division

(Z) CS Leggatt Capt

H.Q. 6' Inf Bde

your G.S. 655/5

Ref. my conversation on telephone
herewith letter confirming that
move is complete & arrangements
made —

W S Hewett Major
Cmdg 6 M.G.C

SECRET
==========

6th Infantry Brigade.
----------M------------

The two machine guns found by your M.G.Coy. at
W.18.b.6.3. will be moved back to their old position at
X.14.b. as soon as possible. They will be so placed as
to cover with their fire the ammunition dumps at X.14.d.
X.20.b. and X.13.a.0.5. Your M.G.Officer must ensure
that communications are re-established between the guns
and searchlight. The two guns at POZIERES will remain
in position. All guns are to be in position by day and night
Please report when this move is complete. Accommodation
for M.G.Section at X.14.b. must be arranged with searchlight Section. ACKNOWLEDGE.

       (sd) C.F.Leggatt Capt.,
     General Staff, 2nd Division

= 2 =

Officer Commanding,
 6th M.G.Company.
=============================

  For your information and necessary action.

  Please report when move is complete and
all arrangements made.

            Captain,

7/3/17.   Brigade Major, 6th Infantry Bde.

"A" Form.
MESSAGES AND SIGNALS.

Army Form C.2121
(in pads of 100).
No. of Message ....

Prefix ...... Code ...... m.	Words	Charge	This message is on a/c of:	Recd. at .... m.
Office of Origin and Service Instructions.	Sent		............Service.	Date ....
SECRET	At ....m.			From ....
	To			
	By		(Signature of "Franking Officer.")	By ....

TO	EF			

Sender's Number.	Day of Month.	In reply to Number.	AAA
* 122	12		

The guns are in position as follows -
4 in GALLOWITZ trench at
M9c 1.3 — M9c 5.3½
These form the GALLOWITZ Group
5 guns in GRUNDY trench from
M8b 6½.9. to M9a 3.8.
These form the GRUNDY Group
3 at M1D 5½ 8½ these form the PYS
Group.
There are 4 guns in reserve in BELOW
The PYS group are manned and
cover from G33 62.8 — G 336 80 —
The GRUNDY Group man 73 guns
and cover from G336 80 to G34 d 1.2
The GALLOWITZ Group man 3 guns

From			
Place			
Time			

The above may be forwarded as now corrected. (Z)

............Censor. Signature of Addressor or person authorised to telegraph in his name.
* This line should be erased if not required.
750,000. W 2186—M509. H. W. & V., Ld. 6/16.

"A" Form.
MESSAGES AND SIGNALS.

and cover from G 34 d 1.2 to past the junction with the division on our right.

The remaining guns of both groups are in dugouts in JALLOWITZ & GRUNDY trenches respectively, with their tripods mounted. It is inadvisable to mount the guns by day as they are in full view of LOUPART WOOD. I am at H.Q. 1st Kings

From EU

"A" Form.
MESSAGES AND SIGNALS.

Army Form C.2121
(in pads of 100).

Prefix......Code.........m.	Words	Charge	This message is on a/o of:	Recd. at.............m.
Office of Origin and Service Instructions.	Sent		.............Service.	Date................
	At............m.			From..............
	To...........			By...............
	By...........		(Signature of "Franking Officer.")	

TO 6th Inf Bde.

Sender's Number.	Day of Month.	In reply to Number.	A A A
*G.I.222	12		

Herewith copy of a lithographed sketch found in a dugout in GRÉVILLERS TRENCH on the 10th. It shows work in progress and contemplated in and around LOUPART WOOD. The original scale was about 1/5000 the attached copy has been reduced to about 1/10000. The spacing cannot be taken as being accurate, it was drawn from our 1/5000 maps & did not compare with certain definite landmarks on the German map. It is accurate enough to serve as a guide to locating dugouts &c. It is thought that this may be of use to you in the future.

From ....
Place ....
Time ....

The above may be forwarded as now corrected. (Z)   A.Hewson Capt.

Censor. Signature of Addressor or person authorised to telegraph in his name.

* This line should be erased if not required.

MW143
15/3/17
4.30 P.M.

   T.D.

Reference your A365 of 14th.
Herewith sketch maps of
Company positions.
Advanced Trench position
already sent by wire

     MWT Wyon ?/Lt.
      A/Adjutant
       RF

Right to Left Front
 D. Coy
 B. Coy
 C. Coy

Company in support
 A Coy

OC 6 M.G. Coy.   P.25

The following is accommodation
of dugouts & reconnoitred this
morning

17th Middlesex Strong Point   = 34.
Coy   IN. G.28.d.6.3.

GUN PITS IN. G 28 a 7.4   – 24
   "   " IN G 28 d 9.2   – 12.
   "   " IN G 27 d 9.5 ✓   – 35
 DOG OUT SHAFTS IN G 34 b 1.6   – 8
   "   "   " G 29 c 2.5   – 15.

16/3/17.   J.P. Roberts Capt
                               6 M.G. Coy

6th Brigade.

2nd Division.

6th MACHINE GUN COMPANY ::: APRIL 1917.

WAR DIARY or INTELLIGENCE SUMMARY

(Erase heading not required.)

Army Form C. 2118

Instructions regarding War Diaries and Intelligence Summaries are contained in F.S. Regs., Part II. and the Staff Manual respectively. Title Pages will be prepared in manuscript.

MACHINE GUN COMPANY
No. 704
Date 1/3/17
6th INFANTRY BRIGADE

Place	Date	Hour	Summary of Events and Information	Remarks and references to Appendices
Nowvey - Crayeux Ourton	1st		Sections are at occupied in the general cleaning ↑ being of guns, lifvers etc in view of forthcoming operations	
	7		The Company moved from Nowvey Crayeux to Ourton	
Acg	10		The Company moved from Ourton to Acg	
Rocincourt	11		The Company moved from Acg to Rocincourt (Reserve Area) Major W. Strutt M.C. proceeded to Courcelles to attend a M.G. Course. Col. J. Phillips assumed command of the Coy & Lieut A.P. Dobson M.C. second in command	
Neuf Bouillett	18		The Coy relieve the 99th M.G. Coy taking over positions on Railway Embankment N. of Bapaume. The position was heavily shelled. 1 O.R. killed.	
	20		2 Vickers Aircraft Guns were mounted, 1 in Sugar Factory N.1 at Bapaume – 9304 Red. The 63rd Div on our right relieved a Colour Guard. The enemy guns retained in time but was enabled up by our Artillery. The Coy stood to then & on the enemy was mopping up men & about Squar C.15.b+d (Sheet 51B n.w.). Enemy Counter attacked about 10 am & again at 11 am at Colour Guard. Our stand to.	
	24		They never amounted to much by our Artillery. The 99th M.G. Coy never relieve 6th M.G. Coy an 26th inst.	
	25		Orders received. Coy was on right at Grivelles 9.15ay	
	26	9.15am 9.30am	2 O.R.s was wounded. Relief cancelled. Orders received to prepare to attack & have positions to be reconnoitred	
	27		Moved to Battle H.Qs in B.Y. D.4.2. (Sheet 51B N.W.). Sections move to Battle positions. Sections were ordered to proceed as follows – No.1 Section under Lieut A.R. Chapman & Lieut R. Ward to advance behind the British West on the right & occupy strong points. No 2 Section under Lieut H. M. Common to advance behind the 17 Middleton Regt and occupy strong points. No 3 Section under & lead with Artillery to occupy position in case of Reserve line & the barrage fire	

1875 Wt. W593/826 1,000,000 4/15 J.B.C. & A. A.D.S.S./Forms/C. 2118.

WAR DIARY
or
INTELLIGENCE SUMMARY
(Erase heading not required.)

Army Form C. 2118

MACHINE GUN COMPANY
No. _____
Date _____
8th INFANTRY BRIGADE

Instructions regarding War Diaries and Intelligence Summaries are contained in F.S. Regs. Part II. and the Staff Manual respectively. Title Pages will be prepared in manuscript.

Place	Date	Hour	Summary of Events and Information	Remarks and references to Appendices
Front of OPPY	27.		No 4 Section less two teams, under Lieut S.M. Nelson and 2/Lieut J.J. Sanders to occupy position on right of Shaven Line and to arrange for two teams to advance or right to have right flank of Rifle Bn. in line. Two advance on left to cover left flank of Rifle Section on ladder positions ready for the attack	
	28	2AM	Attack launched by 12th Division Kings & 10th Essex Regt 8th Bgde & Cobralt as previously described. In retaliation to our Artillery barrage the enemy opened an intense bombardment of our front system of trenches & Gun positions. In spite of this the troops advanced & followed the objective but were compelled to evacuate it later. Lt. Maclean Guns were brought back to our former positions & advance to "Tarn" so as an enemy counter attack was expected. This however did not develop. During the assault severe losses were suffered on the enemy M.G. Casualties were 2/Lieut G.J.G. Cornick (wounded & missing), 1 Offr killed, Belt wounded
		8 AM	Missing	
		9.25 AM	99th Infy Bde attacks on same front as 12th Infy Box yesterday. Lt C/M G.J. Cobralt reinforcement of 4th M.G.Co arrived in the Machine Gun Barrage from reserve trenches, 4 Guns at B17 C.9.9. to B17 C.3.k and R at B23.6.9.5. The enemy Heller front reverse line heavy & continually	
	29	9 PM	The 99 MG Co relieves the six Guns of the 6th MG Co. The remainder of 6 MG Co were withdrawn The Coy spent the night on the Railway Cutting	
ECURIE	30	6 am	The Company moved from its cutting to dugouts East of ECURIE	

OC Colegom Lt
W.C. Enzazy

H.O.
(of Inf Brig)

Reference your 65/g8/25. dated 21st April 15. the M.G. Coy will co-operate as per attached table.

Targets: Full instructions have been issued to officers concerned. Each gun will be in position and ready to fire 1 hour before ZERO.

Ammunition: 14 boxes per gun. 2000 rounds S.A.A. per gun in reserve.

ZERO: ZERO will be notified later.

Opening fire: Rapid rate of fire will be opened at ZERO and will be maintained until ZERO + 30. after which a desultory fire will be maintained.

22/4/17

N. Roberts Capt
M.G. Coy

No of Guns.	Location	Target	Position of Nearest Troops	Range to Target	Height of Tray over Troops
2.	B22.6.9.4	Trench System in C.13.a + d	500ˣ	2600ˣ	200'
2.	B16.6.3.9	Trench System in B.18.d.	400ˣ	2700ˣ	125'
2.	B16.a.9.4	Trench System in B.24.G.	500ˣ	2300ˣ	148'

H.Q 6 Inf Brig/

Herewith suggested scheme for co-operation of 6 Machine gun Coy in forthcoming operations

DISPOSITION OF GUNS.

	Guns for barrage.	Guns for STRONG POINTS	Guns for consolidating 1st Object.
6 M.G.C.	8	6	2
99th M.G.C.	1		
" M.G.C.	7 guns in RESERVE.		

LOCATION GUNS ZERO.

BARRAGE Guns

As shown on attached table

Guns for STRONG POINTS

To be arranged with O.C. units concerned & notified later.

Guns for consolidating 1st Objective

In FRONT LINE TRENCH. One gun will be with RIGHT BATT. 13th Essex
One gun to be with LEFT Batt. 17th Middlesex

RESERVE GUNS 99th M.G. Coy

These guns will take over defensive positions on railway embankment.

ROLE OF Guns/

Guns during barrage work will fire on 1st objective as per attached map until the artillery barrage lifts on 1st Objective. When artillery lifts on first objective the machine gun barrage will lift on to 2nd objective objective when artillery lifts on 2nd objective. M. Guns will cease fire

Guns for consolidating first objective/

As soon as the 1st objective has been taken these guns will move forward and occupy defensive positions on flanks of battalions

Ammunition/

Guns doing barrage work. 14 boxes of ammunition per gun with reserve of 2000 rounds S.A.A.
Guns going forward. 6 boxes per gun.

Opening fire/ Guns will open fire at ZERO and keep up a rapid rate of fire until the artillery lifts on to second objective when they will cease fire

Targets/ All guns will be in position 1 hour before ZERO ready to open fire. Officers in charge of guns will be personally responsible for the correct laying of guns

Communications/ Coy H.Q. B.22.6.7.8.
1 orderly per section will report to Coy H.Q at. B.22 b 7.8.
In addition to this 1 orderly from 6 M.G.Coy will report to Bde. H.Q. B.21 a. 8.7.
In addition again to this 1 orderly will report at H.Q 13th ESSEX. 1 orderly H.Q 17th Middlesex on X day.
Telephonic communications will also be established with nearest Bn. H.Q 13th ESSEX. B.23 a. 6. 8.

24/4/17

J.P.Roberts Capt.
6 M.G. Coy

GUNS FOR BARRAGE.

Location	1st Target	2nd Target	Range 1st Obj.	Range 2nd Obj.	Height of lowest shot. Safety O.F.L. (1400x)
2 guns. B.23.a.5.5.	1st Objective	2nd Objective	2230x	2900x	233 feet
2 guns. B.23.a.1.9.	1st Objective	2nd Objective	2200x	2900x	233 feet
2 guns. B.17.c.1.3.	1st Objective	2nd Objective	2250x	2900x	250 feet
3 guns. B.16.d.9.7.	1st Objective	2nd Objective	2100x	2900x	190 feet

H. Roberts Capt
6th M.G. Coy

24/4/17.

Disposition of Guns. 61 M.G. Coy

	Barrage Guns.	Consolidation S.P.	Consol. F. Oly
61 M.G.C.	9.	8.	2
99th M.G.C.	4		
31st Div.	16.		

In addition to above a Company of the 31st Division will be attached to Brigade for operations.

LOCATION of Guns at ZERO.

			1st TARGET 1st Objective	2nd TARGET 2nd objective
A.	2 guns	B 16 d 0 9	"	"
B.	2 "	B 17 c 0 4	"	"
C.	2 "	B 23 a 5 5	"	"
D.	4 " (99th)	B 23 b 4 8	SUNKEN RD. C 13 b.	Barrage C 14. a

2.

E. Guns going forward for consolidating 1st Objective — FRONT LINE.

F. Guns for STRONG POINTS. To be arranged with OC units.

G. 4 guns of 99th M.G.C. will be in RESERVE in TRENCH running through B 21 a.

H. 16 guns of 31st DIVISION will be about B 23 central
1st Target. 8 guns SUNKEN RD. B 12 d
                                                                 C 7 c
                          8 " TRENCHES in C 13 r & d.
2nd Target. Barrage C 14. a r d.

ROLE OF MACHINE GUNS.

"Guns" doing barrage will open fire at ZERO. When artillery lifts on to first objective the M.G. barrage will be put on 3rd objective. When artillery lifts on 3rd objective. A.B.C guns will cease fire. A & B will move forward 600ˣ and put a barrage down in C 14 a & c. When final objective is gained all guns will cease fire. If S.O.S signal is sent up, barrage will be put down in C 14 a & c.

The two guns going forward to consolidate 1st objective will move forward as soon as 1st objective is taken.

Guns for STRONG POINTS
Time of moving forward to be arranged with OC units concerned.

Ammunition   Barrage guns. 14 boxes
                  3000 Rounds S.A.A
                  Guns going forward. 8 boxes
Targets.   full instructions have been
                  issued to officers concerned
                  Guns to be in position 1
                  hour before ZERO.
Communication.   C.H.Q B 17 d 4.4
                  1 orderly per section C.H.Q Y. DAY.
                  1 "   to report B H Q Y "

J. Roberts Capt
6 M.G Coy.

26/9/17

H.Q. SECRET M.6.16.

1st 6 Inf. Brig.

Herewith scheme for disposal of M.G. going forward with Infantry. This scheme has been approved of by Col Kelly. Will you please forward it to Col Martin for his approval or amendment.

1. At ZERO guns will be formed up as per sketch.
2. When first objective has been taken they will move forward into old German Front line
3. When 2nd objective has been taken they will move forward to first objective and remain there until final objective has been taken when they will move forward to strong points. 1 Gun will move behind 3rd wave of attacking battalion and protect flank of battalions.

5 Guns for left Bn. (17th Middlesex) will be at B.16 central at 12 mid-night. As battalion forms up the officer in charge of guns will report to O.C. 17th Middlesex and then take up their alloted positions.

5 Guns for right Bn. will be at B.22.b.9.1. at 12 midnight. Officer in charge will report to O.C. 13th Essex at a time to be notified later. They will then move into position.

1st WAVE. ▨ ▭ ▭ ▭
2nd "   ▭ ▭ ▭ ▭
3rd "   ▭ ▭ ▭ ▭

ılı   ılı ılı   ılı ılı
FLANK GUN.   S. POINTS   S. POINTS

6th Brigade.

2nd Division.

6th MACHINE GUN COMPANY ::: M A Y 1917.

WAR DIARY
INTELLIGENCE SUMMARY

Army Form C. 2118.

6 M G Coy

MACHINE GUN COMPANY No. M/105
6th INFANTRY BRIGADE

Place	Date	Hour	Summary of Events and Information	Remarks and references to Appendices
ECURIE	May 1		No.1 and No.2 sections moved to Ecurie. No.3 and No.4 sections went up the line. ECURIE. No.3 section (Lieut Antis) and No.4 section (Lieut Nolan) were under Captain Robb and engaged in R27a (51.B.N.W.) into position relative to B17.L. i.e. in order to co-operate with the barrage on the morning of the 3rd.	
L Coy Bray 5 Coy Line	2		The following targets were allotted by O.C. 99. I.B. Coy. 1st TARGET. Trench in C.P.C. & Cross Roads in C.P.a. 2nd TARGET. Barrage across C8.c. S.O.S. Same as 2nd target. Role of Guns All guns opened fire at ZERO and fired according to following table. 1st TARGET ZERO to ZERO + 7 mins 2nd TARGET ZERO plus 7 mins to ZERO plus 12 mins. Artillery fire was kept up on the S.O.S. target during the day. Rate of fire was 1 belt every 6 mins to rate of fire decreasing if: ZERO + 15 mins. About 5 p.m. the enemy was reported to be massing for a counter attack and the guns were ordered to fire down a barrage on trenches in C.P.C. (a of R28a of R.w.1a) The guns remained in position until 10.30 P.M. when 99 I.B. Coy took over the section neglected position where they were withdrawn and moved into dugouts behind ECURIE. The following troops were used on recent operations...	

Army Form C. 2118.

WAR DIARY
INTELLIGENCE SUMMARY.
(Erase heading not required.)

Instructions regarding War Diaries and Intelligence Summaries are contained in F. S. Regs., Part II. and the Staff Manual respectively. Title pages will be prepared in manuscript.

[Stamp: MACHINE GUN COMPANY No. ___ Date 3/5/17 8th INFANTRY BRIGADE]

Place	Date	Hour	Summary of Events and Information	Remarks and references to Appendices
L Coy Fourth L Coy Bray			(1) Guns should be grouped fairly close together for barrage work to facilitate communication	
			(2) All indication of expert on any particular shall be avoided as flash positions dark should be chosen in a neighbourhood shell lit and camouflaged	
			(3) Machine Gun teams should be forward from reliefs 3-4 days earlier than infantry	
			(4) Men should have plenty of trackes in belts ready by hand	
			(5) System of light signals denoting position of the infantry should be established	
			(6) The necessity of chronometers and auxiliary aiming marks for barrage work	
			(7) The M.G. Barrage Guns should be in local support that commands in order to obtain views of the situation to their own as possible	
			(8) A close co-operation should exist between Victor and Lewis Guns	
			Supplement of 50 o/o aimed	
Bray	3rd		No 3 and No 4 sections joined the remainder of the company at Bray while at Bray the company was employed in all defences work on rear of prevention rendered for the following programme of training was carried out while the Coy was at Bray - Physical drill, lug drill, Lewis drill, Storage, Mechanism, Locations, Stoppages, Lire drill, Panorama sketch of range cards, The 9 pound and coves formations and drill, Signals, muster Tell light rifles, Advance stopping, Laying gun to night firing, Squad or Caturantos, Range work, Exchange exercise, Quick loading Fire discharge, NCOs class map reading &c.	

Army Form C. 2118.

WAR DIARY
or
INTELLIGENCE SUMMARY.
(Erase heading not required.)

Instructions regarding War Diaries and Intelligence Summaries are contained in F. S. Regs., Part II. and the Staff Manual respectively. Title pages will be prepared in manuscript.

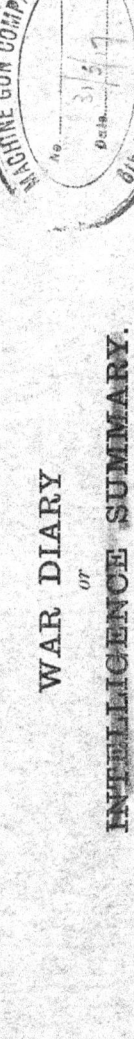

MACHINE GUN COMPANY
No. 31
6th INFANTRY BRIGADE

Place	Date	Hour	Summary of Events and Information	Remarks and references to Appendices
BRAY	13		H.Q. O.C. 2nd.Lieut and 7th. U.S. Bn. joined the Company	
	14		H.Q. 2nd Lieut H.S. Ayres joined the Coy.	
			The Company were from Bray to Corbron-Chateau	
CORBRON CHATEAU	17		Lieut A.P.D.Dowry D.C.L.I. proceeded to Corbron on 1 G.Come.	
	18		The following programme of training was carried out while at Corbron Chateau:	
			Repeat hill Gun Drill, stoppages, Advance stripping Gun and spare parts,	
			Drill and stoppages with Lock cases, Use of Margens Corpons, firing positions,	
			Mane carrying, Use of spare and Gun Gears, Mountings, Register	
			of Section, Laying Gun for angle swing, Lateral swing, Roll swing,	
			Taking cover, range cards, Fire Direction, Indirection, Combinations	
			Indirect Elevation training Construction of emplacements, Use of Auxiliary	
			arms, mask, Use of Lewes, Instruction in Barrage Barbette Gun	
			Rang work, Application for decussive combat.	
			NCO Class firing Guns for indirect fire of Ways at Corbron	
			The Company moved from Corbron-Chateau to Rocquemont in Motor Lorries	
			and photograph films to Corbron took over Command.	
ROCQUEMONT	25		Unit Devices a Reserve at Rocquemont to the Western Company	
	26		Proceeded on with schemes of programme of training were carried out	
			Construction and improvement of trenches, Gas hull Inspection	
			of Staff bobs, immediate action in the village, Panorama cards, Fire	
			Direction, Gas Drill, General Musketry training. McLoman	
	31			McLoman M/G

6th Brigade.

2nd Division.

6th MACHINE GUN COMPANY :::: J U N E 1917.

WAR DIARY
or
INTELLIGENCE SUMMARY.
(Erase heading not required.)

Army Form C.2118.

Instructions regarding War Diaries and Intelligence Summaries are contained in F.S. Regs., Part II. and the Staff Manual respectively. Title pages will be prepared in manuscript.

6 M.G. Coy June 1917

Place	Date	Hour	Summary of Events and Information	Remarks and references to Appendices
Robecq	1st		Hostile aeroplanes very active at night, dropping bombs in close vicinity of Camp	
			In accordance with 64M.G Bde's Operation Order No.160 dated 30/5/17 the 7/9	
			positions in the LEFT SUB SECTOR WILLERVAL FRONT were reconnoitred by the Officers	
			commanding	
			No 1 Section under Lieut. J.S. BOOTH relieved 1 section of the 99th G Coy in position	
1 Section in line	2		in the RED LINE, RIGHT SECTOR, WILLERVAL FRONT.	
			No 2 Section under Lieut. H. Davis relieved 1 section of the 53rd G Coy in position	
			on the RED LINE LEFT SECTOR WILLERVAL FRONT	
HQrs and 2 Sections Robecq LINE.	4		HQrs No 3 and No 4 Sections relieved the 53rd G Coy in the LEFT SECTOR	
			Disposition of Company:-	
			2 Sections in front of ARLEUX LOOP	
			1 Section between Arleux Loop and RED LINE	
			1 Section in position on RED LINE.	
	6.	10.35am	Composite Section of 8 Guns under Lieut P.M. Sanders to Herald cutt	
			INDIRECT FIRE for 12 minutes on enemy roads and Batteries. Barrage Artillery	
			H. Chancellor. Cafe, M Cagla, and Fill Copse	
			As the enemy was expected to withdraw from Lipovetre the following Operation	
			Order was issued:-	
			Reference GRANGUE Map 20000	
			(1) In the event of the withdrawal of the enemy from his present position the C.O.	
			16th G.Bde are ordered to advance and regain lines at once.	
			(2) First advance is to be made by tanks, to objective given below	
			to be secured before proceeding further.	
			(a) First Limit: - Brown line given about C.1.a.5.3. on right Boundary of	
			Brigade Front to Junction Juniper Rd at L.19.d.9.5. on left Boundary	

Army Form C. 2118.

WAR DIARY
or
INTELLIGENCE SUMMARY.

(Erase heading not required.)

June 1917

Instructions regarding War Diaries and Intelligence Summaries are contained in F. S. Regs., Part II. and the Staff Manual respectively. Title pages will be prepared in manuscript.

Place	Date	Hour	Summary of Events and Information	Remarks and references to Appendices
LINE	6.		Operation Order: Cont.	
			(b.) Second Line to GREEN LINE being to FRESNES-POURROY TRENCH from	
			U.17.c.Central and including Boss Bernard - 42.a.	
			3. The C.O.'s G Coy will cooperate in the advance but only after receipt from	
			Bde H.Q. of definite information that the 2 Lines BROWN & GREEN	
			respecting have been taken and firmly secured	
			4. (a.) On information that the BROWN LINE has been consolidated :-	
			(i.) 2 Guns of No. 2 Campbell's Section at B11.9.77 will be at once moved	
			to go forward under Section Officer to position about C.11.6.5.5. on the	
			Right of the NEW LINE.	
			(ii.) Immediately 9 guns from the Section will be advanced to FRESNES	
			LOOP and come under the orders of the O.C. own Section (as below)	
			(iii.) The 2 guns from T.13.d. will be sent forward under their Officer	
			to Brielen about H.19.9.65.10 on the Left of the NEW LINE.	
			(iv.) At the same time the Section in RESERVE will move up from C.11.0s	
			to FRELUN LOOP TRENCH to about B.3.a. CENTRAL to be ready to complete under orders	
			Be ready to complete under regence.	
			(b.) On the LINE of the second banner being taken & consolidated :-	
			(i.) 2 Guns on the right of FRESNES LOOP, viz., 1 from Br. a (Calgara)(Newborn)	
			and 1 from Brielen S. will be sent forward together under their	
			Section Officer to position about C.6.9.2 to hold the R.9 4.F. Flank	
			of the NEW LINE.	
			(ii.) 2 Guns from Left of FRESNES LOOP in Fig.6. will go forward under	
			the Section Officer to position on the Left of NEW LINE about the FRESNES	

WAR DIARY
or
INTELLIGENCE SUMMARY.
(Erase heading not required.)

Army Form C. 2118.

Instructions regarding War Diaries and Intelligence Summaries are contained in F. S. Regs., Part II. and the Staff Manual respectively. Title pages will be prepared in manuscript.

Place	Date	Hour	Summary of Events and Information	Remarks and references to Appendices
LINE			**Arcadia Green (Cont)**	
	7		The rest of the 4 guns in rear of the new forward lines and to be shifted to cover of Red Lines and to enable the C.O.'s of the officers to take up positions and get into action as quickly as possible. Late alternative position should be selected after reconnoitering the ground on the spot. C.O.'s, Officers should, as soon as possible, get and find out each other and learn the plant in view and arrange a concentric scheme of fire to ensure covering the whole of the line front of position.	
	8	3.15am	Composite Section of 3 guns under Lt Saunders cooperates with Artillery barrage.	
		8.35pm	For 12 minutes in conjunction with Artillery barrage.	
		11.45pm	Composite Section of 3 guns under Lt Rindless cooperates with indirect fire.	
	9	10.50am	For 12 minutes in conjunction with Artillery barrage (1 O.R. wounded). Composite Section of 3 guns under Lt Lambern co-operate with indirect fire. For 12 minutes in conjunction with Artillery barrage.	
	11		3 Guns of No 1 Section under Lieut Howell relieve 3 guns of No 2 Section in Right Sub Sector. Remaining team of No 2 Sec remain in Red Line. One gun from B.H.Q. T.C. relieved remaining team of No 3 Sec in Red Line. Team of No 3 Sec move into position selected at Trig. O.O.4.	
	13		Relief orders received in accordance with what the following general order was issued.	
	14		The C.O.s of Gr Coy will be relieved in the line on the night of June 15/16 as follows:—	

WAR DIARY or INTELLIGENCE SUMMARY

Army Form C. 2118.

Place	Date	Hour	Summary of Events and Information	Remarks and references to Appendices
LINE	14th		Poselin No 1 to 8 (Red Line and Intermediate Line) by 105th & 7th Coy Poselin No 9 to 16 (Harlem Loop Line) by 95th & 79th Coy 2) A guard from each gun will report to D Coy HQs and will conduct the respective team to the position on the arrival at Wilkerval. 3) Section Officers will be responsible to handover all Trench Stores, Ammunition, an Bombs, Rifles, lie of wire &c to the relieving officer at Sec HQs. The relieving officer will be conducted to Sec HQs by a guide sent to Coy HQ for the purpose. Section Officers taking over will be responsible for the contents of trench stores, bombs in the forward area by Sec Officers on relief. The lists will be forwarded to Coy HQ and also that relief is complete as soon as possible after Captain of the team reliefs Sect. Bombs will not be exchanged. 5) On completion of relief teams will be marched to Coy HQs where the Lorries will be waiting. Every man later of possible carry out his ablution & cooperation of his rations for breakfast. 6) After loading up, each section will proceed independently to Ecoivres where the company will to the Fields. 7) The Transport Officer will arrange for a Section Leader and the HQs to be on the Famous-Wilkerval Rd near Coy HQ at M.2 Midnight. Each driver having been forwards instructed as to the route to be taken to Ecoivres, on success arrives they will be placed for the Transport Officer will arrange for the Transport less those that	

WAR DIARY or INTELLIGENCE SUMMARY

Army Form C. 2118.

(Erase heading not required.)

Place	Date	Hour	Summary of Events and Information	Remarks and references to Appendices
LINE	14		**Operation Order Cont.**	
			that required by Section to move to ECOIVRES during the day	
			15th June to be afterwards arranged by the OC 15/Royal Scots.	
			All Officers and NCOs not in the line will accompany the	
			advance party, and a complete arrangement for the arrival of the	
			Company made, one will guide party rejoining Sections to	
			the billets.	
			9/ transport Officer will be responsible for bringing men at present	
			at transport lines and at Camp, Steenbecque to OC Company at	
			proper order before leaving Fauquis for Slain Lanquer in	
			Fauquis to be taken.	
			10/ The OC MG Coy will arrange for a provision of a hot meal	
			for the men on arrival at ECOIVRES (expected to arrive at 1pm)	
			11/ Separate orders are issued to the Reserve Section Eure 5 Coy	
			stationed at VILLERVAL	
			12/ The very important that the relief enroute to Complete	
			as expeditiously as possible. The use of Coy is no	
			smoking and men must not be allowed to	
			stand about in groups.	
			In accordance with Operation Order Transport moved to ECOIVRES.	
ECOIVRES	15		Section arrive at ECOIVRES.	
	16	5 am	Orders received to "Stand to" to move.	
	18			
	19		Coy Section conveyed in Motor Lorries to Bethune, Rifles in Salabooms in	
			Coy Transport moved off separately. Reserve Complete Coy.	

Army Form C. 2118.

WAR DIARY
or
INTELLIGENCE SUMMARY.
(Erase heading not required.)

Instructions regarding War Diaries and Intelligence Summaries are contained in F. S. Regs., Part II. and the Staff Manual respectively. Title pages will be prepared in manuscript.

Place	Date	Hour	Summary of Events and Information	Remarks and references to Appendices
BETHUNE	19.		Orders received to relieve the 202nd M.G.Coy in the GIVENCHY SECTOR. Reliefs were reconnoitred by the Officer Commanding and Section Comdrs. and were issued as follows:— The 6th M.G.Coy will relieve the 202nd M.G.Coy on the line or support for Company and Section at 1.30pm and full transport lorries will arrive and will march to GORRE CROSS ROADS where the stop where they will be met by Section guides from 202nd M.G.Coy en route Via CANAL ROAD. (iii) No. 1, 2 and 3 Sections will relieve all the 15 teams manning the line of 202nd M.G.Coy taking 5 guns each and Limbers will be broken accordingly. No. 4 Section will take over the guns & gentlemen? scout transport to Coy HQ at BATH TERRACE GORRE on Reserve. (iv) Reliefs will take place in the following order:— Section to the Right Section 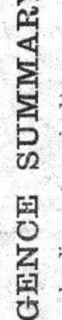 No. 1 CENTRE No. 2 LEFT No. 3 They will be met at Section HQs by guides from the respective gun position and will proceed forthwith to their position. with the exception of No 3 Section which will remain at existing HQs until Section officers taking over 3 isolated positions respectively. 1 Officer will accompany Section on Left over CENTRE Section, N. 2 Officer will accompany Section on Left over Centre Section, N.1 Officer to the Right Sector.	

WAR DIARY
or
INTELLIGENCE SUMMARY
(Erase heading not required.)

Army Form C. 2118.

Place	Date	Hour	Summary of Events and Information	Remarks and references to Appendices
			Operation Order (Cont)	
			(VI) Guns, Tripods and Belt Boxes will not be taken over by the relieving Section but Ayrshires recyds will be given for all such stores and ammunition on S.A.A. boxes. Coopers carts supply for a day will be furnished by No 101 M.G. Cy on each location.	
			(VII) The usual landing over Cookhouse will be given and taken over respective reports complete to C.H.Q. as early as possible.	
			(VIII) Telephone wires will will be handed over to No 101 M.G. Cy in exchange for ours Lines.	
			(IX) 3 Section Officers 1 for each Sector will accompany the O.C. 6" M.G. Coy at 9.30 am 20 June to reconnoitre subsections. Transport Officer will arrange for lorry accordingly.	
			(X) All ranks will concentrate for the day and O.C. M.G. Coys will arrange for the daily supply of rations to Coy H.Qtrs each evening.	
LINE	20.	1.30pm	Battery reports from Bethune. H.Q. are No 110 wk Section took over trench in Gorre. No 1 & over 2 Sections took over section in the Cour Leili Section five scotos employees 7 September in 710.6.55. also tour to our trench pystin in 710. am Cockcatch went Gas projection. Left Sector Trenches 1000 yds on Cross Roads between Singing Station and Flat Farm. S.9. a. 6. 75. Centre Sector June 750 Rds from Jardin in Georges during night on target 75.6.65.95. Right Sector June 1000 yds during night on Puts du Weners 52.6.6. & M. S.19.9.5.5.	

WAR DIARY or INTELLIGENCE SUMMARY

Army Form C. 2118.

MACHINE GUN COMPANY
No ...... Date 1/7/17
6th INFANTRY BRIGADE

Place	Date	Hour	Summary of Events and Information	Remarks and references to Appendices
	23/24		Left Section fired 1000 Rds on Enemy Dumps Pts. a.6.6.10.	
			Centre " " Reserving Fire a.2.8. to 15.a.4.5. (New Cut)	
	24/25		Left Section fires 1000Rds (Gren. Bomb Pt) 1000 Rds on Trench System near A.15.a.15. Redoubt Alley Pt. C.6.	
	25/26	5.30pm	No 1 Section relieves No 1 Section in the Right Sector	
		11.0pm	Centre Section Barrie's Ravelin & Arrybertia fires 750 Rds on Arrybertia Ravt	
	26	5pm	Anti-Aircraft gun engages 3 enemy Scouts driving them back to their lines.	
		6pm	Right Section fires 500 Rds on Crossroads Chille St Foch Pt a.9.7.9	
			from 8pm to 8.40pm also 1000 Rds at Pts on Pt. A.9.95 (S.26 c3. S.27.9.1)	
	26/27	1.00/1.30am	Enemy attempts a new raid, Crew of T.M. Barrage which was returned with Lewis Guns to the enemy. Our casualties were	
			2 O.Rs Killed and 1 O.R. Wounded.	
			Left Section fires 1300 Rds at S Puits etc. 9.4.7.7	
			Left Section fires 1000 Rds at Target S.9. B.2.4. Cross Roads between	
			Running Station and Flat Iron	
			Centre Section fires 750 Rds than Barrier Road Bastion a Sughee (?)	
			Bat HQs on A.15.a.45.45.	
	28/29		Left Section fires 1000 Rds on Ordnance Sergeants on S.18 d.83.d.D.	
			No 1 Section relieves No 2 Section in the Centre Sector.	
	29/30		Left Section fires 1000 Rds on Redoubt Alley North S.28.d.55.5.D.	
			during the night	
			Centre Section fires 500 Rds on Consolidation in Pt. C.1.7.	

6th Brigade.

2nd Division.

6th BRIGADE MACHIME GUN COMPANY ::: JULY 1917.

Army Form C. 2118.

No 19

WAR DIARY
or
INTELLIGENCE SUMMARY.
(Erase heading not required.)

Place	Date	Hour	Summary of Events and Information	Remarks and references to Appendices
GIVENCHY SECTOR	1/3	During night	1000 Yds front are Rue de Mamus Sig 9 n.5; 49.	
	2/3	1000	" RIDOUT ALLEY NORTH S28, a 55.50	
	3/4	1000	" CROSS ROADS between FERNYHUNG SIDING and FLAT IRON	
	4		The following Orders were issued:- (Maps ROBECOURG 35 S.W.2 LA BASSEE 36 N.W.)	

(i) Guns will be moved to new positions today in accordance with the attached diagrams.

(ii) Officers i/c Givenchy Centre and L.F. Sectors will reconnoitre the ground, make all arrangements and personally supervise the actual move.

(iii) A covering party of the 2nd South Staffs Regt will report to Capt Gorre at 7.45 p.m. and will be detailed by Lieut Dobson on orders of the various gun teams to act under the orders of N.C.O. i/c charge of Gun team. Ration carriers will be the people getting parties and will report to Cpl Taylor, LE BARRIN, & Lieut Dobson at 7 p.m. when all rations will all duration tonight.

(iv) Digging parties will also be available to complete to work at Redoubt 12 under Lieut Dobson and at Giveronest 12 under Lieut Booth.

(v) Lieut Booth will take over the O.B.L. and also to the sending New Chipocoder two positions in trenches and the Keep Group and to Redoubts in the Front Centre Sector. N.O.s. the completion of at the improvement of these Redoubts to enter under the supervision of Lieut Booth, to whom the grant measures as they are carried out.

(Cont)

signature

WAR DIARY
or
INTELLIGENCE SUMMARY.
(Erase heading not required.)

Army Form C. 2118.

Place	Date	Hour	Summary of Events and Information	Remarks and references to Appendices
Givenchy Sector	4		(VI) 6th Offrs. 10B3. Group Rights Centre Lgt. Mauer Sensor neg renewed its Laying of the guns on the new positions as soon as possible. The enemy in ascertain this may be owing in occasions etc to Range Card always prepared. Completion of the move must be especially follow up any ly to following Gun words: Centre Through, Right Through Left Through Respectively	
			PRESENT POSITION **NEW POSITION** **TIME OF MOVING**	
			Lowtham E Bantam Rd (Lewis sup) 1000. Complete before Midnight	Thirteen 75 guns and Vickers Guns covered its stages
			Lowtham W O.B.L Ditto	Arrangement by OC within stages
			Pioneer House Ditto Complete before dark	"
			Richmond Ter Pioneer Trench "	
			New Rose Stuart East 10/5 Complete before Midnight	Arrangement by OC within Sector
			George St Stuart West Complete before dark	Ditto
			Scottish Tr. Grenadier East 12.00 Complete 2am	Ditto
			Kings Rd Grenadier West Ditto	Arrangement by OC Givenchy Sector
			Givenchy	

Army Form C. 2118.

WAR DIARY
or
INTELLIGENCE SUMMARY.
(Erase heading not required.)

Place	Date	Hour	Summary of Events and Information	Remarks and references to Appendices
GIVENCHY SECTOR	4/5	During Night	New Colt Gun Team 2000ft on enemy trenches nears Canadian Orchard. 1500 for farm on trenches in S28.6 — in anticipation of a raid on the Portuguese Baton for 5am Jane 5000ft on covering the Portuguese Front. Orders were received that the 1st Cavalry M.G. Squadron were to be relieved except 1 gun of the 247 G. Coy in the Givenchy Sector. Company Standing Order No 9 was issued as follows. (i) The 247 G. Coy (less 16 guns) will be relieved in its turn by the 1st Cavalry M.G. Squadron (12 guns) on July 5th 1917 the guns in Givenchy will not be relieved. (ii) Each flew bank team is to be relieved and send the 1247 Coy guns teams at Left Cay HQr (Tps Hqr Hdq 25.F) at 3.45pm and thence harded over to the following sector:- 1st CENTRE SECTOR 2nd LEFT SECTOR Rifle relieves of 150 Yards. 3rd RIGHT SECTOR The groups will not move until Cycles completed (viii) Releif of CENTRE SECTOR by relief of S.A.A. over Belt Faces and to light on the Lui but all this gun equipment will be overdrawn by the teams relieved (iv) All ammunition Mgs. turn stores old cots crypt signals will be eaubooks and completed stations of energy thing known and signed by Lt. Partial will be forwarded to Cay Hos month to Cdr. fields. Acheul Campbell, by Section Officers as soon as possible. Giles Com Offg	

Army Form C. 2118.

WAR DIARY
or
INTELLIGENCE SUMMARY.
(Erase heading not required.)

Instructions regarding War Diaries and Intelligence Summaries are contained in F. S. Regs., Part II. and the Staff Manual respectively. Title pages will be prepared in manuscript.

Place	Date	Hour	Summary of Events and Information	Remarks and references to Appendices
GIVENCHY SECTOR	5		(9600 a Cont)	
			(v) Transport will proceed to Cateronnet (Ouvry) order will be given for return to Gorre and be loaned at Gorre for return to Gorre	
			(VI) Adv Bd H Qs at H.Q. Co. L.I. will be at Le Faybar of 7th OC. 1 Cavalry M.G.Squadron and all Reserve Squadrons will be assured. Also L'Brie as our reference for rear GPCoys & before leaving Gorre	
			(VII) On rly to 6/M.Gly. Lecomte + Beresneau Reserve (? Pour) will remain available (Mr Gurrue) at all times for Reserve at any point along the Reserve Line and down Orchy by one of our own. No will be no available	
			(VIII) Our Officer on it in Sight the Sector one is O.S.M. will reconnoitre the voltage line of Byrne Prayment the Dec Road and no certain the best lines of approach to it in all Brigade sectors. Also the shortest route to each Brigade HQ.	
			Divisional Order No 57 issued:-	
			(i) No battalion under Mr Stephens will be relieved in the Givenchy Sector in No 1 Section under W Dickson on July C/67	
			(ii) All Guns equipment, stores etc will be handed over by the team relieved. The incoming teams belonging will be given on lathes ageing to new Lorries Tyre will be forwarded to Coy GTrain after completion of relief.	
			(iii) Relieve will be reported complete as soon as possible after the relief.	

Signature

WAR DIARY
or
INTELLIGENCE SUMMARY.
(Erase heading not required.)

Army Form C. 2118.

Place	Date	Hour	Summary of Events and Information	Remarks and references to Appendices
	5		Relieved Claim wood no Divisional Reserve at GONF	July 1917
	6		6th/K.R.R. of No.93 received starting — Their posts has to certain number of flashes batteries have been registering on the circle of our left subsidiary over three of the Brigade are now left in squadrons over S.S.T. the many means that the enemy intends to carry out and attack from the our lines on the Ora. In order to be prepared for eventualities to following preparations: Gun No. S.F. was moved.	
			(1) Relief of No.4 Section through as cancelled	
			(11) No.2 Section under Lieut. Dobson went into out position about 1650 in the O.R.L. to reinforce Right Group of 5 P.O. Cavalry M.G. Squadron 2 guns went in order to entirelying the enemy's front line on day of enemy's S.P.O. and S.S.O.	
			(111) No.2 Section under 2/Lt. Spicer went into out position on the O.B.L. North of POMMERN Ra. their object being:-	
			(a) To protect our Northern Flank in case of the enemy getting through the front line,	
			(b) To strengthen out overhead fire to S.O.S. barrage which in case of attack will be put on to enemy's intended support from by the machine guns. (1)	

R. H. [signature]

WAR DIARY or INTELLIGENCE SUMMARY

Army Form C. 2118.

(Erase heading not required.)

Instructions regarding War Diaries and Intelligence Summaries are contained in F. S. Regs., Part II. and the Staff Manual respectively. Title pages will be prepared in manuscript.

Place	Date	Hour	Summary of Events and Information	Remarks and references to Appendices
GIVENCHY SECTOR	6		Private Crawford 58 Bn.	
			(ii) H.Q. Work and Assembly of Cottom Keys N. on S.O.C.s.	
			and a new set to be acceptable cottom keys N. The whole High Trench	
			also to be examined	
			(V) No 3 Section will be like in Reserve to be immediately	
			available to furnish a team of reserve members (spare) (N)	
			(VI) All Sudden will be Lodged Gun direct and running repairs	
			effected and vices the Reserve System. Extra equipment	
			Officers Kit, SAA and Infantry Complete for Nos 7 & 8. Nos 7. C & 7.	
			(VII) Both Guns and SAA Boxes and all ammunition at all Posts	
			(viii) Special vigilance will be maintained by Officers, learn	
			commanders and Section Officers of No 1 Coy to guard against any	
			hostile offensive in the area.	
			S.O.S. lines on target S.O.S. lines a 70.95	
	6/1		No 1 Gun a 75, 80, 95 sit a 60, 00 sit a 50, 55 sit a 70, 55	
		night	2 — A2 a 60, 00 sit a 85, 85 sit a 70, 55	
			3 — A3 a 05, 95 sit a 10, 05 sit a 50, 55	
			4 — A4 a 05, 95	
			Gun in Pioneer Sgh Jones Scythe or Riviere Trenches S.O.S. a 80, 70 f.e.	
			Gun at No B. Lord Rue de Cailloux firm 750m on Facoboot. Alley S.O.S. 34 T.2.	
		17:00	Operation Order 59 (Relief)	
	7	4:00p.m.	(ii) Lt Griffin and his relieved in the Givenchy sector at 6:30 pm. 70 am	
			by 2nd Lt Nolan	
			(ii) H.Q. Moved over the team quarters at Cailloux North Keys S.O. C.2.a.	
			well be relieved by Mr Park and the Rising Team of No 2 Section	
			at 6:30 pm any Off kit, ammunition to members bedding over and	

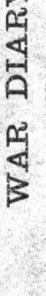

Army Form C. 2118.

WAR DIARY
or
INTELLIGENCE SUMMARY.
(Erase heading not required.)

Instructions regarding War Diaries and Intelligence Summaries are contained in F.S. Regs., Part II. and the Staff Manual respectively. Title pages will be prepared in manuscript.

MACHINE GUN COMPANY
6th INFANTRY BRIGADE

Place	Date	Hour	Summary of Events and Information	Remarks and references to Appendices
GIVENCHY SECTOR.	7	4pm	Shrapnel Barrage Relief O.L. and certificates signed by Coy Officers taken up. Relief completed on return with the down to Bn. H.Q. (iv) Officer to Right and Left Reserve Sections placed exceedingly...	Aug 1917
		5pm	...	
	7/8	During night	... 1000 Pds ... Lewis...	

Army Form C. 2118.

WAR DIARY
or
INTELLIGENCE SUMMARY.
(Erase heading not required.)

Instructions regarding War Diaries and Intelligence Summaries are contained in F. S. Regs., Part II. and the Staff Manual respectively. Title pages will be prepared in manuscript.

MACHINE GUN COMPANY
8th INFANTRY BRIGADE

Place	Date	Hour	Summary of Events and Information	Remarks and references to Appendices
Givenchy Sector	8/9	During Night	Left Sector fired 5000 Rds from Guns in Parapet Targets Tackis. 1200 Rds on Right lines. A combined operation by Coys. inspected by Divnsr Coys. B & D on left of flank of the 5th Infantry Bde on our right with 900 recruits in accordance with Coy. order No. G.S.78/74/2 of 6/7/17. The following Coy. Operation Order No. 20 was issued. (i) The 1st Cavalry of Givenchy Garrison (4 guns) will be relieved on the night of the 6/7th of July 10th July 1917 in accordance with following orders. (ii) All ammunition, Belt Boxes, Maps, Stores and all terrain registers and to take over and certificates in duplicate as given by late officers given and taken. (iii) Reliefs will be reported on completion to Hon HQ as early as possible after completion relief. (iv) The position in Givenchy will be reckoned as "Forward Redoubt" and being vacated and must be left clean and in proper order. (v) The Sector from Givenchy Coy Team become Company Reserve and report to Bn HQrs for further orders. (vi) Section HQ for Right and Centre Groups will be at the junction of File Road and O.23.L of paradis. Left Group HQs as at present. (vii) The Maxim Redoubt guns become a Reserve and remain in order of Officer to Right Group and will be placed in the charge of a senior NCO. Lewis the relieves Lieudenants by extra teams of the Reserve Section	

Army Form C. 2118.

WAR DIARY
or
INTELLIGENCE SUMMARY.
(Erase heading not required.)

Instructions regarding War Diaries and Intelligence Summaries are contained in F. S. Regs., Part II. and the Staff Manual respectively. Title pages will be prepared in manuscript.

MACHINE GUN COMPANY
8th INFANTRY BRIGADE

Place	Date	Hour	Summary of Events and Information					Remarks and references to Appendices
			Section	Team	Present Position	Group	New Position	Time
Givenchy Sector	9		No 1	1	Reserve O.B.L.	Right	Grenadier Trench Lt. Dobson	9 am
			"	1	"	"	O.B.L. New Cut	
			No 2	1	Off Yellow Rd O.B.L.	Left	Pioneer Trench O.B.L.	10 am
			"	1	Pioneer Rd O.B.L.	"	"	
			No 3	1	Resting	Centre	Burton Rd Yellow Rd Stuart Wr Rd West	Lt. Nolan	11 am
			"	1	"	"	"	
			"	1	"	"	"	
			No 4	1	Givenchy Avenue Kilby's Walk	"	Into Coy Room at Hav. Coy HQ	On arrival of Team from Caillous Keep to Marie Redout to be 2nd in Command when required
			"	1	Cellars			
			"	1	Marie Redout			
			"	1	Cailloux Keep		Marie Redout Lt. Dobson	9 am

Note: N° Cailloux Keep's team were captured Guns ammunition etc O. Pow'S.D on their way to Marie Redout to the best of the remaining guns of N°3 section resided all being sent up their position.

Army Form C. 2118.

WAR DIARY
or
INTELLIGENCE SUMMARY.
(Erase heading not required.)

Place	Date	Hour	Summary of Events and Information	Remarks and references to Appendices
Givenchy Sector	8/9/17	Day Night	1200 R.a. fired on targets in S.O.T. 28. 3 Guns on O.B.L. fired barrage fire on S.O.T. targets 500 R.a. per gun 1 Belt per gun fired 750 R.a. on Cross roads Sig. O.16.C.1.8	
"	10/11	Day Night	1370 R.a. fired at Batt H.Q. (Syrhets) Sig. O.16.79	
"	11/12		1500 R.a. fired on tramway behind Seyhens Trench Sig. a-b. 1300 R.a. Batt H.Q.s (Syrhets) Sig. a-16.80 2000 R.a. Tramway on L.B. a.b. Sig 9.a. 1500 R.a. Sig. a.55.55. 500 R.a. Trench Sig. a. S.o.6. a-6.	
"	12/13		1000 R.a. fired on tramway on Sig a-b. S.99.9. 1750 " Batt H.Q.s (Syrhets(W) Sig. a.26.80) 1600 " Bunghalow on 95.0 3000 " Various targets	
"	13/14		1500 " Tramway on L.B. a. S.29.a. Sig 3.0 850 " Seyhens Trench Sin. S22 1000 "	

WAR DIARY
or
INTELLIGENCE SUMMARY.

Army Form C. 2118.

(Erase heading not required.)

Place	Date	Hour	Summary of Events and Information	Remarks and references to Appendices
GIVENCHY Sector	13/7	During Night	1500 Rds fired on S11 A.35.55. 1830 hrs evening targets.	
	14/8	"	0430. Gun fired 500 Rds on Canteleux Alley N (A.10.a.o) New Cut " 3. (A.6.6.95.05) 1000 . Cinque Rue Gun. 1750. Roorst Alley N 2000 Rds fired on evening targets.	
	15/8	6 p.m	New Cut. Gun fired 500 Rds on Canteleux Alley South (A.6.6.95.05) 100 Rds fired at enemy aeroplane	
	16/8	During Night 11.30 pm 11.30 3 am	Yellow Rd Gun fired 1000 Rds on Canteleux Alley North 250 Rds fired at enemy aeroplane fire OBL (near junction of CINQUE RUE) Gun fired 1000 Rds on Roorst Alley North	
	1/9		750 Rds fired on Canteleux Alley South. A.6.6.95.05 1000 Rds fire on Rly & Lenscale & fire from Yellow Rd	
	1/9	5.45pm	500 Rds fired by 4th Aus Capt gun OBL 1000 Rds fired on the Canteleux - Chapelle St Rocke Light Rly from the Cinque Rue Gun. E.95.1.2 (Robert Luff Ho Company to commanders Sgt T G E)	

A7092. Wt. W128.g/M1293. 750,000. 1/17. D. D. & L. Ltd. Forms/C2118/14.

Army Form C. 2118.

WAR DIARY
or
INTELLIGENCE SUMMARY.
(Erase heading not required.)

Instructions regarding War Diaries and Intelligence Summaries are contained in F. S. Regs., Part II. and the Staff Manual respectively. Title pages will be prepared in manuscript.

MACHINE GUN COMPANY
No.........
Date.........
6th INFANTRY BRIGADE

Place	Date	Hour	Summary of Events and Information	Remarks and references to Appendices
Givenchy Sector	18/9		1000 Rds fired at Embrasures on A.5.a given 0084 just near Company Hqrs.	
	19/9		1300 Rds fired on Cantaloup Alley North + junction and Sluice Tap at No 6bg.2 & No c.o.1	
			1500 Rds fired on enemy position on S.9.c.5.4 S.9.cr by gun at Orchard Rue	
			2000 Rds fired on Cantaloup Alley South by New Cut Gun	
			1000 Rds fired at H Chapelle St Roche "Cantaloup" + Railway by the Gun at OP2 near Orchard Rue	
	20/9		1000 Rds fired on Cantaloup Alley North	
			Violaines Trench + Railway hanging to wood	
			1500 Rds " "	
			by New Cut Gun	
	21/22/9		500 Rds fired on Violaines Trench by New Cut Gun	
			750 " Alley Knock and Trench	
			1500 " Space St Roche Cantaloup Sgd Rs No. 6.11	
	22/9		750 " Cantaloup Alley No. Co.1	
			2500 " at Roche Cantaloup during the day	
			300 " on S.19.0.5.1 by New Cut Gun + Spencer Gun	
			1 OR Wounded	

A7092 Wt. W1285.9/M1293. 750,000. 1/17. D. D & I. Ltd. Forms/C2118/14.

AHemingwqt Cpt

Army Form C. 2118.

WAR DIARY
or
INTELLIGENCE SUMMARY.
(Erase heading not required.)

Place	Date	Hour	Summary of Events and Information	Remarks and references to Appendices
Givenchy Sector	23/6/15		2000 Rds fired at 9.9 in German new which had preparing from cut by own Artillery. 1750 Rds fired in diff. a.a. pts. The following operation Order No. N.O. 12 was issued.	
			I. In conjunction with the Artillery of the Division a M.G. barrage will be placed upon the line of enemy trenches running S.E. from A.9.c.5.9. to A.10.c.5.1.	
			II. (a) 8 guns of the 6th M.G. Coy will be laid with lines down on the accompanying table.	
			(b) 3 guns of the 5th M.G. Coy will be, whilst by firing on the flanks about A.6.a.5.9 and so complete the barrage line according to the attached table.	
			(c) 4 guns of the 2nd M.G. Coy will enfilade systems in charge on the parallel line of trenches running S.E. from A.10.a.0.4. to A.10.c.5.4 Lewis at right angles to their lines.	
			(d) 2 guns of the 6th M.G. Coy will cover the approach communication Trenches Cottbus Alley North and South from position in A.d. as shown.	
			The night crews of Guns Nos 1, 3, 6, 7, will be in charge. Of the Artillery officer and 2nd Sections will man the guns in the respective Coy dumps on Zero M/M/MC	
			III.	

Army Form C. 2118.

WAR DIARY
or
INTELLIGENCE SUMMARY.
(Erase heading not required.)

Place	Date	Hour	Summary of Events and Information	Remarks and references to Appendices
Givenchy Sector	14		00 N M O12 Cont.	
			He will be responsible for the feeling out of enemy posts and the accurate fixing of the zone at their respective locations and directions.	
			(6) The Left group of Guns Nos. 11, 5 & 6 will be under the orders of Lieut Glover. He is to lay off posts who will be similarly responsible for all details. Nos. 1 and 5 positions will be occupied by 2 Rescue Gun teams furnished by the Reserve Section under the Lanarkshire Coy. Lieut Glover will be Reserve Section Officer.	
			(7) Positions in F.O.L. will be occupied by the Reserve Gun of N.M. Section and the Res Gun Near Cat. These guns will come under the orders of Lt. Ward who will make all arrangements.	
			IV Zero day and hour will be announced later and every to prevent the getting to higher heads has of utmost importance. No mountains by all guns according to the chelon of their 1/c	
			V On completion of the operation guns 9th & 17th G.T. Coy will be returned to their normal battn as soon as possible and close under to ordinary lines of chelon. The 16 has been done will be put at once to C.Q.M.Os by each officer to be by the code word "England".	

[signature]

Army Form C. 2118.

WAR DIARY
or
INTELLIGENCE SUMMARY.
(Erase heading not required.)

Instructions regarding War Diaries and Intelligence Summaries are contained in F.S. Regs., Part II. and the Staff Manual respectively. Title pages will be prepared in manuscript.

[Stamp: MACHINE GUN COMPANY / 6th INFANTRY BRIGADE]

Place	Date	Hour	Summary of Events and Information	Remarks and references to Appendices
Givenchy Sector	24		Operation Order No 33	July 1917
			I In accordance with 2nd Div order No 59 a section of the 2nd 2 M.G. Coy will be attached to the 6th M.G. Coy from 1st Patrol	
			II No 3 Section of the 6th M.G. Coy will be relieving by a section of the 2nd 2 M.G. Coy on the night of 24/25.15 in accordance with the moving section. Our machine guns and ammunition remaining with the moving section for ammunition purposes	
			III On relief No 3 Section 6th M.G. Coy will not march back to billets tonight by No. 1 Section	
			IV No 1 section will go into Bde reserve at GUARBECQUE	
			V All guns, equipment, ammunition etc will be taken out by the team relieved and the machine guns relieving	
			VI Relief completed will be notified to 6 M.G.Os no parties or parrots by section officers and deficiencies lists of TRENCH STORES to handed in.	W.M.Kenyon

Section	Present Position	Relieved By	Time	New Position	
No 3 Sec 6th M.G. Coy	Stuart East Stuart West Brunton South Brunton North	C. Section 2 M.G. 2nd 2 M.G. Coy	2 a.m. 3 a.m.	Grenadier Trench New Cut Loop R.P. C.H.Qs for Orders	1 Lewis Gun + 2 MGs whilst delivering Gun out of New Station

Army Form C. 2118.

WAR DIARY
or
INTELLIGENCE SUMMARY.
(Erase heading not required.)

Instructions regarding War Diaries and Intelligence Summaries are contained in F. S. Regs., Part II. and the Staff Manual respectively. Title pages will be prepared in manuscript.

6th INFANTRY BRIGADE
MACHINE GUN COMPANY

Place	Date	Hour	Summary of Events and Information	Remarks and references to Appendices
GIVENCHY SECTOR	24/25	During night	600 Rounds fired on Sig. a 3.5. from d'26. a 5.9.	
		"	600 " ranging practice with observation	
		"	4000 " on DOVER Trench from A.9.C.1.9.	
		"	1250 " Artillery targets indicated by C.O.	
	25	10.30pm	Right Battalion (1st King's Liverpool Regt) raided the enemy. Machine Gun Coy cooperated with the Artillery barrage as per 6th G Coy Operation Order No 170.12	
			23,250 Rds were fired, alright during the raid, as follows:-	
			3,250 Rounds fired on barrage line S26. a 75.80	
			4,500 " S.27. a 35.30	
			2,750 " S.26. a 50.75	
			1,750 " S.26. c 05.40	
			7,000 " Cailloux Alley North approach	
			6,000 " Barrage line T2. b. 9.7., T2. b. 8. 60., T2. b. 65. 10., T2. b. 60. 15.	

Army Form C. 2118.

WAR DIARY
or
INTELLIGENCE SUMMARY.
(Erase heading not required.)

Instructions regarding War Diaries and Intelligence Summaries are contained in F.S. Regs., Part II. and the Staff Manual respectively. Title pages will be prepared in manuscript.

Place	Date	Hour	Summary of Events and Information	Remarks and references to Appendices
Givenchy Sector	26	4pm	In accordance with 61st I.G. Coy. O.O. No. 17 O.B.1 No. 1 Section moved into Brigade Reserve at Gorre	
	26/27	1000	Harassing fire on Target 339 at 15.55 (Intermittent firing)	
		1500	Redoubt Alley N	
		1000	Violares Trench	
	27/28	850	Redoubt Alley N.	
		1500	Stink Trench in S28 c	
		1300	Cantelleux Alley North in H10. a	
		1000	Ridley Gorges in S28 c	
	28/29	1000	Rue de Marais & Marais Alley	
		1020	Redoubt Alley North	
		1250	Stink Trench S28 a	
		1250	Cantelleux Alley in H10. b and d.	
	29/30	850	Redoubt Alley N	
		1250	Marais Alley	
		1250	Stink Trench S28 a	
		1250	Cantelleux Alley in H10. c and d.	
	30/31	1000	Cantelleux Abbey in H10. c and a	
		1000	Stink Trench S18 a	
		1000	Rue de Marais	
			Violares Trench	

6th Brigade.

2nd Division.

6th MACHINE GUN COMPANY ::: AUGUST 1917.

H.Q.
6th M.G. Bn.

Herewith diary for the month
of August 1918.

No. 6
MACHINE GUN
COMPANY.
No. 529
Date 1/9/19

J. North Lt.
for O.C. 6th Machine Gun Coy

NO. 6 MACHINE GUN COMPANY Army Form C.2118.

No. ....
Date. 1/9/17

WAR DIARY
or
INTELLIGENCE SUMMARY.
(Erase heading not required.)

August 1.17 Maps. Richebourg 36 SW 3
                   La Bassée 36 I NW 1.

Place	Date	Hour	Summary of Events and Information	Remarks and references to Appendices
Givenchy Sector	1	During Night	4500 Rounds fired on Cateleux Alley and Stork Trench	W20
"	2		2500 " Rue de Marais	
"	"		1250 "	
"	"		750 " Violaines Trench.	
"	3		1250 " Stork Trench.	
"	"		1000 " A.A. and A10	
"	4		750 " Canteleux Alley	
"	5		2500 " Redoubt Alley	
"	"		750 " Stork Trench	
"	"		750 " Rue de Marais	
"	6		1500 "	
"	7		1500 " + Canteleux Alley	
"	"		No 3 Section relieved No 2 Section in the Right Sector. No 1 Section	
"	"		moved into B.E. Reserve, Gorre.	
"	"		Lt G.H. Sharpe (Officer Commanding) admitted to hospital sick	
"	8		Sgt G Le Wallace (142 M.G. Coy) took over Command of Company	

WAR DIARY
or
INTELLIGENCE SUMMARY.

(Erase heading not required.)

No. 6 MACHINE GUN COMPANY. Army Form C. 2118.

No. 599 Date 1/9/17

Maps La Bassée, 36.C.N.W. Richebourg, 36.S.W.3

Place	Date	Hour	Summary of Events and Information	Remarks and references to Appendices
Givenchy Sector	10	During night	1000 Rds fired on Rue de Marais	
	11		1000 Violanes Trench	
			250 enemy Air craft	
			1000 Rue de Marais	
	12		1500 Violanes Trench and Brickfields	
	13		8000 A.10.c.12.85 to A.10.c.u.3	
			2500 A.10.c.10.85 to A.10.c.u.3	
			3000 Brickfields	
	14		3000 Cupola Alley	
	15		4000 A.10.c.3.4 to A.9.a.9.9	
			1000 Violanes Trench and Tramway	
	17		2000 Craters A.10.c.3.4 - A.9.a.9.9	
			1250 Redoubt Alley South	
			500 Enemy T.M.Emplacements A.10.a.	
	18		1500 Craters A.9.a.9.9 to A.10.c.3.4	
			2500 Violanes Trench and Tramway	

No. 6 MACHINE GUN COMPANY

504 /9/17

WAR DIARY
or
INTELLIGENCE SUMMARY.

(Erase heading not required.)

Army Form C. 2118.

Month: August 1917

Place	Date	Hour	Summary of Events and Information	Remarks and references to Appendices
Givenchy Sector	18	During Night	1250 Rounds fired on Enemy T.M. Emplacements if 10.a and if 10.c	
	19.		1200 Brickfields in A.5.a	
			1500 Violanies Trench in A.4.b & and a	
			1500 in Rear of Craters in A.9.9.9.2 B.10.c.3.w	
		By day	750 at Enemy T.M. Emplacement A.4.a 7.8	
	20	During Night	1250 in Rear of Craters in A.9.a 9.2 to A.10.c.3.w	
	21		2700 on Haybealers Anti Tank gun Emplacement A.4. b.6.9	
			3200 Inintables A.11.9.6.5.	
		By day	1000 at Enemy T.M. Emplacements in vicinity of Chalks Sr Rochs	
	22	During Night	1000 Cantelieux Alley South A.17.a	
		By day	250 at Enemy arof Comes	
	23	During Night	300 No 1 Section relieved No 3 Section in the Right sub sector	
			1300 Rounds fired on Enemy Groups at A.2. a 7.1	
			1500 Tracks A.e. c.1.1 & A.4. a 1.5 7.6	
			1500 A.4.d. and A.5.a	
		By day	500 at Enemy T.M. Emplacement in ereinity of Chalk Sr Rochs	

Army Form C. 2118.

No. 6
MACHINE GUN
COMPANY.
509
Date 1/9/17

WAR DIARY
or
INTELLIGENCE SUMMARY.
(Erase heading not required.) August 1917

Instructions regarding War Diaries and Intelligence
Summaries are contained in F. S. Regs., Part II.
and the Staff Manual respectively. Title pages
will be prepared in manuscript.

Place	Date	Hour	Summary of Events and Information	Remarks and references to Appendices
Givenchy Sector	25th	During night	1500 Rds fired on Enemy track in A.4.c.1.1 to A.4.d.15.75	
			1500 Redoubt Alley South	
			1500 Enemy T.M. Emplacement at A.4.c.0.8.7.	
			1500 Violaine's Trench in A.4.c.	
			1500 Brickfields A.u.b. - A.5.a	
	26	By day	1000 Enemy T.M. Emplacement at A.10.a.75.80 and A.4.a.8.7	
			1000 Farm at A.4.C.65.30	
		Night	1500 Turntable - A.11.a.57.51	
			1500 Cybola Alley R.u.a - A.10.b	
			1500 Violaine's Trench A.u.b - A.u.d	
	27th	During day	3000 Enemy T.M. Emplacement & Centre of Activity in A.4.c	
			1500 Stone Trench A.u.b.c	
			1500 Rue de Marais. A.10.a1 x A.4.b.c.	
			1000 Farm (where movement took place) at A.4.b.b. 65.30	
			1000 Redoubt Alley South A.u.a and A.u.b	

Charles

MACHINE GUN COMPANY. Army Form C 2118.

WAR DIARY
or
INTELLIGENCE SUMMARY.
(Erase heading not required.)

August 1917

Place	Date	Hour	Summary of Events and Information	Remarks and references to Appendices
Givenchy Sector	27	During day	3000 Rounds fired on Enemy T.M Emplacements & centres of Activity on A.2.C	
"	"	During night	1500 " " " Stork Trench A.2.b.6	
"	"	"	1500 " " " Rue des Marais A.26.a & A.28.b	
"	"	"	1000 " " " Town Centre (suspected loop-holes) A.2.b.65.30	
"	"	"	1000 " " " Redoubt Alley S. A.4.d	
			No.3 Section relieved No.2 Section in the Givenchy Sector	
"	28	"	1000 Rounds fired on Anti Tank gun emplacement A.5.a.9.0	
"	"	"	1500 " " " Centre of Activity A.4.d. & 9.55	
"	"	"	1500 " " " Anti Tank gun emplacement A.6.6.9	
"	"	"	1500 " " " Cross Roads A.10.a.7.6. Cuhlu - St Roche	
"	29	During day	1000 " " " Enemy T.M. Emplacements & places of movement in A.2.C	
"	"	During night	1500 " " " Strong Point in A.5.d.3.8	
"	"	"	1500 " " " Centre of Activity A.u.d 30.55	
"	30	"	1500 " " " Brickfields A.5.9.	
"	"	"	1500 " " " Volaires Trench A.u.6. & A.u.d.	
"	"	"	1000 " " " Rue de Marais S.29.6.	
"	"	"	1000 " " " Road A.u.0.20 to A.u.c.55.10	

Army Form C.2118.

No. 6 MACHINE GUN COMPANY.

WAR DIARY
or
INTELLIGENCE SUMMARY.
(Erase heading not required.) August

Instructions regarding War Diaries and Intelligence Summaries are contained in F. S. Regs., Part II. and the Staff Manual respectively. Title pages will be prepared in manuscript.

Place	Date	Hour	Summary of Events and Information	Remarks and references to Appendices
Givenchy Sector	31	During day	1250 Rounds fired on Enemy T.M. Emplacements in A.7.c. Marais Alley	
		During night	1500	
			1500 Eitel Alley South	

6th Brigade.

2nd Division.

6th MACHINE GUN COMPANY :::: SEPTEMBER 1917.

Army Form C. 2118.

No. 8 MACHINE GUN COMPANY

WAR DIARY
or
INTELLIGENCE SUMMARY.
(Erase heading not required.)

September 1917 Maps: Richebourg 36.S.W.3
                     La Bassée 36.C.N.W.1

Place	Date	Hour	Summary of Events and Information	Remarks and references to Appendices
Givenchy Sector	September 1		No.2 Section relieved No.4 Section in the Centre Sector	
		During Night	1500 Rounds fired on Brickfields in A.5.a.	
			100·0 Redoubt Alley South Ann Aux	
			300 Hostile Aircraft	
		2	1500 Light Rly 2 Aux Cist Aux C.62	
			1500 Minest Roch. A10.0 6280	
			1500 Brickfields in A.5.a	
			1500 Turntable in A11.9.5752	
		During Day	1000 at Enemy T.M. Emplacement in A11.C	
			300 Hostile Aircraft	
		3	2000 Enemy T.M. Emplacements in A11.c. A10.9	
		During Night	2500 Redoubt Alley South in A.4.b	
			2500 Redoubt Alley North S.28.d	
			2500 Holmes Trench A.4.b	
			2500 Cupola Alley. A10.c.	

Army Form C. 2118.

No. 6 MACHINE GUN COMPANY.
Date: 1/9/17

WAR DIARY
or
INTELLIGENCE SUMMARY.
(Erase heading not required.)

Instructions regarding War Diaries and Intelligence Summaries are contained in F.S. Regs., Part II. and the Staff Manual respectively. Title pages will be prepared in manuscript.

Place	Date	Hour	Summary of Events and Information	Remarks and references to Appendices
GIVENCHY SECTOR	4th	During Night	2750 Rounds fired on Enemy ammunition dump A.4.a.7.1	
			2500 " " " " Salient front A4.c.9.1 - A4.d.10.75	
			2500 " " " " Rue du Marais S.36 - S.29.d	
			2500 " " " " Adelbert Alley S.w.d & S.23.C	
			2500 " " " " Trenches A9.b.9.6 - A.10.a.27 in co-operation with Destructive Shoot	
			2500 " " " " A.10.C.w.5 - A.10.C.77 Ditto	
			3000 " " " " A.10.C.0.95 Ditto	
			500 " " " " Enemy Aircraft	
			5000 " " " " Road in A.10 & A.10.a	
			3000 " " " " Sa A.5 a 5.6 & A.5.a.9	
			3000 " " " " Brickfield A.3.0.	
			1000 " " " " S.O.S. Target Right (Test)	
	6/7	Day	2000 " " " " Enemy T.M's in A.10.a & A.4.c	
			6th Machine Gun Co, relieved by the 99th Machine Gun Company; on relief H.Qs and the four sections moved to billets in ANNEZIN &	
ANNEZIN Transport at GORRE			Transport at GORRE.	

[signature]

WAR DIARY
or
INTELLIGENCE SUMMARY.

(Erase heading not required.)

Army Form C. 2118.

No 6 MACHINE GUN COMPANY.

Place	Date	Hour	Summary of Events and Information	Remarks and references to Appendices
ANNEZIN	8	11.25am	The Officer Commanding inspected the Kits of N°s 1, 2, 3, & 4 Sections	
		3pm/3pm	The Officer Commanding inspected all the Guns and Spare parts	
	9	10am	The Company paraded for inspection by the Officer Commanding. Drill marching order	
		2.10pm	Company Parade for Church Service	
	10	7am/7.45am	Parades Cleaning of Belts & Belt Ammunition	
		8.30-9.30	Arm Drill and Section Drill	
		9.35am-10.30am	Stoppages and IA	
		10.45/11.45am	Practice in the use of Pack Saddles	
		11.50/12.45pm	Packing of Limbers and Cinder Drill	
		8.30am/10.30am	Communication & Arm drill for all N.C.Os	
	11	9.00/9.50	Living Practice on the Range	
		6pm	A team of 147 M.G Coy played a team of "C" Coy 13th Essex Regt on their ground at Association Football. Result: 6-17.G. Coy. 2 goals 13th Essex Regt 1 goal	
	12	9am/9.45am	Gun Cleaning	
		7pm/12.50pm	Route march	

Army Form C. 2118.

No 8
MACHINE GUN COMPANY.
Date: 1/5/17

WAR DIARY
or
INTELLIGENCE SUMMARY.
(Erase heading not required.)

Instructions regarding War Diaries and Intelligence Summaries are contained in F. S. Regs., Part II. and the Staff Manual respectively. Title pages will be prepared in manuscript.

Place	Date	Hour	Summary of Events and Information	Remarks and references to Appendices
ANNEZIN	13th	7am	Gun Cleaning. Demonstration by S/Sgt Lomley (61st MG Squadron) on the best method of fitting and carrying Machine-Guns on Packs	
		8.30/9.30am	Squad Drill	
		9.30/10.30am	Lecture on "Barrage Work"	
		10.15am	Inspection of all guns and gun kit by D.H.O.S.	
		10.45 - 11.45	Practice in Barrage work	
		11.45/12.45pm	Gun Drill and T.O.E.T.	
		10.45/12.45pm	Junior N.C.Os class under the C.S.M. (Communication & Arm Drill)	
	14	8am/9.30am	Cleaning & stoppages practice on the Range	
	15	7am/7.45am	Section Drill	
		8.30/9.30am	I.A. and Stoppages	
		9.30/10.30am	Location & Recognition	
		10.45/11.45	Action from limbers and Limber Drill	
		11.45/12.45pm	Gun Drill and T.O.E.T.	

Signed

WAR DIARY
or
INTELLIGENCE SUMMARY.
(Erase heading not required.)

Army Form C.2118.

No. 6 MACHINE GUN COMPANY.

Place	Date	Hour	Summary of Events and Information	Remarks and references to Appendices
AMMEZIN	16.	10.30 a.m.	The Divisional Commander distributed Medal Ribbons to the Officers & NCOs of the 6th M.G. Coy. the following receiving of the Company were present.	
			No 1706. C.S.M. W.J. AMBROSE Military Cross	
			No 16011 Sgt F. GOLDING. D.C.M.	
			No 17069 Pte. G. GLENN. M.M. with Bar.	
			No 64543 L/Cpl. G.V PROWSER. M.M.	
			No 17088 Pte. E. HORTE M.M.	
	17.	4am	Marcha from AMMEZIN to GORRE.	
		6am	"Halts at GORRE for tea.	
		8am	Marcha from GORRE and proceeded to relieve the 99th M.G. Coy in the GIVENCHY SECTOR (Relief completed 12.30 a.m. 18th inst)	
	18.		No 1706. C.S.M W.J. AMBROSE proceeds to England to join Home Establishment	

Army Form C. 2118.

WAR DIARY
or
INTELLIGENCE SUMMARY.
(Erase heading not required.)

Instructions regarding War Diaries and Intelligence Summaries are contained in F. S. Regs., Part II. and the Staff Manual respectively. Title pages will be prepared in manuscript.

No 6
MACHINE GUN
COMPANY

Place	Date	Hour	Summary of Events and Information	Remarks and references to Appendices
Givenchy Sector	19/9/-	1000	Reconnoitring trenches on recovering through Chapelle St Roche	
		4000	A.11.a.0.7 & A.11.a.8.00.35	
		3000	Redoubt Alley N.	
		3000	La Bassée Alley	
	20/9	7250	A.11.a.1. & A.11.b.1.	
		4350	A.11.c.8.7. & A.11.0.d	
		2000	Redoubt Alley N.	
		250	Points on the La Bassée Rd	
	22/9	2000	La Bassée Alley A.5.C. & Tramway P.5.C	
		2500	Redoubt Alley N.	
		4000	A.11.c & A.11.o.d	
	23/9	2000	Cross Road & Tramway Chapelle St Roche	
		2000	Rue de Marais	
		3000	Road & Ry. crossing from Brickfields to Chapelle St Roche 16.142	
		" 5.10 a.m.	The enemy attempted to raid our trenches in the left sub-sector after intense artillery preparation. He was completely repulsed.	[signature]

Army Form C. 2118.

NO. 6 MACHINE GUN COMPANY.

WAR DIARY
or
INTELLIGENCE SUMMARY.
(Erase heading not required.)

Place	Date	Hour	Summary of Events and Information	Remarks and references to Appendices
GIVENCHY SECTOR	24	5 am	This Company Co-operated with Artillery by firing 5000 R^{ds} on R^d S.O.S. Lines in the Left Sub-Sector.	
		5.30am		
	24/25	During Night	6000 Rounds fired on Shingle and Straw Trenches	
	25		3000 " S.2.2. Central	
			3000 " " "	
			500 " at Hoochi Quichagh	
			No 3 Section relieving No 1 Section in the Centre Sector	
	25/26		1000 Rounds fired on "	
	26		9000 " " "	
			3000 " L.944.R.5 and Road leading from Chasbane St Roette to Brickfields	
	26/27		1000 " " "	
			1250 " Redoubt Alley South Violaines French & Brickfields m.g.nest	
			2500 " Canteleux Alley	
	27/28		3000 " Adolbert Alley searching - rag - d- R.24. S.49 to d-23.6.13.	
			2250 " Rue de Marais & Maras Alley	
			2500 " Canteleux village	
			2500 " Tuna Fork	

(signature)

Army Form C. 2118.

No. 6 MACHINE GUN COMPANY.
Date 1/10/17

WAR DIARY
or
INTELLIGENCE SUMMARY.
(Erase heading not required.)

Instructions regarding War Diaries and Intelligence Summaries are contained in F. S. Regs., Part II. and the Staff Manual respectively. Title pages will be prepared in manuscript.

Place	Date	Hour	Summary of Events and Information	Remarks and references to Appendices
GIVENCHY SECTOR	Sept 1917 28/29	During Night	Capt. G.H.Stonehewer returns from attending any Gas Course. 3000 Rounds fired on Trench Ray Aw 697 to A51933.	
			6000 Tramway Terminus in Aw Central	
		During Day	2500 " " " " Aw Central to Aw 258	
			120 at Hosell's air craft	
		During Night	2500 on Tracks in S.P.A	
	29/30		1500 Trenches, Roads etc N.W. of Canteleux	
			3000 S.E. of Canteleux	
			1750 at Hosell's aircraft	
			No 2 Section relieved No 4 Section in the Right Sector	

6th Brigade.

2nd Division.

6th MACHINE GUN COMPANY :::: OCTOBER 1917.

Army Form C.² 2118.

No. 6 MACHINE GUN COMPANY.
No. ....
Date ....

WAR DIARY
or
INTELLIGENCE SUMMARY.
(Erase heading not required.)

Instructions regarding War Diaries and Intelligence Summaries are contained in F. S. Regs., Part II. and the Staff Manual respectively. Title pages will be prepared in manuscript.

Place	Date	Hour	Summary of Events and Information	Remarks and references to Appendices
Givenchy Sector	1st Oct	During 10th night	Targets Engaged	
			2750 Rounds fired on Marais Crescent Purfing Station S.29.a. Maps Richebourg 36 N.W. La Bassée 36 N.W.	
			4000 Rte Central & Junction Epinette to Turntable	
			7000 Stoneycloop Lamperoots vicinity	
			250 at hostile aircraft	
			1500 on Canteleux Village A.11.C	
			3750 Trenches in A.11.a	
			2250 Yokohama Alley & Brickfields	
	3/4		No 4 Section relieved No 1 Section in the Givenchy Sector	
			2000 Rounds fired on Large Building in A.11.C.9.5	
			2000 Junction in Chapelle St Roch	
			5000 Brickfields & Canteleux	
			2000 La Bassée Alley	
	4/5		4000 Yokama Cuboka Alley to Turntable	
			10000 Large Building in A.11.C.9.5 and Junction in C.2.d. - Fu.C.9.9 Canteleux village in observation and projector types.	
			8250	
			12000 Line Brestsaction to Turntable	
			750 Rte de Marais	

No. 6 MACHINE GUN COMPANY.

No. ....
Date. ....

Army Form C. 2118.

WAR DIARY
OR
INTELLIGENCE SUMMARY.

(Erase heading not required.)

OCTOBER 1917

Instructions regarding War Diaries and Intelligence Summaries are contained in F. S. Regs., Part II. and the Staff Manual respectively. Title pages will be prepared in manuscript.

Place	Date OCTOBER	Hour	Summary of Events and Information	Remarks and references to Appendices
GIVENCHY SECTOR	5/6		Ref. 6th M.G. Bde's ORDER No. S.9 dated 4/10/17 the following Operation ORDER N° 146 was issued:— 1. (a) The 6th M.G. Coy (3 sections) will be relieved on the line by the 7th M.G. Coy on Oct 5.9.17. (b) One section of 242nd M.Gun Coy attached to 6th M.Gun Coy will be relieved on the line by the 7th M.Gun Coy at the same time. (c) No 1 Section 6th M.Gun Coy in Reserve Billets at Gorre will proceed to Bethune and take over the billets vacated by the 7th M.G. Coy under independent arrangement made by O.C. Section. (d) All transport of the 6th M.Gun Coy except limbers for rations and ammunition for H.Q. will likewise proceed to Bethune in accordance with orders to Capt. Q.M. Le Panton. (e) Guides will be sent from Reserve section at Gorre to meet the advance party at Gorre Cross Road at 9 a.m and conduct them early to Capt. Q.M. Le Panton. (f.) Reserve section will also send guides to meet the 7th M.Gun Coy	

NO. 6
MACHINE GUN COMPANY.

Army Form C. 2118.

WAR DIARY
or
INTELLIGENCE SUMMARY.
(Erase heading not required.)

OCTOBER 1917

Place	Date	Hour	Summary of Events and Information	Remarks and references to Appendices
GOEREGHY SECTOR	5/L		GUIDES	
			at GOEREE Drawbridge: ab. 2.30 p.m. an escort conduct them to the Cold. or guide.	
			(b) Guides will be sent from O.C. to GOEREE to conduct the Company	
			sections at short intervals to their respective Section HQrs on arrival of Coy.	
			(c) Section Officers will meet their guides at their Section HQ. to conduct relief	
			to their respective gun position.	
			(d) One guide will conduct O.C. 7th M.G. Coy. to Capt. O.C. his parties	
			(3) TRENCH STORES	
			(a) Section Officers will hand over all M.G.s, turned mountings, and S.A.A. on cases. Walli-comp field Coy. carried	
			the apparatus S.A.A. in cases. Walli-comp field Coy. carried	
			mountings & all trench stores, to be at Sections HQ. and eye Piecemen	
			also Spare parcels of work in progress	
			(b) Certificates in duplicate signed by both parties will be handed	
			in to O.C. on completion of relief as early as possible.	
			(4) ORDERS	
			Section Officers will explain in detail the role of each gun	
			and satisfy themselves before quitting the incoming Officers	

WAR DIARY or INTELLIGENCE SUMMARY

Army Form C. 2118.

No. 8 MACHINE GUN COMPANY.

OCTOBER 1917

Place	Date	Hour	Summary of Events and Information	Remarks and references to Appendices
GWENCHY SECTOR	5/10		Section Orders No. 14	
			1. Covering Officers	
			are duly appointed and conversant with the scheme of defence and	
			S.O.S. arrangements. A reliable N.C.O. per section will be left	
			with the relieving Section Officer (including section of 243 M.G. Coy)	
			The N.C.Os. will report at Coy HQ. to 2/Lieut. P.G. Smooth at 10 am on	
			the 6/10/17.	
			5. MOVEMENT	
			(a) 1 Limber per section will be at Brown's Road Cemetery/corner of	
			Barnton Road at 10 pm where the Lieut/per section of relieved Coy	
			Sections for each section's Limber will be endorsed	
			(b) after issued by Section Officers at HQs the relief is complete	
			each section will proceed independently via Gorre Cross Rds	
			to the Grand Place Bethune where they will be met by guides	
			detailed from No 1 Section to conduct them to billets in Essars	
			(MICHELET Law Square per Section)	
			(c) Section of 243 M Gun Coy after embarking same at mule harness	
			will directly to town its billet at BEUVRY	

NO. 6
MACHINE GUN COMPANY.

No. ....
Date ....

Army Form C. 2118.

WAR DIARY
or
INTELLIGENCE SUMMARY.

(Erase heading not required.)

Instructions regarding War Diaries and Intelligence Summaries are contained in F. S. Regs., Part II. and the Staff Manual respectively. Title pages will be prepared in manuscript.

OCTOBER 1917

Place	Date	Hour	Summary of Events and Information	Remarks and references to Appendices
GIVENCHY SECTOR	5/10		Operation Order No. 97/14 Cont.	
			5. MOVEMENT Cont.	
			(a) 1 Limber typed at O.H.Q le Ratin at 10p.m.	
			6. Hqrs P.G.SMITH will remain at Coy HQ once the attack to	
			177 Coy Coy will convey Hqrs he will keep in view that	
			7. Consolidation	
			O.C. 177 Coy Coy will have seen all maps, plans, photos and	
			retirement schemes, aeroplane photos, pasition cards etc.	
			Starting gears.	
			8. LMGs improvised when all hands had fallen, deposit on a	
			emplacements should be left un altered by clean and	
			sanitary condition so that the tradition of the Division	
			& Company considered he exploited	
			5/10/17	
			Signed. G.H. Stompe Capt.	
			Commanding 6 Machine Gun Company	
BETHUNE	6. Day	Movement as per Operation Order No. 97/14 complete.	
	7.	5.50am	Company paraded complete.	
HURIONVILLE		8am	March from BETHUNE to MICHELET Training School to HURIONVILLE	

No. 6.
MACHINE GUN COMPANY.

Army Form C. 2118.

WAR DIARY
or
INTELLIGENCE SUMMARY.
(Erase heading not required.)

OCTOBER 1917

Place	Date	Hour	Summary of Events and Information	Remarks and references to Appendices
HUNIONVILLE	7		Sections occupied in the general cleaning up & refitting of pulls	
	8		Col. G.H. Wallace proceeded on leave	
	8/14		Training Company etc. in accordance with the attached programme	
			of training	
	15		Inspection of 6th Infantry Brigade by General Sir H. S. HORNE K.C.B.	
			Commanding First Army at BUSSURE	
			Reserved of the 6th Machine Gun Coy however for new section	
			under the command of Lieut A.P. DODSON M.C. in accordance	
			with attached sketch	
	16		2nd/Lieut Gunning commences an advance scout to attend programme	
	20		Lieut A.P. Dodson M.C. proceeded to U.K. to join the Corps establishment	
	21		Capt G.L. Wallace returned from leave	
	22		Capt G.L. Wallace took over command of the Company during	
			the temporary absence of Lieut Col G.H. Stobo	
	24		Brigade tactical exercise took place 6th Gun Coy co-operated	
	26		Capt G.H. Stanhope proceeds to country	

Army Form C. 2118.

No 6, MACHINE GUN COMPANY.

WAR DIARY
or
INTELLIGENCE SUMMARY.
(Erase heading not required.)

OCTOBER 1917

Instructions regarding War Diaries and Intelligence Summaries are contained in F. S. Regs., Part II. and the Staff Manual respectively. Title pages will be prepared in manuscript.

Place	Date	Hour	Summary of Events and Information	Remarks and references to Appendices
HURIONVILLE	26/5		TRAINING was carried out in accordance with the attached programme	

NO. 6
MACHINE GUN
COMPANY.

No. ....
Date ....

Trenches = 100 yards.

→ To Burange

→ To Willonophie

2nd Kings

250 ×

19th Essex

× 250

17th Middlesex

100 ×

2 F Staffs

6th Scot Gr M Btn

Rate Signal Section 250 ×

205

Bombs of
15 Kings
2 F Staffs
19 Essex
17 Middlesex.

Road

6th Machine Gun Company — 2nd Week

Training Programme for week ending Oct 21st 1917

Day	9 to 9.30	9.45 am / 10.30 am	10.30 am / 11.15 am	11.30 am / 12.30 pm	12.30 pm / 1.15 pm
Monday	← ... Baths ... →		Barrage Drill [By Sections]	← No. 1 – 30ᵗʰ Range → No. 2. I.A. No. 3 Pack Animals No. 4 J.D.	No. 2 Box Respirators & Gun Drill No. 3 I. & R. No. 4 I. A.
Tuesday	Physical Training	Packing and Unpacking of Limbers	Barrage Drill [By Sections]	No. 1 Belt Filling No. 2 I. & R. No. 3 J.D. No. 4 Tripylines	No. 1 I. R. No. 2 R.G.D. No. 3 I. & R. [with gun] No. 4 Box Respirators & Gun Drill
Wednesday	Ditto	Barrage Drill [Company]	No. 1 Tripylines No. 2 Under S.O. No. 3 R.G. Drill No. 4 Lecture on I.R.	No. 1 Box Respirator & Gun Drill No. 2 Barrage No. 3 M.G. Signals No. 4 R.G. Drill	No. 1 Pack Animals No. 2 Gun Mounting Drill No. 3 Box Respirator and Gun Drill No. 4 I. R. [with Gun]
Thursday	Ditto	No. 1 Under S.O. No. 2 Tripylines No. 3 Gun Mounting Drill No. 4 Pack Animals	No. 1 Barrage Drill No. 2 Pack Animals No. 3 Use of Ground and Cover No. 4 Under S.O.	No. 1 M.G. Signals No. 2 R.G.D. & Stoppages No. 3 Barrage Drill No. 4 Gun Mounting Drill	No. 1 J.D. on 30ᵗʰ Range No. 3 Under S.O. No. 4 Use of Ground & Cover
Friday	Ditto	← ... 30ᵗʰ Range ... →		No. 1 R.G.D No. 2 M.G. Signals No. 3 C. & C. No. 4 C. & C.	No. 1 C. & C. No. 2 C. & C. No. 3 I. & R. with gun No. 4 M.G. Signals
Saturday	Part II on Long Range Combined with Action from Limbers.				
Sunday	Inspection by O.C.	Route March with Pack Transport			

Competition on Thursday for Prizes in:
- Pack Transport.
- Immediate Action
- Belt Filling
- T.O.E.T.

Abbreviations:
- G.D. — Gun Drill.
- R.G.D. — Rough Ground Drill
- I.R. — Inspection Recognition
- C.C. — Care & Cleaning.
- J.D. — Judging Distance.

No. 6 MACHINE GUN COMPANY.

No. 6 MACHINE GUN COMPANY.

3rd Week

Programme of Training for week ending August 2nd

Day	9 to 9.15	9.15 to 10.30	10.30 to 11.30	11.45 to 12.30	12.30 to 1 p.m.
Monday	Physical Training	Barrage Drill by Sections	No.1 Lays the Gun. No.2 M.G. Signals. No.3 Pack Saddlery No.4 Rest Mountings	Barrage Drill by Company	No.1 R.G. Drill No.2 Pack Saddlery No.3 S.L. No.4 M.G. Signs.
Tuesday	"	Tactical Schemes by Sections	—	—	—
Wednesday	"	Barrage Exercises	Field Day	—	—
Thursday	"	Barrage Drill by Sections	Fire Mounting No.2 Vehicles. No.3 Sandbags. No.4 First Aid	No.1 Indirect S.C. No.2 S.L. No.3 A.A. with Guns. No.4 Construction	No.1 Topography No.2 Use of Ground and Cover No.3 Points B.G.R. No.4 First Aid
Friday	"	Long Range Barrage Fire and action from trenches	—	—	—
Saturday	Physical Training	No.1 Gun Drill on Lewis Registration No.2 Topography No.3 Telephone Notes No.4 Use of Ground and Cover	No.1 Indirect Fire and Observation of same. No.2 Gun Drill No.3 Gun Position No.4 Telephones	No.1 Use of ground and Cover No.2 R.G. Drill No.3 Range Finding	No.1 Pack Saddlery No.2 Points B.G.R. No.3 Topography No.4 Telephones
Sunday	Inspection of Company by Commanding Officer				

vi. The Mobile Guns will form up temporarily in rear of the respective Infy Battⁿ detailed for the Sauge Area and will go forward with them for a short distance when they advance.

When the Subsection officer is satisfied that the Battⁿ has definitely secured their objective he will go forward and select the firing positions for the guns, and will have regard to

(a) Any Strong Points or points of tactical importance in the Area captured.

(b) Defence against hostile counter attacks from any likely direction:-
Area C. valley in C.9.b and C.9.d
Area D. Eastern Edge of Rainbert Wood. C.16.a and C.

(c) Defence of the Area in depth as far as possible
Subsection Officers should report to the O.C of the Battⁿ of their areas.

(a) To ascertain his exact disposition

(b) To ensure the closest co-operation with the Infantry

(c) To inform him of his proposed methods of advance and positions

VII. <u>Barrage Machine Guns</u>
The remaining 8 guns of the 6ᵗʰ M. Gun Coy Sections 3 & 4 will form a Battery under Lieut Arthur and will put down a creeping barrage with a final S.O.S line in conjunction with the 16 guns of the 242ⁿᵈ M.Gun Coy which are at the disposal of the 6 Infy Bde for the day. — The whole comprising a Group of 24 guns under orders of O.C 6ᵗʰ M.Gun Coy

The Lifts & Times will conform to those of the 18 Pdr Barrage and definite Orders together with fighting Maps will be issued later.

VIII. Subsection Officers/c Mobile Guns will each arrange direct with T.O. for half a Limber per Subsection and will make all necessary arrangements for getting into position & disposition of Transport on ZERO day

IX. Zero hour and Day will be 10am 30th Oct 1917 and all teams will be in position at ZERO-30.
X. All men will wear Fighting Order.
XI. Coy H.Q. will be at C.15.a.m.
After Zero messages should be sent to Bde. Advanced Report Centre at C.10.d.5.4.
XII. Appendices are issued to Section Officers dealing with administration notes

S H Campbell
Capt
Comdg 6th Machine Gun Coy

Issued 27hrs
28/10/17

6th Machine Gun Company
Appendix No 1 to Operation Order E2.   29.10.17

Arrangements [imaginary] have been made by the Corps M.G.O. for a group of 8 guns to put down an Enfilade M.G. Barrage in co-operation with 6th Infy Bde. attack along the valley in C.9.d. & C.15.b. from Zero to Zero+60 from positions immediately North of village of BURBURE
With a view to breaking up formations for counter attack under cover of the steep reverse slope during the advance.

S H Campbell
Capt
Comdg 6 M. Gun Coy

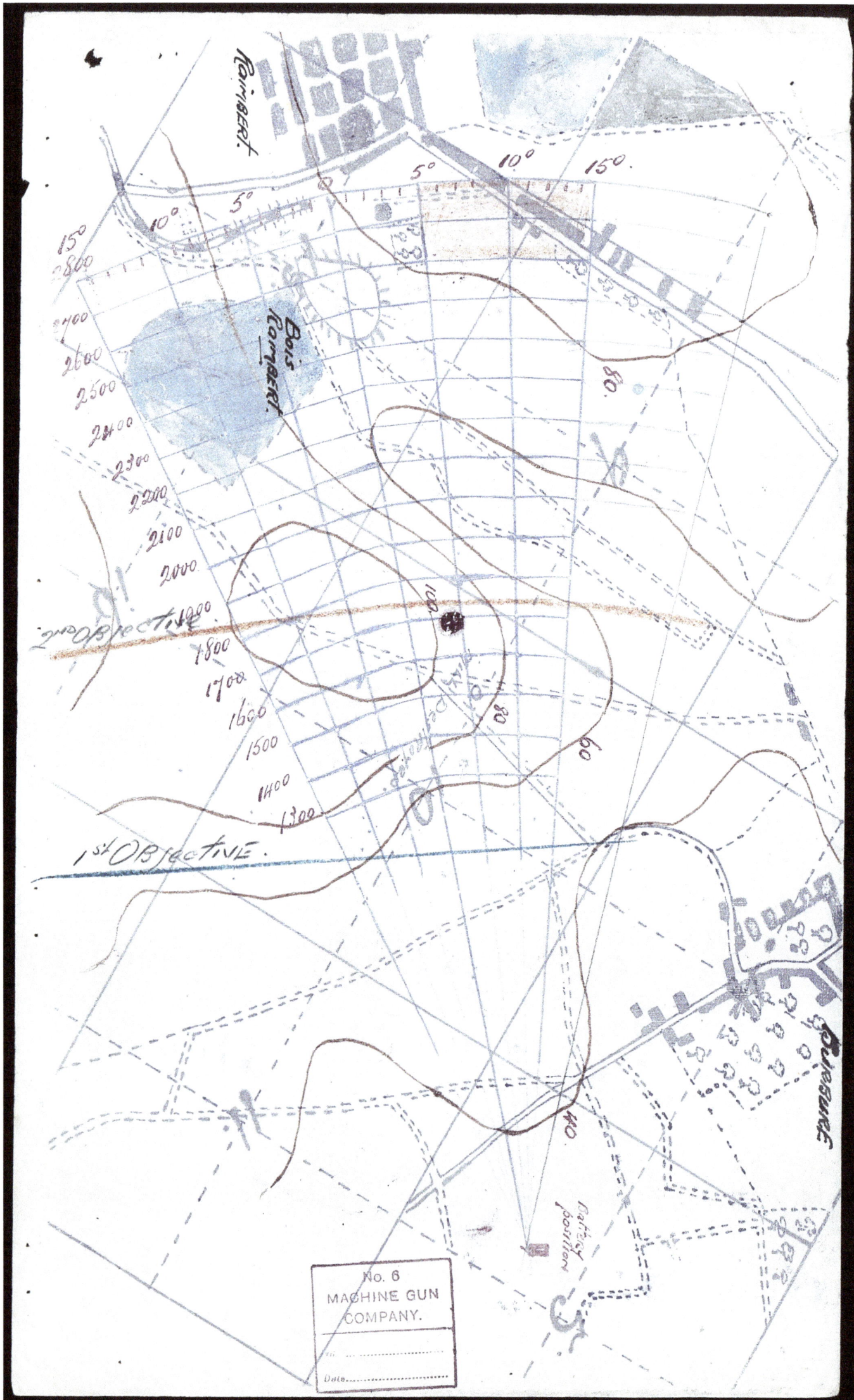

6th Brigade.

2nd Division.

6th MACHINE GUN COMPANY ::: NOVEMBER 1917.

10th MACHINE GUN COMPANY

Army Form C. 2118.

WAR DIARY
INTELLIGENCE SUMMARY.
(Erase heading not required)

November 1917

Instructions regarding War Diaries and Intelligence Summaries are contained in F.S. Regs., Part II. and the Staff Manual respectively. Title pages will be prepared in manuscript.

Place	Date	Hour	Summary of Events and Information	Remarks and references to Appendices
	November			
Hurionville	1		5th Week's Training Commenced in accordance with attached programme.	Re: Major Holdsworth S.Y. Lewis 11 Voluntaires to
Steenbecque	5	830	Company marched from Hurionville to Steenbecque	
Eecke Area	6		" " " Steenbecque to Eecke Area	
Houtkerque Area	7		" " " Eecke Area to the Houtkerque Area	
	8		Lieut B.S. Hynes left the Company & proceeded to the Machine Gun Corps Base Depot.	
	11	1130	Company attend Church Service at Houtkerque	
	12		Training commenced in accordance with attached programme	
	19		2nd Week's Training commenced	
	23	6.30am	Company marched to Roven when they entrained & were transported	
	24		Company detrained at Miraumont and were conveyed in motor	
Rocquigny		3pm	lorries to Rocquigny (re- Mr Lewis 11)	
Dorgnies	25	6.30am	Company marched from Rocquigny to Dorgnies (Re- Mr Lewis 11)	
	27	10am	Transport moved to Hermes (May Bee released 10 May Bee (3.50))	
	28	30p	Company moved up to the line & relieved 105 M.G. Coy at St Croix	
			and took up Encen positions — on 2 Battns of E. Lancs each	

WAR DIARY or INTELLIGENCE SUMMARY

Army Form C. 2118.

No. 6 MACHINE GUN COMPANY.

November 1917

(Erase heading not required.)

Instructions regarding War Diaries and Intelligence Summaries are contained in F. S. Regs., Part II. and the Staff Manual respectively. Title pages will be prepared in manuscript.

Place	Date	Hour	Summary of Events and Information	Remarks and references to Appendices
LINE	28		Have "C" section and "B and D" section "B and D" section completed today	
"			"D" Battery was hastily dug during the night. (One killed & several wounded)	
"			"D" Battery proceed to new position and was not recurred — one Gun of No. 2 Section of "D" Battery covered in with 6 hour defence	
"	29			
"	30	7.30 am	Reports that enemy was to be seen moving about Quesnoy Wood and Lilli Rd. Large numbers were seen in bag of POPLARS Village. Both Batteries fired at K.3 & 9. & 8 Quesnoy Wood & Grove	
"			R. C. Sections over "D" at L.26 c 33 (8 guns of "B" & "D" Section were fired. (R.R. Chapman) was wounded and S.O. Hand was Queen. Now as follows "C" Battery line East of Cash between	
"			Squares 15 and 21. "D" Battery line West of Farm Keep Trenches village between squares 14 and 20. 2nd Lt Gun & was "D" Battery at about L.26 d 33 were also wounded and fires 15 & continue to battery line Eastward in Square L.26 cent 233	

WAR DIARY or INTELLIGENCE SUMMARY

Army Form C. 2118.

No. 6 MACHINE GUN COMPANY.

Date: November 1917

Place	Date	Hour	Summary of Events and Information	Remarks and references to Appendices
LMS	30		Nos 1, 2 Batteries at 6.27 C.3.3. Cobb were to thicken fire west of Moeuvres and ws also to keep off flanks of front of Brigade S.O.S. and to get to bear Bombardment of whole front all guns shewed plainly and many west targets were attacked. No enemy came over the slope we were to sweep. Nos 1 AR. Cholm. swept 20000 of his left to get clear of the wire. Village of Moeuvres had been shelled & was clear & the enemy trenches made at Bricks down to front & rear by Quarry Wood and was shelled as to bring fire to bear Artillery was seen my Lovers Bomb 17 — These three were heavily knocked out by new heaviest artillery. 21 Pdr Guns C1 had done some knocked out and crippled "B" Battery to benefit of which was noted Infantry were sure front and firm line in front of village line that also took & were further that our was also lost all along the front of Div on its left	

Instructions regarding War Diaries and Intelligence Summaries are contained in F. S. Regs., Part II. and the Staff Manual respectively. Title pages will be prepared in manuscript.

WAR DIARY
or
INTELLIGENCE SUMMARY.
(Erase heading not required.)

No. 6 MACHINE GUN COMPANY.
No. ....
Date ....

Army Form C. 2118.

NOVEMBER 1917

Place	Date	Hour	Summary of Events and Information	Remarks and references to Appendices
LINE	30		Very heavy fighting was experienced on Right of Canal and some ground was lost. Machine Guns in front line on Right Bde in Batteries made excellent shooting as enemy came over in 10 successive waves down the slope and valley in Squares F.21 and 22. The fighting along this front was particularly desperate and some guns were knocked out and Officers & men killed. Attacks were renewed again and again with the greatest violence but everywhere the line held and except for certain front line position the hostile advance was successfully resisted. 6th M.G. Coy had only slight casualties and about 100 000 rounds were fired during the day.	
			At night the company was ordered to co-operate in a projected counter attack to retake LOCK 6 in Square F.21. a Artillery barrage scheme was got out and about 22 Machine Guns were given barrage tasks in conformity therewith. Guns were laid and all ready, but a necessary preliminary attack	

D. D. & L., London, E.C. (A7883) Wt. W803/M1672 350,000 4/17 Sch. 52a Forms/C/2118/14

WAR DIARY or INTELLIGENCE SUMMARY

No. 8 MACHINE GUN COMPANY.

Month and year: November 20th 1917

Place	Date	Hour	Summary of Events and Information	Remarks and references to Appendices
Little	20		Attack	
			on the Bourlon at 6.20 A.M. 8 of 16 guns of No. 8 Machine Gun Company opened fire barrage on Tadpole Copse. The right half of 8 guns fired the barrage throughout. The left half of 8 guns were to advance with the infantry & were to take up positions later. These 4 guns advanced with the Brigade and were eventually abandoned by our infantry by reason of very heavy fighting. Throughout the night & the following day fighting guns of 8 M Gun Coy were supplied throughout on 2 Batteries of 6 guns each. One Coy being at Boulon Wood & Bourlon and OC Left Group of Artillery and numerous Battery & Brigade HQrs. Every company exchanges at Crosse Roads. Fire was maintained throughout the day except when an SOS line was given about either hostile counterattack and an SOS line an infantry measures. This Pr. Suggests over the Artillery Power. The scheme worked excellently and it was clearly shown that this organization of guns & lines was necessary to allow the infantry & alternative telephone lines were amply possible.	

NO. 6 MACHINE GUN COMPANY.

6th Machine Gun Company

Programme of Training for week ending Sat Nov 24th 1917

Day	9 to 9.30	9.30 to 10	10 to 10.45	10.45 to 11.30	11.45 to 12.30	12.30 to 1.15pm	
Monday Nov 19			Company Route March with Transport. Return from Limbers en route				Night Operation p. with 17th Middx
Tuesday Nov 20th	Physical Training	Whale Oil Drill	A. Barrage Drill B. Barrage " C. I.A. D. Revolver Shooting	A. Barrage Drill B. Barrage " C. I.A. D. Revolver Shooting	A. Revolver Shooting B. " " C. I.A. D. German Gun	A. German Gun B. Revolver Shooting C. Inspection & Recognition D. " " "	
Wednesday Nov 21st	Physical Training	Whale Oil Drill	A. Gun Drill B. Gun Drill C. Barrage Drill D. " "	A. I.A. B. T.O.E.T. C. Under Sec Officer D. Field Day with 17th Middlesex Regt.	A. Squad Drill with arms B. Squad Drill with arms C. Under Sec Officer D. " "	A. Lecture by O.C. Coy.	
Thursday Nov 22nd	Physical Training	Whale Oil Drill	A. } B. } C. } D. }	Barrage Scheme under O.C. Company Batteries by Sections with Telephonic Communication Barrage Charts and Detailed Fire Organisation			
Friday Nov 23rd	Physical Training	Whale Oil Drill	A. Under Sec Officer B. Under Sec Officer C. Lecture by D. O.C. Company	A. Under Sec Officer B. Under Sec Officer C. Gun Drill D. I.A.	Company Drill under O.C. Company		Night March By Compass By Sections 5.30pm to 7.30pm
Saturday Nov 24	Physical Training	Whale Oil Drill	A. I.A. B. Laying guns for Indirect Fire C. " " " D. Gun Drill	A. T.O.E.T. B. Field Day with C. Laying Guns for D. German Gun	A. Laying Guns for Indirect Fire B. 17th Middx Regt C. T.O.E.T. D. Laying guns for Indirect Fire	A. Under Sec Officer B. " " C. Squad Drill with Arms D. T.O.E.T.	

6th Brigade.

2nd Division.

6th MACHINE GUN COMPANY :::: DECEMBER 1917.

WAR DIARY or INTELLIGENCE SUMMARY

Army Form C. 2118.

No. 9 MACHINE GUN COMPANY.

DECEMBER 1917

Ref Maps: Special Sheet (Parts of Sheets 57c NW & NE & 51b SW & SE) issued 25th Sept 1917

Place	Date	Hour	Summary of Events and Information	Remarks and references to Appendices
CAMBRAI front MŒUVRES SECTOR	1	8:50 am	Warned all Batteries Enemy massing in E.15.a & c	
			Batteries were engaged as follows —	
			'A' Battery Exp 6. 25.25 8 Guns 24hrs M.G.Coy, Capt Bates	
			'B' " Exp 6. 3. 5. " Do	
			'C' " K.3. 6.8. 8. " 6" M.G.Coy Capt K.2.a.4.8.	
			'D' " Exp 6. c.3.3. 8. " Do Lt Glover } Battery HQ and	
				Mr Chapman } Telephone Exchange
		9:0	All Batteries firing on engaged S.O.S lines	
		9:35	All carriers sent up to Batteries to report in Bell Ferme	
		9:40	"D" Battery ordered for the day from newest Canal & Quietistesp	
		10	S.O.S. in village	
		10:50	'C' Battery on 26 Parallel trenches in 15.C & d. 2.3a & c, for Bourgogne	
			Heavy concentration of enemy	
		11:12	Line down — Runner to D'Battery — were range to 1600 over fire	
			all guns out	
		11:18	Lahor S.O.S reported to Batteries	
		11:30	Barrages commence coming on Jalloure	
			1. All signallers to be kept for event and lines at Rate	

WAR DIARY or INTELLIGENCE SUMMARY

Army Form C. 2118.

NO. 6 MACHINE GUN COMPANY.

DECEMBER 1917

Place	Date	Hour	Summary of Events and Information	Remarks and references to Appendices
CAMBRAI FRONT MOEUVRES SECTION	1.	11.30	Communication: 2. Coy pioneers at Batt HQs with O.C. Coy.	
			3. "C" & "D" Batteries to keep 2 gunners each at Coes.	
			4. Recce HQs to supply their own pioneers.	
		3.30	Fire prepared. "D" Battery all guns 1800 fuse fires on village.	
		3.40	"C" Battery all guns full fires at own trenches and E15 c16 and D21 c23.	
		3.45	"B" Battery fires on E.16	
		4.04	Attack developed on left & immediately afterwards enemy seen massing on Moeuvres Village. All guns on village & canal and to the right of it — Lopra Lane.	
		5.04	"A" and "B" Battery fires off and stand by. Asked Sydney Coy (Bycourses) to keep right Batty available to fire over Moeuvres if required.	
			"D" Battery reports that the 2 guns had been withdrawn back to Battery and could be replaced on the left immediately if required — By friend.	
	2.	9.50	Warned Battery of heavy movement in F.16	
		10.20	Information that enemy were concentrating in large numbers on ...	

Army Form C. 2118.

No 6
MACHINE GUN
COMPANY.

DECEMBER 1917

WAR DIARY
or
INTELLIGENCE SUMMARY.
(Erase heading not required.)

Place	Date	Hour	Summary of Events and Information	Remarks and references to Appendices
CAMBRAI FRONT MOEUVRES SECTOR	2		Several hunks on S.p E.14.15 v.16. 20.21 v.22. General pattern	
			to be on two hunks and x road leading to the	
			D'Bty left of Canal C' Right of Canal B Battery (less M.G.Co.)	
			forward to enlarge this when to the right	
			Dy Enemy reported massing down everlooking road in 15th Coke's area ready	
			to cross this reed walk Bgrn at once and continue to do so	
			they bombed to do so at once	
	11.25		All guns "steady fire" eng. points that enemy must unmass for attack	
			Steady fire maintained on areas mentioned	
	1.00		When all Bts. cease fire and stood by	
	1.50		Mobile barrage reported on Tadpole Copse. Ordered D Batty to	
			sweep with right Guns 20° left and gradually reach elevation 2500	
			on our artillery opening. But to ready to return to S.O.S on	
			our front in case of need	
	2.23		Ordered D Batty Parkay on Moeuvres S.O.S	
	4.59		S.O.S Canal - M.L Lines down	

Army Form C.² 2118.

No. 6 MACHINE GUN COMPANY.

DECEMBER 1917

WAR DIARY
or
INTELLIGENCE SUMMARY.
(Erase heading not required.)

Instructions regarding War Diaries and Intelligence Summaries are contained in F. S. Regs., Part II. and the Staff Manual respectively. Title pages will be prepared in manuscript.

Place	Date	Hour	Summary of Events and Information	Remarks and references to Appendices
COMBRAI FRONT				
MOEUVRES SECTOR	2	5.40	Barrage guns fired - L.G's inrange from M. Elene, M.15.b.b.1.2. gun knocked out & 2 men casualties. 4.7m L.Melan into L.Melan has caused.	
"	"	"	Command of D. Battery taken over by M. Chapman has been [illegible] & several casualties. Both sections heavily shelled.	
"	"	"	Owed thereat to move to D. Battery to assist the Hotchkiss 2nd/c to relieve O.C. Coy at Group H.Q. at 5.30am 3/17 - with a view to recovering the gun and examining the situation of Luke Battery positions (where 6 O.D.D.'s & Luke guns) are.	
"	"	5.45	Revised S.O.S. lines issued (Bynner)	
			Battery	S.O.S.
			D¹ Fordis barrage australia	1798 Ref.
			D² Fordis barrage australia	E.20.a.0.5 - E.20 & 6.5 General S.O.S.
			C¹	E.13.c.4.9 - E.13.6.1.2	By the turn of telegram just
			Barrel wire Ypres avenue tr.	E.19.a.5.4 - E.16.a.2.2	If General are to fall.
				E.19.a.5.5 - E.16.a.1.3	

No. 6 MACHINE GUN COMPANY.

Army Form C. 2118.

WAR DIARY
or
INTELLIGENCE SUMMARY.
(Erase heading not required.) DECEMBER

Place	Date	Hour	Summary of Events and Information	Remarks and references to Appendices
CAMBRAI FRONT MOEUVRES SECTOR	2/12/17		S.O.S. 7:05 P.M.	
			"C" Battery C.O.S. - Ed. a.o.S. - Ed. b.o.S. General S.O.S	
			"B" Battery B¹ 3 Guns { Landed barrage distribution	
			B² { Bd. b.o.S. - Ed. b.5.5 } barrage to guns	
			Machine gun village { barrage	
			"A" Battery A¹ Scarpe – Lumsden road 2.5.6 { E.W. a.S.O. – Canal General S.O.S	
			A² { Ed. b.7 – Ed. b.4.9 General S.O.S.	
			Revised organisation of Carriers (Attached)	
			1. 1st bay to be next Section – kept at Hem	
			2. 2nd bay to come up every Sgt Ferror each night with limbers to Graticabolishing ambii.	
			3. Each Battery to send the O.M. Carriers another N.C.O. to meet limbers at Graticis each night. Dawnation supplies ammunition etc and return to Battini limbers return under Sgt Ferror to Hem with limbers	

No. 6
MACHINE GUN COMPANY.

Army Form C.2118.

WAR DIARY
or
INTELLIGENCE SUMMARY.
(Erase heading not required.)

Month: DECEMBER

Place	Date	Hour	Summary of Events and Information	Remarks and references to Appendices
CRAMBROOK FRONT MOEUVRES SECTOR	2		Nil. Charge over very 3 days.	
"	3		S.O.S. Situation reported all carried to be ready to Batteries. Wire down a good deal of the day. Sundry communications however to divisions to Batteries but fire direction has to be left largely to Battery Commanders who were in front with Infy Bne.	
"			Some observing however. Day a good deal quieter. Overreviewed that Infy Bne was to be relieved that night but	
"	4		17 Guns not be following day enough.	
"		10.30am	Received orders of G.O.C. 5th Infy Bne who relieved 6th Infy Bne never orders of G.O.C. 173rd. No orders available until afternoon.	
			conference with G.O.C. 2nd Div.	
		12 noon	Conference of M.G.Coy Commanders ever O.M.G.O 17 Guns of 5 Coy & 2nd M.G Coy allotted to defend new front to take up position in advanced of frontages over boundaries 6th M.G Coy to maintain guns at disk and proceed to Locre 17th Cey to act as Reserve with annual lotr of 2nd & 3rd Coy's of guns.	

No. 8 MACHINE GUN COMPANY.
Army Form C. 2118.

WAR DIARY or INTELLIGENCE SUMMARY.

(Erase heading not required.)

DECEMBER 1917

Place	Date	Hour	Summary of Events and Information	Remarks and references to Appendices
CAMBRAI FRONT MOEUVRES front	14	2pm	Orders issued by D.I.R. to transport & Battery O's. "D" Battery to proceed at once to cross roads K.1.9 once from Turbeau Fen on road to LA BUCQUIERE. All mgns, equipment, stores etc to be removed from position which is to be abandoned. "C" Battery to move to Lock No 6 at dusk to where pack animals are to be in waiting to transport Kit to Lock No 7 (as above) stables at LA BUCQUIERE. Position to be abandoned – all mgns etc to be removed. O.C. Coy transferring H.Q. at Lock No 6 & wires withdrawn with "C" Battery.	
	12 Midnight		Withdrawal carried out according to plan except that transport failed to arrive – other means found. Reported to D.M.G.O. & G.O.C. 51st Bn at Lock No 6. Handed over 6 guns, tripods etc complete to 2nd M.G. Cy to work up.	

No. 6 MACHINE GUN COMPANY

WAR DIARY or INTELLIGENCE SUMMARY

Army Form C. 2118.

(Erase heading not required.)

DECEMBER

Place	Date	Hour	Summary of Events and Information	Remarks and references to Appendices
CAMBRAI FRONT Nov 30/ MOEUVRES SECTOR	Dec 4		**LESSONS LEARNT FROM RECENT OPERATIONS**	
			(1) Battery organisation of M. Guns is an effective method of employment of M. Guns. The organisation as used in offensive operations were when the machine gun has an opportunity to engage targets on the most approved methods viz. Guns laid on true and exact traversen obtained.	
			(2) The Battery method is effective mainly because of the co-ordination & control allowed for it, but it is largely dependant upon efficient communication which must be by wire — by runners rarely being quick enough to be of use. Hence the need of the importance of duplicate or ladder wires from M.G. Battery.	
			(3) Guys Commanders must be in direct touch with R.A. Groups Commanders such as M.G. Bn. H.Q. to get information at the earliest possible moment.	
			(4) Selection of Battery positions is of utmost equal importance to this being so to be overturned steadily & carefully & careful consideration of casualties & applic. its Ballistic must be allowed out of the time of the probable hostile barrage.	
			(5) More signallers and linesmen are required than the 5 at present allowed. Lyscon Establishment, in order to undertake the increases.	

WAR DIARY
or
INTELLIGENCE SUMMARY.
(Erase heading not required.)

NO. 5 MACHINE GUN COMPANY. Army Form C.2118.

Month: DECEMBER

Place	Date	Hour	Summary of Events and Information	Remarks and references to Appendices
	5		(5) increasing & important part of M.G. work	
			(6) The value of having personnel including attached carriers, highly frightened on building was shown as the consumption of ammunition was enormous & few rounds at a very rapid rate.	
			Signed G.K. Stampe Captain	
			Commanding 6th Machine Gun Company	
La Bucquiere	5.		Section billeted in huts. Lengagoh on Velu Wood	
	6		Hostile artillery fairly active at intervals chiefly in vicinity of billets (1 oto killed.) Section moved to huts in another part of village	
		7-8ᵖᵐ	Section were down every 4 hours to have a much rest as possible after the heavy fighting of the last week	
			6th M.G. Coy relieved the 262/17 Gun Co. in Hd Battery position	
Manures Sector	9/10		Indian camp & Canal as far as the Karp South of Lock 407	
			Two section "C" & "D" took up outpost position in front of Manu line of Resistance	
	10.		Quiet day, intermittent shelling of Lock 407 ones Trenches in vicinity	

Army Form C. 2118.

MACHINE GUN COMPANY.

WAR DIARY
or
INTELLIGENCE SUMMARY.
(Erase heading not required.)

Instructions regarding War Diaries and Intelligence Summaries are contained in F. S. Regs., Part II. and the Staff Manual respectively. Title pages will be prepared in manuscript.

DECEMBER 1917

Place	Date	Hour	Summary of Events and Information	Remarks and references to Appendices
MOEUVRES SECTOR	10		No casualties. At night line outpost guns were withdrawn A Section holding position on Main Line of Resistance on left bank of canal and D Section came back to C.H.Q. The Battery position shelled slightly.	
	11		Recommenced forming section for 8 gun Battery - Finally took over position vacated by 253rd MGC. "B" Sector from "B" Battery. "C" Sector formed the rear battery of 8 guns. Two guns of A Section withdrawn from Main Line of Resistance to the battery positions and formed 6 gun Battery with C Section. A Section withdrawn from line had one gun blown up. No times by Trench mortar - gun left damaged. Another gun was issued causing nuisance to stopped bullet and casualties.	
	12		Quiet during day - slight shelling. Great hostile activity on both sides LOCKNOT sector in evening hostile barrage opened. B Section had 1 O.R. killed and 2 O.Rs. wounded (gas) own guns firing line gun hit by M.G. bullet - no damage - target constantly swept by M.G. fire from the left.	

Army Form C 2118.

WAR DIARY
or
INTELLIGENCE SUMMARY.
(Erase heading not required.)

No 6 [ ]NE GUN [ ]Y.

November 1917

Instructions regarding War Diaries and Intelligence Summaries are contained in F. S. Regs., Part II. and the Staff Manual respectively. Title pages will be prepared in manuscript.

Place	Date	Hour	Summary of Events and Information	Remarks and references to Appendices
MOEUVRES SECTOR	13		Quiet – Heavy wind all day. A.D Battery fired shell and front-mortars – no damage and no casualties. Intermittent shelling at night about Heavy bombardment on right and left. Reserve Staff made up to 10,000 rounds per gun. B Battery advanced water from Sucreft B leading from Fremicourt to Bapaume - Cambrai Rd. (near Les Jeux)	
	14		Quiet and misty. Slight enemy activity. Front line shelled – no damage to gun position. Col. Wolstenholme came in for later to (a.m.?) take charge in particular. Capt Watson unable to take duties (sick)	
	15		Quiet – observation good. Artillery actively front fairly on playing everywhere on left side.	
		1.30pm	B.M.G.O. visits. C.H.Q. who is site Y. Battery and decided to have a new front made and guns in line with site on Slag Heap on left of Canal (K10.a.6)	
		9pm	New site Y. Battery completed	

WAR DIARY
or
INTELLIGENCE SUMMARY.
(Erase heading not required.)

Army Form C. 2118.

No 6 MACHINE GUN COMPANY.

Instructions regarding War Diaries and Intelligence Summaries are contained in F.S. Regs., Part II. and the Staff Manual respectively. Title pages will be prepared in manuscript.

Place	Date	Hour	Summary of Events and Information	Remarks and references to Appendices
MOEUVRES SECTOR	16		Early over. Guns reported - one was found defective in HQ Battery	
			No guns were sent down and to be replaced	
			Arrived at HQ Battery made out Lewis gun report	
			Moved CHQ and exchanged to report AHK & 15.D. Enemy	
			aeroplanes very active. Engaged them from HQ position at	
			17 Battery. Heavy shelling on Right 6.15pm. Our troops	
			shewn during evening - HQ Batteries all Gns - in communication	
			again. By 9.7pm this was OK	
	17		Light shelling through evening. Enemy barrage formed	
			Kerves sent up from Batt HQ. Enemy began barrage Ref gun	
			inspection and found carried out one working order 5pm	
			Enemy T.Q. sent to HQ Battery position at intervals. Artillery retaliation	
			on Right on 59" DIN front. Infantry firing action available.	
	18		Guns sent up from No HQ to complete HQ Battery	
			Intermittent artillery actively throughout morning. Enemy	
			nearly to start again and harassed HQ Battery	

WAR DIARY
or
INTELLIGENCE SUMMARY.
(Erase heading not required.)

Army Form C. 2118.

No. 6 MACHINE GUN COMPANY.

DECEMBER 1917

Instructions regarding War Diaries and Intelligence Summaries are contained in F. S. Regs., Part II. and the Staff Manual respectively. Title pages will be prepared in manuscript.

Place	Date	Hour	Summary of Events and Information	Remarks and references to Appendices
MOEUVRES SECTOR	18.		Had Liaison Officers at A. Battery getting left gun oral has Liaison Officer to Bull Barack.	
		11.15	Together with D.T.G.O. recommended position for forthcoming Gas Operation at A2 BATTERY. Gas liberation happened with on account of wind being unfavourable. Hence at A2 position was supplied with more camouflage. He should during the day & evening.	
			To A2 Battery finally reported during the evening. Selected alternative positions and D.T.G.O. them and finally settling upon site recommended tomorrow (19" inst) before position	
			prepared positions.	
		10.0 p	Received Operation Order re Gas Operation. The guns (K1 and K2) have to side slip to the right to L.H. Canal bank for same, from the Battery position (A2) and move forward to Bullion Trench and to A3 position to fire over on the Slag Heap at ZERO +12 guns will be taken in section at A1 Battery. To remaining two guns will "Stand Fast"	

Army Form C. 2118.

No. 6
MACHINE GUN
COMPANY.

No. ....
Date. ....

WAR DIARY
or
INTELLIGENCE SUMMARY.
(Erase heading not required.) December

Instructions regarding War Diaries and Intelligence Summaries are contained in F. S. Regs., Part II. and the Staff Manual respectively. Title pages will be prepared in manuscript.

Place	Date	Hour	Summary of Events and Information	Remarks and references to Appendices
MOEUVRES SECTOR	18	4pm	Information received that the Germans were bombarding with Gas this place	
	20		B.M.G.Os and M.G.Os conference at H.Q. 99th M.G.Coy. O'Group regarding dispositions and activities covering of Companies made by O.C. 5th M.G.Coy. commanding Relief. Reconnaissance made from B.M.G.O and Cabinet by every Section Officer interviewed by this Officer — Reconnaissance for this Inspection on our front to take place tomorrow. Guns of A Battery to move — M.Gs over M.Gs to go up and fire, crew of B Battery to go to Bullen Trench. Section No 2 and No 3 to take Garrison Cover for relief from 5 M.G Bn. to over duties of Liaison Officer.	
	21		Relieved by 5th M.G.Coy. Relief complete by 5.35pm. To Couverslie.	
VELU WOOD			Received at reserve billets VELU WOOD Company billeted in link Capt. G. le Wallace taken sick — Lieut. M. Melia assumed command.	
	22		Accident base in arms to O.O. Capt. G. le Wallace admitted to hospital	ML

WAR DIARY or INTELLIGENCE SUMMARY

Army Form C.2118.

No. 6 MACHINE GUN COMPANY

DECEMBER

Place	Date	Hour	Summary of Events and Information	Remarks and references to Appendices
Velu Wood	25	10am	Inspection of transport by A.D.V.S. Church Service at 100th Field Ambulance. Lieut E.M. Grose (2nd i/c "17 M.G. Coy") took over duties of Commanding Officer in absence of Capt G.H. Sharpe. Lieut P.H. Hall joins the company. (Reinforcement)	
	26		Lieut E.M. Grose visits Bde H.Q. and D.T.G.O. Section Officers reconnoitre Sections whom we are relieving to 2nd "17 M.G. Coy". Operation Order 17th/17/16 issued. (1) The 6th M.G. Coy will relieve 8 guns of the 2nd "17 M.G. Coy" and 8 guns of the 99th M.G. Coy on the line on the night Dec 27th/28th 1917. (2) "A" Section will relieve a Section of the 2nd "17 M.G. Coy" in B1 Battery Position "B" and "D" Sections will relieve 2 Section of 16th 2nd "17 M.G. Coy" in B2 Battery Position. "C" Section will relieve a Section of 16th 2nd "17 M.G. Coy" with H.Q. of Group. (3) Group H.Q. will be at K.14.b.10.00 with H.Q. 4 Group. (4) B.L. Boxes will be taken over as Trench Stores. Keys will be taken for all Trench Stores. (5) Guide will meet incoming teams at Rmp.K.14.c.2.6. for B1 and B2.	

Army Form C. 2118.

No. 6 MACHINE GUN COMPANY.

WAR DIARY
or
INTELLIGENCE SUMMARY.
(Erase heading not required.)

Instructions regarding War Diaries and Intelligence Summaries are contained in F. S. Regs., Part II. and the Staff Manual respectively. Title pages will be prepared in manuscript.

Place	Date	Hour	Summary of Events and Information	Remarks and references to Appendices
Mœuvres Sector			O.O. No 16 Cont.	
		(6)	Signallers will go to Group HQ on the morning and will reconnoitre routes to B1 and B2 Batteries	
		(7)	H.Q. Officers servants will go up under C.S.M. and be billetted	
		(8)	Our numerous from each Battery will report at Group HQ	
		(9)	Tenders CQMS and I am am to proceed to reconnoitre by road to R.V. at C.1.6 in the morning	
	27	(10)	Relief complete will be reported to Group HQ by town wire 28 Feb 17	
			Signed D. 1st Batt 4 Hunts	
			Relief took place last night B1, B2 & C1 Battery Bose to C Battery were relieved to be known as B3 Battery. B Group HQ at HQ R Goose	
	28		Day fairly quiet all guns fired on trade and known schemes German front line as follows	

Battery	No of Guns	Targets	Rate of Fire	Times
B1	1	Trenches in E.26.a.	2 Belts per hour	5 - 11 pm
B2	1	Trenches in E.26.c + D		2 - 6 am
B3	2	Lock N° 6		

Army Form C. 2118.

NO. 6 MACHINE GUN COMPANY.

WAR DIARY
or
INTELLIGENCE SUMMARY.
(Erase heading not required.)

DECEMBER 1917

Instructions regarding War Diaries and Intelligence Summaries are contained in F. S. Regs., Part II. and the Staff Manual respectively. Title pages will be prepared in manuscript.

Place	Date	Hour	Summary of Events and Information	Remarks and references to Appendices
MOEUVRES Sector	28		Two more guns were added to B.3 Battery making 7 list of 8 guns at firing S.O.S. lines and/or 100 yards	
	29		Fairly normal. Went routine and night firing as per programme shot	
	30		Artillery activity slight. German attack to our right – stood to everything developed – unable to fire as attack was made on our front	
			Enemy shelled our back areas with Gas Shells about midnight causing just received from B.3. Very slight effect. No casualties.	
	31		Some night firing. Decrease in activity – no firing	

6th Machine Gun Company.

Summary of Operations : Cambrai Battle Front — Moeuvres Sector.
Nov. 30 — Dec. 4. 1917

Ref: MOEUVRES. Special Sheet (Parts of Sheets 57c. NW, NE, SW & SE.
$\frac{1}{20,000}$ Ed: S.F. corrected to 1/11/17.

---

1. 6th M. Gun Coy. went into the line on the night Nov. 28/29 with 16 guns & took up two Battery positions for 8 guns each as follows—

    (a) A & C Sections (C Battery) in a trench E.25.b.9.2 — E.25.b.7.4.
    This was a new position & emplacements were prepared by the teams during the night. It had been previously reconnoitred & was designed to afford protection by direct fire of the left flank of the Brigade front, the boundary of which ran through . . . . also at village of Moeuvres & to the left over left Bgde front to Tadpole Copse.

    (b) B & D Sections (D Battery) in the trenches & saps at about E.26.c.3.3.
    These positions were taken over from the 109th M. Gun Coy. & allowed of a very fine sweep of direct fire in a N.E. direction, East of the Canal towards Quarry Wood, into & beyond village of Moeuvres & up the Canal.

    (c) The two positions together commanded the whole of the left Bgde front by direct fire & afforded exceptional opportunities for observation of fire & hostile movement; & further, for long range work into the areas of hostile concentration.

    (d) The 242nd M.G. Coy. (Divl. Coy.) put in 8 guns as a battery, at ~~E.26.b.~~ E.26.d.8.7, relieving 109th M.G. Coy., from where they could search the Canal & command all the ground in front of the right Bgde. East of the Canal.
    This was B Battery.

    (e) The remaining battery of this series, A battery, was also provided by 242 M.G. Coy., relieving 107 M.G. Coy. at E.27.b.25.25 on the right Bgde front. They swept the open ground to the Canal into Moeuvres & up towards Quarry Wood to their front.

2.

2. Left Group comprising C & D Batteries, 16 guns of 6th M.G. Coy
had its H.Q. at 6th Bde. H.Q. at K7d03 where the O.C. Coy
was in direct touch not only with his Brigadiers, but also the O.C.
Left Group R.A. who also had his H.Q. in the same dugout
thus providing unique facilities for information of all movements.

Both batteries were in telephonic communication by direct wire
to a forward M.G. Exchange at the centre K2a18 thence back to
H.Q. by direct wire.

When the wires were cut each battery sent 2 runners to Advanced
Bde. H.Q. at Lock VI K3a & communication was maintained
thence with C.H.Q. by Coy. or B'gde Runners who were always moving to & fro.

3. (a) On the night of arrival C Battery were heavily shelled, killing &
wounding a number of the personnel & destroying the emplacements;
during the 29th therefore the Battery was moved to K2b98
a group of trenches South of Cambrai Rd. with better accommodation
for the teams & also affording excellent facilities for observation of
fire up the Canal, to the right of Rd. & towards Quarry Wood.
Also our Nocures.

(b) When this had been done D Battery Commander knowing the
importance of the Valley to the left of Bde front pushed out 2 guns
to his left to sweep up into Nocurels & so secure the flank.

(c) B Battery also heavily shelled had to move & they took up a
position at E26d33. This battery was repeatedly
deputed to cover certain vulnerable points & certain guns were
detached for various duties, also they had 2 guns knocked out
reducing the battery to 3 guns & thereby the battery method had to
be abandoned during the operation & the remaining guns thickened
the fire or extended the barrage lines put down by C & D Battys
at the request of O.C. 6th M.G. Coy.

4. Following is a summary of O.C's diary kept throughout the operations & includes most of the orders issued or information obtained from Group H.Q. and 6th Inf. Bde. orders:—

30/11/17.

7.50 a.m. Enemy seen massing about Quarry Wood & leaving Mosinees village in large numbers.

Following S.O.S. lines laid down for batteries:—

C. Batty: line E. of Canal about Sqs. 15 & 21 (grid line)
D. do.   W. of Canal through Mosinees village about Sq. 12 & 20
242 Coy B. Batty: to extend barrage line Eastward in Sqs E15c & 22a
D. A. Batty: to thicken fire into Mosinees & establish right flank of bde.

S.O.S. after heavy hostile bombardment of whole front.

All guns opened rapid fire & many direct targets were obtained as enemy came over the slopes & in waves after waves.

Field artillery seemed to have come into action in E. Gonnelieu & was promptly knocked out by our howitzer & field arty.

Though sheer weight of numbers enemy succeeded in penetrating our front line along 6th Bde front & his tanks along whole front, but the volume of arty. M.G. fire & the desperate resistance of the Inf. broke the force of the attack & it got no further. Enormous casualties being inflicted right along the line.

Very hard hand to hand fighting continued in the front by Inf. throughout the day & night & Lock 7 was lost & retaken round about.

Throughout the day D. batty. fired 1000 rounds into & around Mosinees & the Canal area.

Most excellent work was done by both batteries & the system of controlled & coordinated M.G. fire by the battery buckled was amply justified.

The necessity for multiple telephone wires was brought out as the efficiency of the method depends largely upon reliable & quick communication.

4.

1/12/17

8.55 am. Warned all batteries. Enemy massing in E15a & b
Batteries now organised as follows:

A. Batty. E27 b 75.25. 8 guns. 242 M.G. Coy. Capt Borlace
B - E26d 3 3   6 -   Do.   H.Q. at K3. a 6 7
C - K2 b 8 9   8 -   6 M.G. Coy   Lt. Glover   } cyclists
D - E16 c 3 3   8 -   do   Lt. Chapman   K2 a 4 8
                                                    (Batty H.Q.)
                                                   + telephone exchge.

(9.25 All carriers sent up to Batteries to assist in belt filling.)

9.0   All batteries firing on various S.O.S. lines as before

9.40. D Batty ordered to thicken fire round Canal & quicken up.

10.0   S.O.S. in Village.

10.50 C. Batty on to parallel trenches in 15 c & d & 21 a & b
       for 15 minutes rapid.   heavy concentration of enemy.

11.12. Line down — Runner to D. Batty — reduce air range to 1600ˣ
       & fire all guns all out.

3.0 pm. Line repaired.
       D. Batty all guns 1800ˣ full speed on Village.

3.40. C Batty. all guns full speed on trenches in E15 & 16, 21 & 22.

3.47. B Batty trenches E.16.

4.0   Attack on left developed & large concentration in Moeuvres Village
       All guns on Village & Canal & Infil. gul — Rapid fire.

5.0.   Wired both batteries: Ease off & stand by.
       Asked 242 Coy (by runner) to keep Right Batty available to
       fire over Moeuvres, if reqd.

       D. Batty reported that the 2 guns had been withdrawn back to Batty
       but could be replaced on the left immediately if reqd.
       Confirmed.

5.

2/12/17.

9.50 a.m.   Warned batteries of enemy movement in E.4

10.30   Informed that Enemy were concentrating in very large
            numbers in parallel trenches to Sys. E.14. 15 & 16
                                              & 20. 21. 22
            Ordered all batteries to lay on their trenches & report when
            ready to fire.
                        D left of canal   C right of canal
            B. bty. (302 Bty.) promised to extend their line to the right.

10.48   Enemy reported moving down Sunken road to 15.b.
            Asked 302 Bty. to search this road with 2 guns at once
            & to continue to do so.   They promised to do so at once.

11.25   All guns "steady fire" on spots all enemy were massing
            for attack.
            Steady fire maintained on areas mentioned.

1.24.   Wired all batteries. Cease fire & stand by.

1.53.   Hostile barrage reported on Tadpole Copse.
            Ordered D battery to switch 4 left & open fire
            with elevation of 2500° on our artillery opening.
            But to ready to return to S.O.S. on our front the case of need.

2.23.   Ordered D battery to relay on Normal S.O.S.

4.39.   S.O.S. Canal.
            — All lines down —

5.40   Barrage quietened.

Later message from Lt. Glover that he had 2 guns knocked out & some
casualties — from Lt. Nolan, who had assumed command of D Bty,
that 2/Lt. Chapman had been killed & several casualties.
Both positions heavily shelled.
Ordered 2/Lt. Welch to proceed to D.Bty. to assist Lt. Nolan
2/Lt. to relieve Lt. Coy. at Group H.Q. at 8.30 a.m. 3/12/17 with a view to
reconnoitring the ground & examining the situation at both battery positions.
Wired to D.a.D.O.S. for issue form.

6.

2/12/17.

Revised S.O.S. lines issued at 5.45 p.m. by Special Runner

Battery	S.O.S.	Map Ref	
D	D.1. Frontal barrage Distributed	E.20 a 0.5 – E.20 b 6.5	General S.O.S
	D.2. do	E.13 c 4.9 – E.13 b 1.2	by 4 guns if village S.O.S.
C	C.1. 2 parallel lines of enfilade fire	E.22 a 6.4 – E.16 d 2.2 E.22 a 5.5 – E.16 d 1.3	If canal area is S.O.S.
	C.2. Frontal barrage Distributed	E.21 a 0.5 – E.21 b 0.5	General S.O.S.
B. (Remaining 3 guns)	B.1. Frontal barrage	E.21 b 0.5 – E.21 b 5.5	If village S.O.S.
	B.2. thicken fire into village	E.14 d 5.0 – Canal	General S.O.S.
A (Remaining 2 guns)	A.1 branch sunken road E.21 b	E.21 b 7.1 – E.21 b 4.9	General S.O.S.

Revised Organisation of Carriers. (Attached men)

1. Half to be with Sections – half at Rear.
2. Rear half to come up under Sgt. Trenner each night with limbers to Ceulet : distributing centre
3. Each Battery to send their other carriers under an N.C.O. & meet limbers at Ceulet each night; Draw rations & supplies, return to Batteries: Remainder return under Sgt. Trenner to rear with limbers.
4. Change over every 3 days.
5. If situation requires it all Carriers to be sent up to Batteries.

3/12/17

Wires down a good deal of the day.

Sundry communications from D.H.Q. direct received to Batteries; but few deputations had been left behind to Battery Commanders who were in touch with Infy. units & were observing themselves.

Day a good deal quieter.

Orders rec'd that 6th Infy Bde was to be relieved that night but M. Guns not till following day or night.

4/12/17

Placed under orders of O.C. 5th Infy Bde who relieved 6 Bde

10.30 am Reported to him at Lock VII
No orders available until after conference with G.O.C. 2nd Div.

12 Noon Conference of M.G. Coy Commanders under D.M.G.O.
12 Guns of 6 Coy & 242 Coy allotted to defend the new front to be taken up after readjustment of frontages & boundaries
6 M.G. Coy to withdraw 8 guns at dusk & send 8 to Lock VII to act as reserve until arrival later of 242 Coy 8 guns.

2 pm Orders issued by D.H.Q. to Transport & Bullry O.Cs.
D Bttry to proceed at dusk to cross Rd. K.1.a & join Limbers there march to Labreguière. All maps, documents, stores & kit to be removed from position which is to be abandoned.
C. Bttry to move to Lock VIa at dusk where pack animals are to be in waiting to transport Kit to Lock VII (as above) & later to Labreguière.
Position to be abandoned — all maps etc. to be removed.
O.C. Coy & my H.Q. at Lock VI - will withdraw with C Bttry.

12 midnight Withdrawal carried out according to plan except that transport failed to arrive — other means found.
Reported to D.M.G.O. & G.O.C. 5 Bde at Lock VII
Under new 6 gun bipods etc. complete to 242 Coy to make up.

Lessons learnt from recent Operations.

1. Battery organisation of M.G. Fire is an effective method of employment of M.G. Guns for defensive as well as offensive operations, either when there is either time nor opportunity to organise batteries on the most approved methods - of Guns laid out in line, true parallelism obtained.

2. The Battery method is effective mainly because of the coordination & control obtained by it - but it is largely dependent upon efficient communication which must be by wire - Runners not being quick enough to be of use. Hence the first-rate importance of duplicate or ladder wires from H.Q. to Batteries.

3. Group Commander must be in direct touch with R.A. Group Commander, & with Infy. Bde H.Q. to get information at the earliest possible moment.

4. Selection of Battery positions is of almost equal importance, if the firing is to be maintained steadily & casualties avoided the batteries must be sited out of the lines of the probable hostile barrage.

5. More Signallers & linesmen are required than the 8 at present allowed to M.G. Coys in order to maintain this increasingly important department of M.G. work.

6. The value of having all personnel, including attached carriers, highly proficient in belt-filling was shewn, as the consumption of ammunition was enormous & for periods at a very rapid rate.

6.12.17.

J. H. Stample Capt.
Commanding C" M. Gun Coy.

B.G.C.
6th Infy. Bde.

Sir,

I have the honour to submit the attached narrative of the operations recently undertaken by this Company in conjunction with the other units of the Brigade in the Mormores Sector.

I have appended a summary of the Casualties suffered by the Coy. & the lessons learnt from the operations.

Extracts from my own diary compiled during the operation are included in the narrative.

I should like to add, Sir, that such services as was rendered during these operations by my Company, was entirely due to the Valour of the Officers & N.C.O's their cool & clearheaded direction & the complete & magnificent devotion of the men — none of whom ever faltered in the prompt discharge of his duty, without any regard to personal danger or probable consequences.

I have the honour to be, Sir,
Your obedient servant

J. H. Stringer Capt.
Commanding 6th Rifle Coy.

In the field.
7/12/17.

6th Machine Gun Company

Casualties sustained during Operations Nov 28th – Dec 4th 1917

KILLED	WOUNDED	N.Y.D.M.		
2/Lt. A.R. Chapman 2 ORs. M.G.C. 2 ORs. Attached.	12 ORs. M.G.C. 3 ORs. Attached.	4 ORs. M.G.C. 2 ORs. Attached.		
1 Officer. 4 ORs.	15 ORs.	6 ORs.		

1 M. Gun knocked out
1 do badly damaged. } both brought out of action on withdrawal.

SECRET

6th Machine Gun Company

OPERATION ORDER No. 1715.   dated 8/12/17

Ref. Maeuvres Special Sheet Ed.n 5.F. 1/20000
France Sheet 57c Ed.n 2   1/40000

1/ The 6th M Gun Coy will relieve 16 guns of the 5th M Gun Coy & the 2nd 2nd M Gun Coy in the line on the night 9/10 Dec according to the appended table.

2/ On completion of relief the 2nd 2nd M.G. Coy will be withdrawn to rest billets & the 5th M.G. Coy will co-operate in the defence of the Bde front with 8 guns in position & 8 guns in Reserve at Coy HQ at K.14.d.45.80.

3/ Guides from each gun position will be at the cross Canal Side (Sunken road immediately west of canal) at S.15.a.2.5. at 6 pm on the 9th inst. to which point all guns, tripods &c will be brought by limbers.

4/ All belt boxes, ammunition, maps, orders etc of the guns in the line will be taken over by the incoming teams & receipts given in duplicate for everything including all Trench Stores.

5/ All belt boxes in possession of this company will be returned at the Transport Lines & handed over on request of the relieved Corps receipts in duplicate being taken.

6/ Section Officers will proceed to reconnoitre the ground & as many positions as possible during the day 9/12/17 & will conduct their Sections into position from billet later — leaving Camp at 4 pm in column with intervals of 50 paces between Sections. They will reconnoitre the route to follow from LA BUCQUIERE to HERMIES, thence via CEMETERY & along Canal bed.

7/ All attached men will accompany their respective Sections into the line to assist with the improvement of the positions, erection of shelters & preparation of such new positions as will be required.

8/ Coy Sgt Major & Signallers, runners will be stationed at CHQ at K.14.c.45.80. where OC Coy will be.

9/ Rations & Supplies will be delivered nightly at the Ramp S.15.a.2.5 & Transport Officer will reconnoitre the route & supervise all arrangements therefor.

10/ A minimum of 14 full belt boxes & 5000 rounds S.A.A. should be maintained at each gun & a return is to be rendered by S.O. on the morning after relief shewing the amount of ammunition available at each gun.

11/ Water for drinking & for guns can be drawn at Lock VII K.4.c. & there is a Bde amm'n Dump there.

12/ Relief complete will be reported by the Code word "Splendid" as early as possible to CHQ.

13/ Duplicate receipts & list of stores etc taken over will be sent to CHQ by noon on the day following.

14/ Table of reliefs attached.

Copies to
Section Officers
TO
6 Infy Bde.
OC 5 MG Coy
OC 2 MG
DMGO
War Diary

Capt
Comdg 6th Machine Gun Coy

Relief Table 9/10 Dec 1917

Nos of Guns & approx Map Ref

Battery K9.c.5.9	Main Line of Resistance	Outpost Line	At Present Found by	Relieved by	Remarks
8 Guns			2nd MG Coy	6th MG Coy	8 & C sections reverse of 9/10 Oct covered by 2nd Sections. 3 Guns. 5th Section Lewis Gun Supports. 5th Section now being released before Co in support.
1 K9.b.1.7			5th Coy	6th Coy	5th Section 4th Wants
2 K9.a.6.6					
3 K9.a.5.5					
4 K8.b.3.9					
5 K8.a.5.5			No Relief 5th Coy		
6 K8.b.9.3.5					
7 K7.b.8.5					
8 K7.b.6.5					
9 K7 Cotton					
10 K7.a.6.4					
	1 K3.c.95.20		2nd Coy	6 Coy	D Section } New Molars
	2 K3.c.85.20			6 Coy	D Section }
	3 K8.a.6.9			6 Coy	F Section } 4/4 Wants
	4 K1.a.8.4			6 Coy	F Section }
				6 Coy	D Section } Lr Molars
				6 Coy	D Section }
Coy HQ 1 at K3. a.3.0			2nd Coy	6 Coy	A Section } 4/4 Wants

Remaining Guns of MG Coy to go to Left Battery L.O. as Reserve in Reserve
Bat moves out C.H.Q.

G.H. Stanbroks Capt
O.C. 6th MG Coy

2ND DIVISION
6TH INFY BDE

NO. 6 MACHINE GUN COY.

JAN - FEB 1918

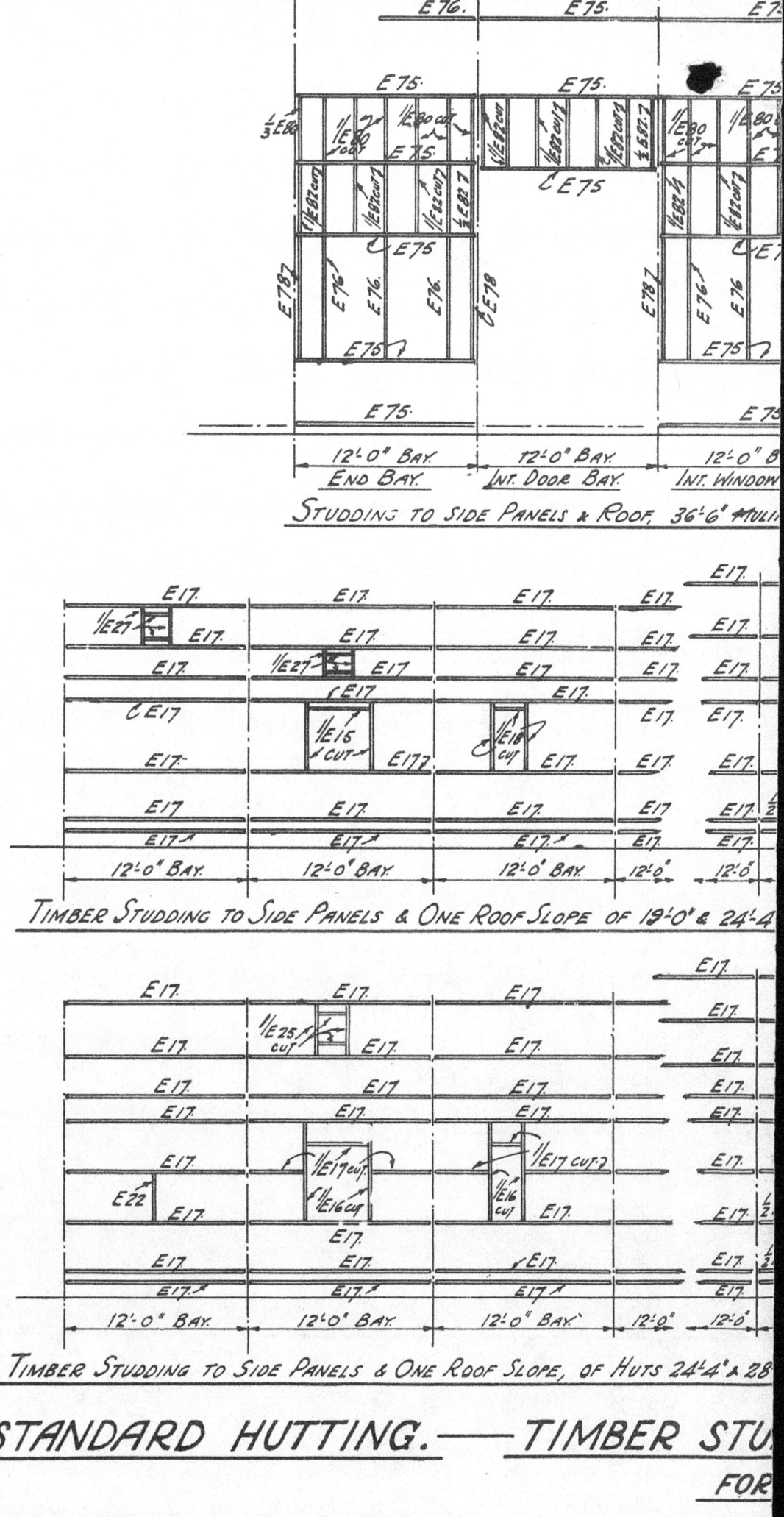

STANDARD HUTTING. — TIMBER STU

6th Brigade.
2nd Division.

No. 6 MACHINE GUN COMPANY

JANUARY 1918.

Army Form C. 2118.

No. 6 MACHINE GUN COMPANY.

WAR DIARY
or
INTELLIGENCE SUMMARY.
(Erase heading not required.)

January 1918

Place	Date	Hour	Summary of Events and Information	Remarks and references to Appendices
Cambrai Front				
Maurices Section	1		About quiet all day carrying a considerable amount of work to be done. Early in the evening the message "SOS" was received on the telephone later it was counter to "Bosch". Nothing was noted in the vicinity of our batteries	
	2		Quiet during the day. Would about 5.30pm when the enemy heavily shelled mortared a part of our front system. B and B3 Batteries at once about fire on seeing the "SOS" signal. B3 Battery was heavily shelled & unable to see the signal from its position - no casualties	
	3		About 1 pm received orders from 17 G.L.D. to "Stand by ready to fire on "SOS" lines from B2 and B3 Batteries. Orders received to draw new about 10 am he was ordered immediately over rifle as unable to see our	
			2000 rounds ammn fired. Capt G.H. Stamp returned from Hospital O.C. 51st M.G. Coy inspected the Batteries Brew - to taking over	
			Operation Order No. P.K. was issued	
			c/o L. 679 Gun Coy relieved in the line by 6 Guns of the 51st M.G.C. on the night 4/5 Jan 1918.	

Army Form C. 2118.

No. 8 MACHINE GUN COMPANY.

WAR DIARY
or
INTELLIGENCE SUMMARY.
(Erase heading not required.)

January 1918

Instructions regarding War Diaries and Intelligence Summaries are contained in F. S. Regs., Part II. and the Staff Manual respectively. Title pages will be prepared in manuscript.

Place	Date	Hour	Summary of Events and Information	Remarks and references to Appendices
Central Front			O.O. No. B.M.	
			(2) The distribution will be as follows:-	
			(a) 2 Guns of 51st M.G. Coy will relieve B1. Battery 4 guns	
			(b) 2 Guns — — — — — B2 —	
			(c) 2 Guns — — — — — B3 8 guns	
			(3) The 51st M.G. Coy will take over 2 Tripods & twenty eight Belt Boxes from each Battery. The guns and remainder of tripods and Belt Boxes will be taken out on relief.	
			(4) All Lunch Stores including Dressings and bandages will be handed over & receipts given and taken & duplicate copy will be sent to Orderly Room by 12 noon 6.1.18.	
			(5) Two limbers per Battery will be at the Broken Wooden Bridge on Canal at K.14.a.95.65. at 4.45 p.m. Each gun & each limber, a slip of paper showing his Battery position.	
			(6) On relief all guns & gun kits will be taken to the Barrier & H.W.C.1.7. and loaded on limbers	
			(7) On limbers for scalier serves to [illegible] up to [illegible] dump	

No. 8 MACHINE GUN COMPANY.

Army Form C. 2118.

WAR DIARY
or
INTELLIGENCE SUMMARY.
(Erase heading not required.)

January 1918

Instructions regarding War Diaries and Intelligence Summaries are contained in F.S. Regs., Part II. and the Staff Manual respectively. Title pages will be prepared in manuscript.

Place	Date	Hour	Summary of Events and Information	Remarks and references to Appendices
			(1) Things at the usual time	
			(2) Signals will move out with the company, the unshaded call attacker squad of 6 Inf Bde	
			(3) Ref arnold will report to CHQ by sick card "ORDER"	
			(10) On relief the company will assemble near Div Office Roe at L.135.a.5.6.	
			(11) The company will move to Roquigny by team having L.34.a.7.4 at 7.30 p.m.	
	4		Materials holds aircraft activity. Boma B3. AA guns fire on planes during the morning. B of G guns claimed a hit.	
Roquigny	5	5.30 p.m.	Relieved by Coms of 51st G Ct.	
	6	12.45 a.m.	Arrived in billets Roquigny. Day spent in straightening up the camp. Lieut Ph.Lee joined the company	
	7		Company attended Church Service. Capt G.H. Smith proceeded on leave	
	8		Day was spent in cleaning guns, equipment & refitting of personnel	

Army Form C. 2118.

No. 8 MACHINE GUN COMPANY.

WAR DIARY
or
INTELLIGENCE SUMMARY.
(Erase heading not required.)

January 1917

Instructions regarding War Diaries and Intelligence Summaries are contained in F. S. Regs., Part II. and the Staff Manual respectively. Title pages will be prepared in manuscript.

Place	Date	Hour	Summary of Events and Information	Remarks and references to Appendices
Rocquigny	9		All guns were inspected by OC Coy. Parades were 9.30 Physical Training 9.45-10.30 Squad Drill 10.30-11.15 Stoppages 11.30-12.15pm Mechanism 12.15pm-1pm Guns were dry cleaned and each crew for inspection.	
	10	3pm	Lieut Field Assistant Inspector of Armourers, Third Army inspected all guns. Parades: 9.30am Physical Training 9.45-11.15 am Immediate Action & Gun Drill 11.30-12.15. Squad Drill with aims 12.15pm to 1pm Gas Helmet Drill and inspection of Box Respirators.	
	11		Sections were occupied in the morning erecting southwards funnel huts etc as protection against hostile aircraft.	
	12		During the evening the Company was presented with a horse drawn Char being the first opportunity the Company had of keeping up the national custom since Dec 25th). The dinner was organised by Capt G.H. Stampe prior to his going on leave & R.S.M.G.Smith took over the organising of the dinner in the absence of Capt G.H. Stampe and succeeded in producing a real good dinner for the men	

(A5883) Wt. W30/M1672 350,000 4/17 D. D. & L., London, E.C. Sch. 52a. Forms/C/2118/14

No. 6 MACHINE GUN COMPANY.

Army Form C. 2118.

WAR DIARY
or
INTELLIGENCE SUMMARY.
(Erase heading not required.)

January 1918.

Instructions regarding War Diaries and Intelligence Summaries are contained in F. S. Regs., Part II. and the Staff Manual respectively. Title pages will be prepared in manuscript.

Place	Date	Hour	Summary of Events and Information	Remarks and references to Appendices
Rocquigny	12		The Nurses was followed by a concert which was quite a good show. Several of the men had composed various "Parodies" and "Trench Songs" for the occasion which were very amusing.	
	13		Lieut. J. M. Nolan relieved from Cave.	
	14		All Sections passed through the Gas Chamber on the Rocquigny - Barastre Rd.	
	15		"A" "D" Sections firing on Range. B Section Firing Practice C. Packsaddlery	
	16		Parades were carried out in accordance with Programme	
	17		The Company had Baths during the morning.	
	18	2.30pm	attended a Flammenwerfer Demonstration	
			Parades were carried out in accordance with Programme	
	19		Coy. and Horse Lines inspected by the Major General Commanding 2nd Division	
	21		Parades were Physical Training, I.A. Stoppages, Gun Drill. Gas Drill Revolver	
			Drill, Action from Limbers & Packsaddlery.	
			B. C. Sections firing on range. "A" Section Packsaddlery & Squad Drill	
	2		D Section. I.A. Stoppages. Gas Drill & Revolver.	

No. 6 MACHINE GUN COMPANY.

Army Form C. 2118.

WAR DIARY
or
INTELLIGENCE SUMMARY.
(Erase heading not required.)

January 1918

Place	Date	Hour	Summary of Events and Information	Remarks and references to Appendices
Rogugny	23		Operation Order No. 85 issued:-	
			(1) The 6/7 G. Coy will relieve the 5/7 G. Coy in Divisional Reserve Billets at Metz tomorrow Jan 24th.	
			(2) Transport (less fighting limbers) will move off independently under 2nd Lt. Booth to V.11.d.8.8. They will not arrive at Equancourt before Noon. Route Metz Rd - Manancourt - Etricourt - Equancourt.	
			Fighting limbers and H.Q. limber will proceed direct to Metz using the same route. Route through Fins.	
			(3) Company will move on M.G. Team leaving Rogugny Bn 55 at 1.45pm Company will parade ready to "March Off" by 1 pm Dress - Full Marching Order (Pack Slung).	
			(4) All blankets and Officers valises will be dumped outside O/M Stores by 8.30am.	
			(5) An advance billeting party of 1 Officer (Lt. McMahon) and 3 ORs will proceed to Metz at 7.30am. Bicycles will be provided for the same. Agnus from this party will be at Etricourt for the party in the afternoon	

No. 8 MACHINE GUN COMPANY

Army Form C. 2118.

WAR DIARY
or
INTELLIGENCE SUMMARY.
(Erase heading not required.)

January 1918.

Instructions regarding War Diaries and Intelligence Summaries are contained in F. S. Regs., Part II. and the Staff Manual respectively. Title pages will be prepared in manuscript.

Place	Date	Hour	Summary of Events and Information	Remarks and references to Appendices
Rocquigny	23		Relieving	
			Point Ors. L.5.9. at 2.45pm to guide the Company to Billets	
Metz	24		Company moved to Metz in accordance with O/O N° B5.	
			Lieut N.V. OXENDEN (5th M.G. Coy) took over 2 in Command of Company	
	25		Capt G.H. Stamfer returned from leave	
	26		Lieut R.S. Robertson joined the Company from Base Depot	
			Lieut Hewitt proceeded on leave	
	29		Lieut H.F. Antill proceeded to M.G. Training Centre Grantham to attend a 9th Instructional Staff Course	
			All Officers reconnoitred positions on the line preparatory to taking over	
		8pm	Cavalier Qrs. 170 B.6. assumed:-	
			(1) Top La Vacquerie Special Sheet 1/10000	
			(2) The 6th M.G. Coy being relieved the 5th M.G. Coy in the La Vacquerie Sector	
			on night Jan 30/31st	
			The position after relief will be as follows:-	

Army Form C. 2118.

No. 8
MACHINE GUN
COMPANY.

WAR DIARY
or
INTELLIGENCE SUMMARY.
(Erase heading not required.)

January 1918

Instructions regarding War Diaries and Intelligence Summaries are contained in F. S. Regs., Part II. and the Staff Manual respectively. Title pages will be prepared in manuscript.

Place	Date	Hour	Summary of Events and Information	Remarks and references to Appendices
Metz			Section Relieving Section Relieved Position	
			A Section 61st M.G.Coy D Section 51st M.G.Coy 1.3 (Right) Groups	
			B B 1.4 (Centre)	
			C C 1.5 (Left)	
			D A R3 Battery	
			The Section of 242nd M.G.Coy at R.H. Battery will come under orders of O.C. 61st M.G.Coy after completion of Relief.	
			(1) S.M. Turney will relieve a Sgt. of 51st M.G.Coy at Ration Hut in R.12.b.7.6.	
			(2) Only guns, spareparts, A.A. Sights will be taken up. Tripods, 1st Belt Boxes and 10,000 Rds. S.A.A. per gun will be handed over by 51st Gun Coy.	
			(3) 4 men per gun, 2 effective N.C.O's and 2 men per section will go into the line.	
			(5) Company will parade ready to move off at 2.15am on morning of 31st Jan. Breakfast 1am.	

No. 8 MACHINE GUN COMPANY

Army Form C. 2118.

WAR DIARY
or
INTELLIGENCE SUMMARY.
(Erase heading not required.)

Instructions regarding War Diaries and Intelligence Summaries are contained in F. S. Regs., Part II. and the Staff Manual respectively. Title pages will be prepared in manuscript.

January 1918

Place	Date	Hour	Summary of Events and Information	Remarks and references to Appendices
Metz	29		Operation Order No. B.6 Cont.	
			(6) Rations, Limbers etc and 1 set of guides per team issues to Packet and 2 Limbers	
			(7) Guns will meet incoming teams at the Ration Hut Pt. B.7.b. at 4.30 am. 13 3rd Guides 1st Guides 15.2 Guides B.1 Guide	
			(8) Relief to be complete by 6.30am and reported to Co. M.G.	
			Signed.	
	30.		Sections were occupied during the morning packing limbers etc ready for going into the line.	
La Vacquerie	31	2.15 am	Company relieved 54th Gun Coy. in La Vacquerie Sector in accordance with operation Order No B.6	

6th Brigade.

2nd Division.

Reorganised in March & formed part of
2nd Divisional Machine Gun Battalion

No.6 MACHINE GUN COMPANY

FEBRUARY 1918.

NO. 6 MACHINE GUN COMPANY.

Army Form C. 2118.

WAR DIARY
of
INTELLIGENCE SUMMARY.
(Erase heading not required.)

FEBRUARY 1918.

Instructions regarding War Diaries and Intelligence Summaries are contained in F.S. Regs., Part II. and the Staff Manual respectively. Title pages will be prepared in manuscript.

Place	Date	Hour	Summary of Events and Information	Remarks and references to Appendices
La Vacquerie Sector	1		Reg¹ Maps La Vacquerie 10,000 Refg¹ Maps La Vacquerie billeted in Metz	
			All sections in the line. Q.M. Stores and details billeted in Metz	
	2	During Night	Harassing Fire on the line Q.M Stores and details billeted in Equancourt	
			1000 Rds. fired on suitable targets in R.10	
	3		1500 " " " " " R.16 (Road & Railway crossing)	
	4		1000 " " " " " R.16	
			Attached carriers from 13th Essex Regt. & 17th Middlesex Regt. reported this Unit	
	5		Lieut. H. A. Murray joined the Company	
		During Night	2000 Rds fires on Cross Rd. La Vacquerie	
			1500 " " " " "	
	6		6000 Rds from 2nd Batt⁰ South Staff⁵ Regt. 6000 from 17th Royal Fusiliers and	
			5000 from 1st Bn. King's Liverpool Regt joined the Company as carriers	
	7		2000 Rds fired on suitable targets in R.10	
		During Night	1500 " " " Cross Roads La Vacquerie	
	8		2000 " " " " "	
	9		1500 " " " Road & Railway crossing in R.16	
		7.30pm	Operation order No V. issued	

WAR DIARY
or
INTELLIGENCE SUMMARY

Army Form C. 2118.

No. 6 MACHINE GUN COMPANY 1/3/18

Place	Date	Hour	Summary of Events and Information	Remarks and references to Appendices
	9		**C.O. M.O.V.I.**	
			(1) On the reorganisation of the Brigade front the following M/Guns relief will take place on the night 10/11 inst:—	

Position	No. of Guns	Relieving Coy	Coy to be Relieved	Remarks
(a) T3.	4	5th Coy B Section	6th Coy A Section	Relieved Sections to move to villas in Metz
(b) R3.	4	5th Coy D Section	242nd Coy C Section	Div. Reserve.

(2) (a) Guides for 13 Battery will meet incoming Section at Rotten Dart Alley B.13.b.55.65. at 6.30p.m.

(b) The guides for R3 Battery leave will report at Coy HQ at 6.45 at 6.30p.m.

(3) (a) Tripods, T. Bases Ammunition, 14 Lilles Belt Boxes & 14,000 Rds S.A.A. per gun will be handed over, all guns and spare parts being taken over.

(b) 99th M.G. Coy will hand over to 6th M.G. Coy at war HQ. at Tripods and 56 Belt Boxes.

(4) Section Officers will hand over all empty orders S.O.S.

No. 6 MACHINE GUN COMPANY

Army Form C. 2118.

WAR DIARY
or
INTELLIGENCE SUMMARY.

(Erase heading not required.)

Instructions regarding War Diaries and Intelligence Summaries are contained in F.S. Regs., Part II. and the Staff Manual respectively. Title pages will be prepared in manuscript.

Place	Date	Hour	Summary of Events and Information	Remarks and references to Appendices
La Vacquerie Sector	9	00 M 00	(4) SOS arrangement for each gun emplacement will be kept the one covering	
			zone on Infantry arrangements on right and for action Lights	
			quitting the position	
			(5) Relay complete will be sent in reports to CHQ in person by section officer on withdrawing	
			(6) Transport will be at Ratonville R.13.6.55.65 for guns etc	
			(a) for 2nd M.G.Coy at 19h 00(5) to 6th M.G.Coy at bottom of Ravine. Railway Rd R.8.C.65.45 at 4h 00	
			(7) Signallers on duty at CHQ once S Battn will come under the arrangements of OC 5th M.G.Coy who will retire them from the 13th just ourselves	
	10/11		A Section relieved by B Section 5th M.G.Coy moved into Div Reserve	
	11	During night	1000 Rounds fired on Coose Lane on R.33.a.47.2	
	12	1500	" " "	
	13	1500	Rear of Railway Crossing on Ribert	
	14		Section in Div Reserve and details moved into front sub-sum MG5	

No. 8 MACHINE GUN COMPANY. 1/3/18

Army Form C. 2118.

WAR DIARY
or
INTELLIGENCE SUMMARY.
(Erase heading not required.)

Instructions regarding War Diaries and Intelligence Summaries are contained in F. S. Regs., Part II. and the Staff Manual respectively. Title pages will be prepared in manuscript.

Place	Date	Hour	Summary of Events and Information	Remarks and references to Appendices
La Vacquerie Sector	14	During Night	3000 Rounds fired on Junction of Tramway & Sunken Road R.10.b.6	
			3000 Junction of Sunken Road R.10.b.x	
			1000 Road and Tramway Crossing R.16.a.3	
			1000 La Vacquerie Cross Roads R.15.d.99.45	
	15/10		The following movement of guns took place	
			No of Guns	Present Posn	Moved to		
			1	C.2	C.3	R.9.b.31.70	R.9.b.38.60 to
			1	C.2	C.2	R.9.b.20.60	R.9.b.33.51
			1	Sg.	F.1.	Red Welsh Support	To Bring emplacement to bear in front of Welsh Support Trench
			1	S.10	C.4	R.9.a.15.80	R.9.a.CH Batteries
		During Night	1000 Rounds fired on Road Junction R.10.b.x	
			1000 Cross Roads R.10.b.7	
			1000 La Vacquerie & Roads R.15.d.99.45	
			1000 Trenches & Roads Junction R.a.B.7.6	
	16		B Section relieved by A Section from 147 MGCoy relieved under A.P.I.1.25	

No. 8 MACHINE GUN COMPANY.
Date: 1/3/18

WAR DIARY
or
INTELLIGENCE SUMMARY.
(Erase heading not required.)

Army Form C. 2118.

Place	Date	Hour	Summary of Events and Information	Remarks and references to Appendices
La Vacquerie Sector	17	During	Round as usual in Cross Roads La Vacquerie	
	18	1000	Raw Railway Crossing in Rt. 2	
	19	1000	Trenches and road junction Rt. 20.96	
	20	For	Covering Operation Order no.51 issued	

(1) The following reliefs and redispositions will take place on the night 20/21.2.18.

	Position	M.g.Bt.	No.of Guns	Present Coy.	Relieved by	Remarks
(a)	R3	Rf.9.a.75.55.	4	5th Coy	242 Coy	This section of 2 H.P. coy comes under orders of 8 Coy.
(b)	B3	R.15.a.10.40.	2	5th Coy	6 Coy	1 Gun from 6. C Section. 1 Gun from Ch. D Section. Proving this position to 2 guns.
(c)	F3	R.9.c.35.96.	1	6 Coy A Section	6 Coy D Section	Date of Gun will move from Bottom R.H. section to the R.H. gun in the return to existing Position B3. pill emplacement at R.93.
(d)	C2	R.9.d.20.60.	2	6 Coy C Section	6 Coy B Section	B. Section from Reserve Billets. C Section to Reserve Billets.

Note:- H.Q. check of H.L.H. Plat. to move with two H section gun from Coy position to Section HQ for use at B3.

(2) Reliefs (a)(b)(c) will be complete by 8pm and will be reported to Coy. HQ. Relief (d) will be complete on left of Cross roads "Jury".

WAR DIARY
or
INTELLIGENCE SUMMARY.
(Erase heading not required.)

No. 6 MACHINE GUN COMPANY. Army Form C. 211
Date 1/3/18

Place	Date	Hour	Summary of Events and Information	Remarks and references to Appendices
La Vacquerie Sector	20		(2) Relief (?) will be fully completed by 9pm and covered by moonlight.	
			(3) No Lipods or ammunition will be moved. Guns and Shaupars are being taken up by relieving teams.	
			(4) Guns and Shaupars of "B" Section 679 Coy will be taken up with limbers. The team will go up to the position under Mr Hunt before dusk.	
			(5) On every case all Maps, Trench Stores, Orders, SOS arrangements etc will be handed over to a Section Officer who must put the position until all details of the scheme of defence are thoroughly understood by the incoming team. Pressures eup of Store will be forwarded to Coy HQ by 10am 21st inst.	
			(6) CM Drummers at Coy Rear HQ, Company ration dumps and advanced Stores under Coy Sgt Major is now on Bray Road at R.8.C.7.4 near derelict tank.	
			(7) Following exchange of Bell Boxes and Tripods will be actualed at Rear HQ. 2 Tripods and 28 Bell Boxes 6 Coy will hand to 3rd Coy. 5th Coy to Tripods and 36 Bell Boxes 242nd Coy.	
			Officers NCO's to accompany 679 Coy Operators over was. Positions and Sections will be greyled as followers (next Page)	

NO. 8
MACHINE GUN
COMPANY. Army Form C. 211

WAR DIARY
or
INTELLIGENCE SUMMARY.
(Erase heading not required.)

Instructions regarding War Diaries and Intelligence Summaries are contained in F. S. Regs., Part II. and the Staff Manual respectively. Title pages will be prepared in manuscript.

Place	Date	Hour	Summary of Events and Information				Remarks and references to Appendices
			Group	Position	Map Ref.	M.G./Guns.	
La Vacquerie Sector.			Section and H.Q.				
			1.	R.3.	R.7.9.95.55.	4	and M.G.D. Section Lt Brewster with Dufosse Bat? R.7.9.55.25
			2.	R.4.	R.9.a.65.60.	3	
			3.	R.3.	R.15.9.10.40	2	D.Section Lt Nolan R.9.a.9.1.
				S.11.	R.9.C.05.65	1	Lt Waite R.9.C.05.65
				S.12.	"	1	
			4.	C.7.	R.9.C.20.60.	2	B. " R.9.C.20.?
				C.H.	R.9.9.15.80	2	Lt Hals. "
			5.	F.3.	R.9.9.3.6	1	D. Under supervision of officers to 4 Groups seem to be arranged in their own M.G. Section. Gun not to be moved except in relief of Section or Pt.
	20/9.		C Section relieved by B Section and moved up to Div? Reserve Pt 2				
			Hostile artillery shelled Villers in Metz, killing 10th Devons and R.16.6.				
	21.	During night	2000 Rds fired on Cross Roads La Vacquerie on R.9.a and R.16.b.				
			Capt. G.H. Stansbie left the company to join the 2nd Div. M.G.Batt?				
		During night	3000 Rounds fired on Cross Roads La Vacquerie & Rase & Railway Crossing R.16.a. Copy H. @ under was with 6thy Box 40 & 9.17 a.65. Lieut H.V. Osborne MC took over Command				
	22.	During night	3000 Rounds fired on Cross Roads La Vacquerie and Road fasty crossing R.16.a.				
	23.		Section in Reserve & details moved out of Metz into Tents Reinforcement of 10 O.Rs arrived.				

No. 8
MACHINE GUN
COMPANY. Army Form C. 211
No. ....
Date. 1/3/18

WAR DIARY
or
INTELLIGENCE SUMMARY.
(Erase heading not required.)

Army Form C. 211

Instructions regarding War Diaries and Intelligence Summaries are contained in F. S. Regs., Part II. and the Staff Manual respectively. Title pages will be prepared in manuscript.

Place	Date	Hour	Summary of Events and Information	Remarks and references to Appendices
La VACQUERIE SECTOR.	23	During Night	2000 Rounds fired on Road & Railway crossings R.16.a.9 & X Roads La Vacquerie Emden Support R.10.C.3.6.10	
			1750	
	24	8am	400 at hostile aeroplanes	
			C Section relieved D Section on completion of relief D Section moved into Divl Reserve	
	25	During Night	2500 Rounds fired on Cross Roads R.16.b.30.17 and Track R.16.c.35.10. Lieut. F.M.Richardson joined the Company and took over the duties of Officer Commanding.	
	26	During Night	1000 Rounds fired on X Roads at R.16.b.30.17	
			1500 " " " X Roads R.10.a.7	
			100 " " at hostile aeroplanes	
	27	During Night	2500 " " on Emden Support and Light Railway in R.10.a	
	28		2000 " " " X Roads La Vacquerie	
		5.55am	18000 " " in response to S.O.S	
			2000 " " at hostile aircraft	
			D Section relieves C Section. C Section moves into Divl Reserve	

F.M.Richardson Lt
OC 8th M.G. Coy

Ref Map.
LA ACQUERIE
1/10,000

SECRET
Copy. No 8

6th M. G. Coy.
Operation Order No. VI.

1. On the reorganisation of the Bgde fronts the following M.G. relief will take place on the night 10/11 inst.

Positions	No of Guns	Relieving Coy.	Coy to be relieved	Remarks.
(a) I₃	4	5th Coy B Sect	6th Coy A Sect	Relieved sections to move to billets in METZ to DIV. RES.
(b) R₃	4	5th Coy D Sect	242nd Coy C Sect	

2. (a) Guides for I₃ battery will meet incoming sections at Bottom Dart Alley B.13.b.55.65. at 8.30 PM
   (b) No Guides for R₃ battery. Teams will report at CHQ R.7.d.65.45 at 8.30 PM.

3. (a) Tripods T bases, Ammn 14 filled belt boxes + 10000 rds SAA per gun will be handed over, all guns and spare parts being taken out.
   (b) 99th M.G. Coy will hand over to 6th M.G. Coy at Near HQ 4 tripods + 56 belt boxes.

4. S.O. will hand over all maps, orders, SOS arrangements for each gun + will see that the incoming teams are properly acquainted with all fire orders before quitting the position.

5. Relief will be reported complete to CHQ in person by S.O. on withdrawing.

6. Transport will be at Ration Hut R.13.b.55.65. for guns etc.
   (a) for 242nd M.G. Coy at 10pm (b) 6th M.G. Coy at bottom of Ravine Railway Rd. R.8.c.65.45. at 11 PM.

7. Signallers on duty at CHQ + I₃ battery will come under arrangements of OC 5th M.G. Coy. will ration them for the 13th inst + onwards.

S.H. Stampe
Capt.
Cmdg 6th M.G. Coy.

8. Acknowledge:-

7.30 PM
9/2/18

Copies to. 1 ——— S.O. A Sect 6th Coy.
2 ——— OC. 5th Coy.
3 ——— OC. 242nd Coy
4 ——— OC. 99th Coy.
5 ——— B M G CO
6 ——— D M G CO
7 ——— 5th Infy Bgde
8 ——— 6th Infy Bgde
9 ——— TO
10 ——— War Diary
11 ——— Office

SECRET   6th Machine Gun Company.
Map.   Operation Order No. 51.   Copy No. 10
La Vacquerie. 10,000.

1. Following Reliefs and redispositions will take place on the night 20/21st Feb.

Position	Map Ref.	No. of Guns	Present By	Relieved By	Remarks
(a) R.3.	R.7.d.75.55.	4.	5th Coy.	242 Coy.	This Section of 242 Coy comes under orders of O.C. 6th Coy.
(b) B.3.	R.15.a.10.40.	2.	5th Coy.	6th Coy.	1 Gun from F.3. A Section. 1 Gun from C.4. A Section. Reducing this position to 2 guns.
(c) F.3.	R.9.d.35.95.	4.	6th Coy. D Section.	6th Coy. D Section.	D Section Gun will move from Battery C.4. Reducing it to 3 guns. A Section gun will return to Section HQ for employment at B.3.
(d) C.2.	R.9.b.20.60.	2.	6th Coy. C Section.	6th Coy. B Section.	B Section from Reserve Billets. C Section to Reserve Billets.

Note:- At dusk 2/Lt. Holate will withdraw A Section gun from C.2 position to Section HQ for use at B.3.

2. Reliefs (a) (b) & (c) will be completed by 8pm. and will be reported to CHQ over the wire by code word "JERRY". Relief (d) will be reported complete by same code word by midnight.

3. No tripods or ammunition will be moved. Guns & spare parts only being taken in by relieving teams.

4. Guns and spare parts of B Section 6th M.G Coy will be taken up with ration limbers. The team will go up to the position under Lieut. Hall before dusk.

5. In every case all Maps, Trench Stores, Orders, S.O.S arrangements etc will be handed over & no Section Officer must quit the position until all details of the scheme of fire are thoroughly understood by the incoming teams. Duplicate lists of Stores will be forwarded to CHQ by 10am. 21st inst.

6. CHQ remains at 6th Infy Bde H.Q. Company Ration Dump & advanced store under Coy.Sgt.Major is now on Railway bed at R.8.c.7.4. near derelict tank.

7. Following exchange of Belt Boxes and tripods will be adjusted at Rear H.Q
6th Coy will hand to 5th Coy 2 tripods & 28 Belt Boxes.
242nd Coy. - 5th Coy 4 tripods & 56 Ditto.

8. Acknowledge.

Issued at 7am. 20.2.18.
Copies to:- 1.2.3.4. Sec Officers 6th M.G Coy.
5. O.C. 5 M.G Coy.
6. 242
7. O.C. H.Q.

H.Q. 6th Infy Bde

Herewith:- War Diary for
the month of February 1918

M.V. Xende Lt
for O.C. 6 M. Gun Co.

Appendix A. to accompany 6th M.G Coy. O.O. No 51.

Positions & Sections will be grouped as follows
after relief 20/21st

Group	Position	Map Ref.	No of Guns	Section & H.Qs
1.	R.3	R.7.d.75.55	4.	2nd M.G Coy D Section Lt Birdseye with Support Bn H.Q. R.7.d.55.45.
2.	R.W.	R.8.a.65.6a	3.	D Sec. Lt Nolan R.8.a.9.7.
3.	B.3	R.15.a.10.10	2.	A . 2/Lt Waite R.9.c.05.65
	S.11	R.9.c.05.65	1.	"
	S.12	Ditto	1.	"
4.	C.3	R.9.b.20.60	2.	B. Lt Hall. R.9.d.2.70.
	C.4	R.9.a.15.80	2.	"
5.	F.3	R.9.d.3.6	1.	D Under supervision of Officer i/c 4 Group – Team to be changed daily before dawn from its own section. Gun not to be moved except on relief of Section at R.H.

2 DIV 6 INF BRIGADE-

1/17 ROYAL FUSILIERS.
1918 FEB TO 1919 FEB.

6 MACHINE GUN COMPANY.
1916 JAN TO 1918 FEB.

1363

2 DIV 6 INF BRIGADE-

1/17 ROYAL FUSILIERS.
1918 FEB TO 1919 FEB.
6 MACHINE GUN COMPANY.
1916 JAN TO 1918 FEB.

www.ingramcontent.com/pod-product-compliance
Lightning Source LLC
Chambersburg PA
CBHW080803010526
44113CB00013B/2318